Understanding
The Scarlet Letter

The Greenwood Press "Literature in Context" Series

Understanding *To Kill a Mockingbird*: A Student Casebook to Issues, Sources, and Historic Documents
Claudia Durst Johnson

UNDERSTANDING
The Scarlet Letter

A STUDENT CASEBOOK TO ISSUES, SOURCES, AND HISTORICAL DOCUMENTS

Claudia Durst Johnson

The Greenwood Press
"Literature in Context" Series

GREENWOOD PRESS
Westport, Connecticut • London

Library of Congress Cataloging-in-Publication Data

Understanding The scarlet letter : a student casebook to issues,
  sources, and historical documents / Claudia Durst Johnson.
      p. cm.—(The Greenwood Press "Literature in context"
  series, ISSN 1074-598X)
    Includes bibliographical references and index.
    ISBN 0-313-29328-7 (alk. paper)
    1. Hawthorne, Nathaniel, 1804–1864. Scarlet letter.
  2. Massachusetts—History—Colonial period, ca. 1600–1775—
  Historiography. 3. Mothers and daughters in literature.
  4. Puritans in literature. 5. Adultery in literature. 6. Women in
  literature. I. Johnson, Claudia D. II. Series.
  PS1868.U53   1995
  813'.3—dc20   94–39083

British Library Cataloguing in Publication Data is available.

Library of Congress Catalog Card Number: 94–39083
ISBN: 0-313-29328-7
ISSN: 1074-598X

First published in 1995

Greenwood Press, 88 Post Road West, Westport, CT 06881
An imprint of Greenwood Publishing Group, Inc.

Printed in the United States of America

The paper used in this book complies with the
Permanent Paper Standard issued by the National
Information Standards Organization (Z39.48–1984).

10 9 8 7 6 5 4 3 2

Contents

Introduction

The nineteenth century was a time of great prudishness in America. Women's dresses came all the way to the ground, and to allow a gentleman to glimpse a black-stockinged ankle while climbing into or out of a horse carriage, by accident or on purpose, was to risk getting a reputation for moral looseness. Similarly, a genteel young lady risked losing her good name permanently if she were ever discovered to have spent time alone in the company of a man who was not a relative. It was called the Age of the Euphemism, when so-called prettier, "nicer" words were coined or substituted for "unpleasant" ones: the word "limb" seemed nicer than "leg"; "white meat" on a cooked chicken seemed more genteel than the older term, "breast"; a drunk person was invariably described as being "unwell" and a dead person as having "passed away." The prudishness of the age would lead Nathaniel Hawthorne's widow, Sophia, to erase completely his rather tame journal description of a prostitute before allowing it to be published. So it is no surprise that many pious readers and critics in the nineteenth century found Hawthorne's first novel, *The Scarlet Letter*, to be shocking and unfit for publication—not only because of its subject, but because of his treatment of it. Hawthorne tells the story of a married woman who has a child by someone other than her husband. She keeps the child, raising it herself in the community where her situation is known, never revealing the name of her lover. Many critics found the novel objectionable because her secret lover is the saintly, idolized young minister of the community, because they didn't believe the adulterers were ever really sorry for what they had done, and because the author seemed to be sympathizing with them rather than frowning on their actions.

Even in the last decades of the twentieth century, issues raised by *The Scarlet Letter* are still controversial. In our much more tolerant age, when huge numbers of children are raised by single mothers, the controversy rages on over whether children should be reared without fathers and whether society is doing enough to discourage the increasingly high percentage of out-of-wedlock births. Respected men of God, like Hawthorne's minister, the Reverend Dimmesdale, have created public commotions with sexual misconduct fully as scandalous as that in *The Scarlet Letter*. None have been more notorious than those created by two famous televangelists in the late 1980s. And *The Scarlet Letter* is pertinent to other timely issues: corporal punishment, the separation of church and state, and child custody—all of which have been hot topics in the 1990s.

Despite its shocking subject matter, *The Scarlet Letter* entered the canon of American masterpieces almost from its first appearance in 1850 and has remained there for over 140 years. No college course in nineteenth-century American fiction is complete without it. And though its subject matter was once considered inappropriate for secondary school students, it is now one of the ten most frequently read novels in junior and senior high schools in the United States. Another illustration of its popularity is the frequency with which the novel is dramatized for film and stage. In the 1970s the National Endowment for the Humanities funded a highly publicized and carefully researched production of *The Scarlet Letter* that attracted one of public television's largest audiences. Summer stock theatrical companies, in New England in particular, mounted successful adaptations of *The Scarlet Letter* with regularity in the 1980s and 1990s. In 1994 a major motion picture of *The Scarlet Letter* was planned starring Demi Moore, a respected and popular young box office attraction.

As might be expected, in the years since its first appearance *The Scarlet Letter* has been one of the most frequently analyzed works of American literature and one of those novels chosen most often as the subject of doctoral dissertations. Literary critics have studied it in the context of Hawthorne's life, in the context of themes in his other works, as a reflection of nineteenth-century social history, and in its historical context of Puritanism. It has been examined from every conceivable point of view: the religious, the psychological, the mythological, the historical, and the sociological. It has even been the subject of an article in the *New England Journal of Medicine*. This interest is a testament to the richness and variety of human exchange and intellectual breadth offered by the novel.

The Scarlet Letter contains universal themes concerned with, among other things, fate, free will, and human nature. As a story of the settlement of America, it also has a thoroughly national theme. New England Puritanism was a natural topic for Nathaniel Hawthorne to undertake, for his family had been at the center of developments in America's early history from the days of the Puritans' reign in New England. One ancestor lives in historical annals as a persecutor of Quakers, and another as one of the investigating magistrates and then a judge in the Salem witch trials. In *The Scarlet Letter*, as in many of Hawthorne's shorter works, he makes abundant use of the Puritan past: its peculiar exclusionary religion, its harsh code of law, its preoccupation with sex and witchcraft. He often incorporates into his fiction figures from American history: Anne Hutchinson, who was tried for heresy by the Puritans; Governor Bellingham, and his sister, Mistress Hibbins, who was executed for witchcraft; the Reverend Wilson, who figured in the persecution of Quakers; John Endicott, who was once governor of the territory; Roger Williams, who was expelled from the Massachusetts Bay Colony; and many others.

At the same time, *The Scarlet Letter* has as much to say about the history of Nathaniel Hawthorne's own time as about the seventeenth century of his Puritan ancestors. Imbedded in the story of Hester Prynne are nineteenth-century controversies about what constitutes human nature (Is it basically good or bad?), about the nature and place of women, about sexual repression, child-rearing, and fictional art. The autobiographical preface to *The Scarlet Letter*, entitled "The Custom-House" (about Hawthorne's mundane job in a government office, which interferes with his real vocation as a writer), makes unmistakable the connection between the seventeenth-century setting of the novel and Hawthorne's own day. For these reasons, the novel is an invaluable key to American history, and American history is an invaluable key to *The Scarlet Letter*. With this in mind, the foundation of this study of the novel is largely interdisciplinary; historical, theological, biographical, literary, and sociological documents are brought to bear on the fiction.

The first chapter is a literary analysis of *The Scarlet Letter*, with attention given to the meanings of the central symbol as they are manifested in the interactions of the four main characters and the Puritan community. The novel lends itself to such a study, which makes little reference to elements outside the fiction, because it is so tightly structured and so carefully balanced. Hawthorne seems to have chosen every word with great care, and there are no digressions, unnecessary bits of dialogue, or superfluous descriptions. He never wanders from the main themes of his fiction.

Chapters 2 through 6 focus on the novel's historical context and issues: the seventeenth-century Puritan background; the place of the wilderness and nature; the Puritans' code of crime and punishment; their basic beliefs and habits of mind; the Antinomian controversy involving Anne Hutchinson; and the witchcraft trials of 1692.

Chapters 7 and 8 are historical in a biographical sense; they examine the preface to *The Scarlet Letter*, for the "complete" *Scarlet Letter* is more than the Puritan-era story of Hester Prynne. Both novel and preface can be read as separate works that stand on their own. Essential links will be made between *The Scarlet Letter* and "The Custom-House," that is to say, the characters in Hester Prynne's seventeenth-century story and the nineteenth-century narrator in the introductory sketch who resembles Nathaniel Hawthorne. To complete this picture, one must also take into account the strong influence on the novel of Hawthorne's own family past in Puritan times, his own life as an artist, and the negative attitude toward fiction with which he had to struggle.

Chapter 9 examines twentieth-century issues pertinent to *The Scarlet Letter*, with emphasis on the unwed mother and the immoral clergyman.

Excerpts from a variety of documents, all bearing on issues related to *The Scarlet Letter*, are included here:

- two literary studies
- bodies of law from the seventeenth century

- historical reports
- private journals
- nineteenth-century magazine articles
- lines of poetry
- sketches
- newspaper stories

Each of the major topics and each document or set of documents is introduced by an essay linking it to *The Scarlet Letter*. Some topics or sections include chronologies. Also included are topics for written or oral exploration, suggestions for further reading, bibliographies, and a glossary of terms.

Chapter 1 is intended to inspire close readings of *The Scarlet Letter*, to help the reader develop a thorough familiarity with the text itself. Chapters 2 through 6 provide the reader with information about America's past, especially that Puritanism with which Hawthorne himself was thoroughly familiar and out of which he fashioned his historical novel. The author's choice of material and his adaptation of it for his art throw light on the meaning of the work. The material presented in Chapters 7 and 8 reveal the various nineteenth-century forces at work on the author's life and art. Chapter 9, by examining issues from *The Scarlet Letter* and Puritan history that remain current in the twentieth century, illustrates the universality of the novel.

The introductory essays are designed to place the documents that follow in context, to give the reader sufficient information to make sense of the primary material. In most cases, the documents should be augmented by supplemental readings in Hawthorne which reflect his further use of the same historical materials. The projects and questions that follow each group of documents have no "right" or "wrong" answers. Instead they are designed to encourage the reader to engage the material and think for himself or herself.

Numbers in parentheses in the text refer to the Signet Classic edition of *The Scarlet Letter* (1959) and the Library of America collection of Hawthorne's *Tales and Sketches* (1982).

Whenever possible, older spellings have been retained to give the reader a sense of the language at the time. However, some spelling has been modified for greater ease of comprehension.

Understanding
The Scarlet Letter

1

A Literary Analysis of
The Scarlet Letter

The Scarlet Letter is one of those novels that so often lingers on the library shelf like a collection of sermons: forbidding, leather-bound, perhaps embossed with gold. We approach it reluctantly, not as a pleasure, but more as a challenge and a duty. It is a book we feel we *should* read—one of these days—if not to strengthen our character, then certainly to round out our education.

Yet, as the introduction suggests, beneath Hawthorne's genteel nineteenth-century language is no humdrum story, but one considered indecent by many readers of his time. Furthermore, the novel raises issues that are just as controversial today as they were two hundred years ago.

The story is simple and dramatic. A young and beautiful woman, Hester Prynne, bound by marriage to an old man supposedly somewhere far away or perhaps even dead, has an illicit—adulterous—affair with an unknown member of the small frontier village to which she has gone. There is no way for her to hide the affair, for she becomes pregnant with a child, and is imprisoned for her sin. The actual narrative begins after the child is born, on the day she emerges from prison to begin enduring her public punishment. The aging husband (much too old for the healthy young bride) comes out of the forest into town on this very day—to see his lovely (and lonely) wife standing on the public scaffold with an "A" for adultery sewn on her dress and a baby in her arms. The wife refuses to reveal the name of her lover, and promises her husband that she will help him keep his identity secret from the community as well.

That is the situation when the story begins. But what, in reality, is *The Scarlet Letter* "about"? It has all the ingredients of a soap opera, but it is far more than that. It could be a Puritan sermon, but it is surely not that, for the Puritans are not the heroes here. It is a story of passion, but the reader never sees what we would call an explicit sexual scene.

It is about the *consequences* of breaking the moral code, in this case a moral law. What happens to human beings as a result of such transgressions?

It is also about failing to be true to human nature. There are, in fact, many failings in this story: the failure of the Puritans; of the leaders; of the young wife, who thinks charitable actions coming from an uncharitable heart will make up for her moment of illicit passion; of the minister, her lover, who lies first to his community and then to himself; of the cold old man who seeks to ruin his young wife's lover.

It is a story about a terrible and cruel revenge worked out as the wronged old husband (who never reveals his true identity or his purpose) slowly injects his poison into the minds and the lives of all those around him.

It is about the hypocrisy of members of a community who refuse to acknowledge that each of them is just as human, just as subject to passionate feelings as the woman they label an adulterer. If any novelist, any book can be said to have ripped the mask off Puritan pretensions, it is this writer, this book.

The Scarlet Letter is also about creativity—a person's attempt to see his or her own artistic side survive in a community that disapproves of the use of the imagination.

Furthermore, *The Scarlet Letter* is one of the earliest psychological novels in modern literature. It is one of the first works of fiction to probe the underside of human character—what lies unseen and unsaid beneath the surface.

This story of passion and chaos is highly structured. Its action begins and ends on the scaffold in the Boston marketplace. At the exact center of the novel is another scaffold scene, set in the middle of the night. The first half of the novel is an examination, first, of Hester, as she attempts to live with her punishment, and then of Dimmesdale, who attempts to live with his guilt and with his companion, Chillingworth, who has successfully kept his relation to Hester secret. In the middle of the first half of the novel is a key scene in which Hester has to defend her right to keep her child.

The second half of the novel includes a look at what seven years have done to each of the lovers. The key middle scene takes place between the lovers in the forest.

Despite its multiplicity of subjects and themes, Hawthorne's novel is surprisingly focused on the scarlet letter itself, an image which, while fraught with many meanings—all of which bear on the overarching moral, "Be true!"—remains steadily at the center of the work as a representative of Truth.

THE MEANINGS OF THE SCARLET LETTER

To get at the many meanings of the scarlet letter, it is useful to see, first, how it is represented in the child Pearl, who, the author tells us, is a little scarlet letter herself. Then the discussion will turn to the letter's meaning for the community, and finally, to its specific relationship to Hester, Dimmesdale, and Chillingworth.

While the letter has many *implied* meanings, it also has particular and explicit meanings. The first and most obvious is that Hester's "A" stands for adultery and, as the narrator puts it, "women's frailty and sinful passion" (83). But the "A" on her breast begins to represent different things as Hester's story unfolds. For example, as a result of her charitable acts in the community, some people begin to think the "A" stands for able. And when the community sees a scarlet "A" in the sky on the night of John Winthrop's death, they believe it stands for angel. So, in the course of the novel, the "A" seems to encompass the entire range of human beingness, from the earthly and passionate "adulteress" to the pure and spiritual "angel," taking into account everything in between.

One begins to see many other human elements that the scarlet letter represents as the novel moves along. Pearl, for example, who is neither adulteress nor angel, is described as the living scarlet letter, and she embodies a full range of human characteristics: "Pearl's aspect was imbued with a spell of infinite variety; in this one child there were many children, comprehending the full scope between the wild-flower prettiness of a peasant baby, and the pomp, in little, of an infant princess" (92). Furthermore, Hester begins to sense that many people besides herself wear scarlet letters on their breasts, even those with reputations for piety and purity:

> Could they be other than the insidious whispers of the bad angel, who would fain have persuaded the struggling woman, as yet only half his victim, that the outward guise of purity was but a lie, and that, if truth were everywhere to be shown, a scarlet letter would blaze forth on many a bosom besides Hester Prynne's? . . . Sometimes the red infamy upon her breast would give a sympathetic throb, as she passed near a venerable minister or magistrate, the model of piety and justice, to whom that age of antique reverence looked up as to a moral man in fellowship with angels. . . . Again, a mystic sisterhood would contumaciously assert itself as she met the sanctified frown of some matron, who, according to the rumor of all tongues, had kept cold snow within her bosom throughout life. That unsunned snow in the matron's bosom, and the burning shame on Hester Prynne's—what had the two in common? Or, once more, the electric thrill would give her warning—"Behold, Hester, here is a companion!"—and, looking up, she would detect the eyes of a young maiden glancing at the scarlet letter, shyly and aside, and quickly averted, with a faint, chill crimson in her cheeks as if her purity were somewhat sullied by that momentary glance. (90)

The scarlet letter, in addition, has many implied meanings. "A" stands for Arthur Dimmesdale, for Hester's art, for Chillingworth's black or magical art. "A" can stand for atonement, which is what Hester is trying to do—atone for her sin with charitable acts. It also represents avenger or avenge, which is the whole purpose of Chillingworth's life. "A" represents the authority of the community that hypocritically condemns Hester for the rest of her life. It stands for Dimmesdale's ambition, as well as his anguish and agony. "A" represents the community, which is frequently characterized as aged or ancient.

PEARL

Much of the meaning of the scarlet letter resides in Pearl because she is the result of Hester's adultery. Hester dresses the child in scarlet, presenting her as a little scarlet letter. Moreover, Pearl has a morbid obsession with the scarlet letter. The connection is first made in the chapter entitled "The Governor's Hall," where her red dress is described:

But it was a remarkable attribute of this garb, and, indeed, of the child's whole appearance, that it irresistibly and inevitably reminded the beholder of the token which Hester Prynne was doomed to wear upon her bosom. It was the scarlet letter in another form; the scarlet letter endowed with life! (103)

Pearl's obsession with the letter her mother wears on her breast begins in infancy as her eyes focus on it. Then as a tiny girl, Pearl evinces a fascination with the letter and continually touches it and throws wild flowers at it:

In the afternoon of a certain summer's day, after Pearl grew big enough to run about, she amused herself with gathering handfuls of wild-flowers and flinging them, one by one, at her mother's bosom, dancing up and down like a little elf whenever she hit the scarlet letter. (98, 99)

Later, she begins to pester her mother with questions about why she wears the letter and what it means. In the forest scene when Hester takes off the scarlet letter, Pearl becomes frantically disturbed and won't quiet down until Hester has it back on her dress, as if by discarding the letter Hester has discarded Pearl. Pearl even makes herself an "A" from green seaweed:

As the last touch to her mermaid's garb, Pearl took some eelgrass, and imitated, as best she could, on her own bosom, the decoration with which she was so familiar on her mother's. A letter—the letter "A"—but freshly green, instead of scarlet! (171)

How does Pearl's connection with the scarlet letter bring us closer to its meanings? If she is identified with the scarlet letter, then the reader needs to consider her characteristics to determine some of the letter's meaning. First of all, Pearl is uncontrollable, subject to hyperactivity, bad temper, even behavior that could be classified as cruel. But for all her childish cruelty and hyperactivity, she is always depicted as nature's child. While the other children in the community play games taught by society and their parents, such as scourging Quakers and having prayer meetings, Pearl plays in the forest and by the seashore with living flora and fauna. The letter "A" she makes for herself is not red, but green—nature's color. These observations lead to the conclusion that the "A," rather than being exotic and lurid, as the community sees it, is in fact natural, and that those things associated with it—passion and sexuality in particular—are natural to human nature, not scarlet and demonic, as the community sees both the letter and Pearl herself. This would explain why Hester, metaphorically speaking, sees an "A" on many breasts other than her own: because passion exists as a natural part of human nature in every human being.

A second characteristic of Pearl shows that the scarlet letter means truth as well as nature. For all her faults, Pearl is the hardest truth-sayer in the novel. It is she who immediately recognizes Chillingworth as the "Black Man," or devil, in the community, telling Hester, "Come away, Mother! Come away, or yonder old Black Man will catch you! He hath got hold of the minister already" (132). And it is she who suspects that Dimmesdale has a scarlet letter over his heart, asking Hester if she wears the scarlet letter for the same reason "that the minister keeps his hand over his heart!" (171). She also knows intuitively that Hester is not telling her the truth about the letter. After Hester has lied about its meaning, Pearl will not let the matter drop.

Two or three times, as her mother and she went homeward, and as often at suppertime, and while Hester was putting her to bed, and once after she seemed to be fairly asleep, Pearl looked up, with mischief gleaming in her black eyes.
   "Mother," said she, "What does the scarlet letter mean?" (174)

Not only does she speak the truth, but she pursues the truth in continually questioning Hester about the meaning of the symbol she wears and the reason why Dimmesdale keeps his hand over his heart. From this connection of Pearl to truth, it is obvious that the scarlet letter, which Pearl embodies, is also a totality of truth about human nature and relationships. That at the end of the novel Pearl leaves America never to return suggests that those aspects of human nature on which the cold Puritans frown—in this case, creativity, passion, and joy—will not be acknowledged in New England for many years to come.

THE PURITAN COMMUNITY

The religious society of Boston, even though it is located in the New World, on the edge of uncharted wilderness, has little other affinity with nature and the natural; nor has the community acknowledged the full truth of the scarlet letter; nor is it tolerant of the whole range of human faculties, from angel to adulteress, that the letter represents. The people of the community, like their harsh ancestors whose portraits hang in the governor's mansion, gaze "with harsh and intolerant criticism at the pursuits and enjoyments of living men" (106). Hester wears an "A" for her passion, but despite a theology that teaches that *all* people are innately, or by nature, evil, the community does not recognize that they themselves are sexual or passionate.

The narrator makes the reader aware of this secret, subtle intolerance early in the novel with stories of the Puritan community's suspicious intolerance of human nature, of those they see as different from themselves. This becomes dramatically clear in the harsh punishments imposed for trivial, natural human behavior:

It might be that a sluggish bond-servant, or an undutiful child, whom his parents had given over to civil authority, was to be corrected at the whipping-post. It might be that an Antinomian, a Quaker, or other heterodox religionist, was to be scourged out of the town, or an idle and vagrant Indian, whom the white man's firewater had made riotous about the streets, was to be driven with stripes into the shadow of the forest. It might be, too, that a witch, like old Mistress Hibbins, the bitter-tempered widow of the magistrate, was to die upon the gallows. (57)

The Puritan harshness of the community is reflected even in the play of the little children who imitate the actions of their elders. In marked contrast to Pearl, these children play at "scourging Quakers; or taking scalps in a sham-fight with the Indians; or scaring one another with freaks of imitative witchcraft" (96).

Because they despise so many human traits, while at the same time failing to recognize those same passionate traits in themselves, Hester, always wearing the badge of adulterous love, becomes a target for their cruelty. It is almost as if the community can better deny the passion of their own nature by projecting it onto Hester and despising her for it. Even though, as we have seen, Hester perceptively senses the lust in the heart of even the most pious man of God and the purest maiden, the community acts as if she alone has passion in her heart:

Clergymen paused in the street to address words of exhortation that brought a crowd, and its mingled grin and frown, around the poor, sinful woman. If she entered a church, trusting to share the Sabbath smile of the Universal Father, it was often her mishap to find herself the text of the discourse. (88)

The community members hide in their hearts and refuse to acknowledge passion, which is one trait represented by the "A." At the same time they value other characteristics represented by the "A," such as age. The community leaders are repeatedly referred to as "aged" or "ancient." They adhere to a system "of ancient prejudice, wherewith was linked much of ancient principle" (159). In this community, reverence, the narrator tells us, was bestowed "on the white hair and venerable brow of age" (222). Repeatedly, the age of community leaders like Chillingworth, Governor Bellingham, and the Reverend Wilson is impressed upon the reader. The very foundation of the community, usually associated with iron and rigidity, rests so heavily on age that characteristics of youth, such as joy, passion, and creativity, are destroyed.

While to Pearl, the truth-sayer, the scarlet letter is green or natural, to the community, which is led by old men who have lost all connection with creativity, it is red or devilish. To the townspeople, the letter "seemed to derive its scarlet hue from the flames of the infernal pit" (74) and "was red-hot with infernal fire" (91). The ancientness, along with the sterile, stultifying control of this community of old men, is emphasized throughout the novel. This constant emphasis on age and intellect, with no room in the heart for joy or tolerance, compels the community to despise virtually the entire range of creative human faculties. Several scenes reveal just how the community has come to despise the youth and feeling—the female principle—the letter represents. In the very first scene, while Hester is standing on the scaffold, we note that the leaders of this harsh community are all old. The Reverend John Wilson is an old man, indeed, "the eldest clergyman of Boston" (71). The colony's governor, Mr. Bellingham, is "a gentleman advanced in years," a fitting governor for a society that owed its development "not to the impulses of youth, but to the stern and tempered energies of manhood and the sombre sagacity of age" (70). The narrator says of the men who pass judgment on Hester that though they were basically good men, "out of the whole human family, it would not have been easy to select the same number of wise and virtuous persons who should be less capable of sitting in judgment on an erring woman's heart" (70). Even most of the women in the town, who express themselves with such authority on the day Hester is sentenced, are old and cruel. They are described in the first marketplace scene as "old dames" (61), "autumnal" (59), and "of mature age" (59). In fact, they want to see

Hester executed instead of just being made to wear the scarlet letter.

There are two exceptions to the old men and old women who look on Hester's punishment on the scaffold in the marketplace. One is the Reverend Dimmesdale who, though he is young by comparison, has already begun to act like an old man. The other is a young woman with a baby, who speaks briefly and sympathetically in Hester's behalf. Yet in this community, old age tends not only to deny and suppress the passions, sexuality, and pleasures of youth, it actually destroys youth itself. For the narrator shows the three young people in the first marketplace scene to be radically altered seven years later. Dimmesdale's youth has vanished. He has become more decrepit and halting than much older men: "The aged members of his flock, beholding Mr. Dimmesdale's frame so feeble while they were themselves so rugged in their infirmity, believed that he would go heavenward before them" (139). The sympathetic young mother of the early scene is the only one among them who has died: "Hester saw and recognized the selfsame faces of that group of matrons who had awaited her forthcoming from the prison door seven years ago; all save one, the youngest and only compassionate among them, whose burial robe she had since made" (230). And Hester has been driven to turn herself into a sexless woman who dresses in drab gray and hides her hair under her cap. Thus youth and femininity do not survive in a community that does not value them.

This lack of sympathy with Hester and those qualities represented by the scarlet letter is also occasioned by the overwhelming intellectuality of these old men. Invariably, their minds far overweigh their hearts. Their spiritual leader, the Reverend Wilson, is described as a great scholar whose kind heart "had been less carefully developed than his intellectual gifts" (71). Dimmesdale, whom they value as a son, is also described as a man of "scholarlike attainments" (72). At one point Chillingworth, himself a man of the library, even pretends to blame Dimmesdale's ill health on his studies: "Aha! see now, how they trouble the brain—these books!—these books! You would study less, good Sir" (152).

Joy is frowned upon in this community as well. No entertainments, especially those that make people laugh, are allowed at the Election Day festival: "All such professors of the branches of jocularity would have been sternly repressed not only by the rigid discipline of law, but by the general sentiment which gives law its vitality" (217). One need only compare Pearl's joyous play with the other Puritan children's grim games. Furthermore, the narrator remarks that this suppression of an essential part of human nature continues well into the nineteenth century:

> Their immediate posterity, the generation next to the early emigrants, wore the blackest shade of Puritanism, and so darkened the national visage with it, that all the subsequent years have not sufficed to clear it up. We have yet to learn again the forgotten art of gayety. (218)

HESTER

It is such a community that compels Hester Prynne to wear a scarlet letter as punishment for giving birth to an illegitimate child. In examining the meaning of the scarlet letter to Hester and her lover, Dimmesdale, it is important to note their relationship to both the letter "A" and to little Pearl, who so often represents the letter. It is appropriate that Hester, unlike the child's father, has to wear the badge of her passion for all to see, for by virtue of her biological nature, she cannot, as he can, hide the consequences of giving way to that desire. From the first, everyone sees that she is pregnant and that she gives birth to a child who then lives by her side, a reminder of what she is and has done always in full public view.

Hester gives the reader an important clue to her attitude when she immediately and richly embroiders the scarlet letter with gold thread. The community is outraged that she has made a mockery of her punishment by making this plain symbol of adultery into a gorgeous decoration:

> On the breast of her gown, in fine red cloth surrounded with an elaborate embroidery and fantastic flourishes of gold thread, appeared the letter "A." It was so artistically done, and with so much fertility and gorgeous luxuriance of fancy, that it had all the effect of a last and fitting decoration to the apparel which she wore; and which was of a splendor in accordance with the taste of the age, but greatly beyond what was allowed by the sumptuary regulations of the colony. (60)

The women in the community recognize the impertinence of what she has done to negate the awful meaning of the letter:

"She hath good skill at her needle, that's certain," remarked one of her female spectators; "but did ever a woman, before this brazen hussy, contrive such a way of showing it! Why, gossips, what is it but to laugh in the faces of our godly magistrates, and make a pride out of what they, worthy gentlemen, meant for a punishment?"

"It were well," muttered the most iron-visaged of the old dames, "if we stripped Madam Hester's rich gown off her dainty shoulders; and for the red letter, which she hath stitched so curiously, I'll bestow a rag of mine own rheumatic flannel, to make a fitter one!" (61)

If the "A," as we have seen, is a symbol of the full range of human nature, both of its base and its angelic qualities, then in assigning her an "A" of scarlet to wear as punishment, the community shows that it regards human nature, especially passion, to be devilish. And Hester, in embroidering the letter in gold, is trying to change her human reality, to make it prettier than it really is. She also is ashamed of her human nature. This can be seen in the way she dresses to present herself to the community, in somber gray hues and with her hair hidden under her cap:

There seemed to be no longer anything in Hester's face for Love to dwell upon; nothing in Hester's form, though majestic and statue-like, that Passion would ever dream of clasping in its embrace; nothing in Hester's bosom to make it ever again the pillow of Affection. (158)

Even though she doesn't remove the scarlet letter publicly when Chillingworth tells her seven years later that the townspeople say she may, she does take it off privately in the forest. This action and Pearl's violent reaction to the removal of the letter seem to suggest that, even after seven years, she has not accepted the truth of her passionate nature (which is, of course, the truth of every person's nature, not just hers).

Hester's scarlet letter represents not only her creativity as a mother but her creativity as a seamstress. "A" also stands for her artistic nature. As the narrator writes of her sewing, "It was the art,—then, as now, almost the only one within a woman's grasp—of needlework" (85). Yet, tutored as she is by her Puritan contemporaries, she also feels guilty about her art, and, in fact, about anything that gives her pleasure, as her art does: "Like all other joys, she rejected it as a sin" (87).

So, as the narrator tells us, "the scarlet letter had not done its office" (160). The community had intended that wearing it would

cause Hester to feel repentant. But she doesn't. Rather than coming to believe that she must accept her true nature and love others
in order to repent (in other words, that repentance must come
from within), she believes that change should come from society,
not within herself.

Hester's greatest self-deception, however, is believing that
through her charitable acts within the community she can change
her human nature and make up for what she is and has done. She
has become a sister of mercy, ministering to the sick and dying,
but she has no charity in her heart. To Dimmesdale in the forest
she says, "Is there no reality in the penitence thus sealed and wit-
nessed by good works?" (183). In the same scene, the narrator
concludes that the trials that Hester has endured because of the
scarlet letter have "taught her much amiss" (190).

Yet, ironically, it is what the scarlet letter represents that saves
her: her pride, her passionate love for Dimmesdale, the child that
she has created and embraced, and her vocation as an artist. As
she tells the three men in the governor's mansion, "Pearl keeps
me here in life!" (112). Just after this visit, she declines old Mistress
Hibbins's invitation to a witches' meeting, saying that if Pearl had
been taken from her, she would have succumbed: "Even thus early
had the child saved her from Satan's snare" (116). These things
make it possible for her to survive the isolation and humiliation
heaped upon her by the community and to have a greater hold on
truth than her unfortunate lover has.

DIMMESDALE

"A" also stands for Arthur; whether actually or metaphorically,
Dimmesdale also wears a scarlet letter over his heart and is constantly aware of it. He knows that it is there, but he refuses to
acknowledge it to the rest of the community, and rather than ac-
cepting the truth of his nature, he is tortured by it and tries to
change it. This refusal is consistent with his rejection of Hester as
his lover and Pearl as his child. But passion is nevertheless a decided part of Dimmesdale's basic nature. Indeed, "passion" is a
word frequently used in describing what in most respects is a pale,
passive man. When he loses his temper at Chillingworth, the old
physician observes: "But see, now, how passion takes hold upon
this man, and hurrieth him out of himself! As with one passion, so

with another! He hath done a wild thing ere now, this pious Master Dimmesdale, in the hot passion of his heart" (34). In the forest with Hester, Dimmesdale's fury upon learning that Chillingworth is her husband is described as "the violence of passion" (185).

The ultimate proof that Dimmesdale denies the truth of his nature, as represented by the scarlet letter, lies in his pretense of saintliness, even though he has felt sufficient sexual passion to father a child with a woman who is married to someone else. One of his most dishonorable half-measures at attempting to confess the truth of his passionate nature as well as his passionate act comes when he tells his congregation from the pulpit—in comfortably safe and general terms—that he is a sinner:

> The minister well knew—subtile, but remorseful hypocrite that he was!—the light in which his vague confession would be viewed. He had striven to put a cheat upon himself by making the avowal of a guilty conscience, but had gained only one other sin, and a self-acknowledged shame, without the momentary relief of being self-deceived. He had spoken the very truth, and transformed it into the veriest falsehood. (140, 141)

At the same time, he also—in secret—attempts to literally beat his passion out of himself in his closet. Even his midnight vigil on the scaffold is a way of trying to give himself peace without showing the public his scarlet letter. The narrator says: "Was it but a mockery of penitence? A mockery, indeed, but in which his soul trifled with itself! A mockery at which angels blushed and wept, while fiends rejoiced with jeering laughter!" (144).

Still, the fact of Dimmesdale's human nature remains. It surfaces when he leaves the forest after his talk with Hester and begins to fantasize about behaving indecently. When he encounters a young parishioner who seems to be in love with him, he thinks of taking advantage of her:

> As she drew nigh, the archfiend whispered him to condense into small compass and drop into her tender bosom a germ of evil that would be sure to blossom darkly soon, and bear black fruit betimes. Such was his sense of power over this virgin soul, trusting him as she did, that the minister felt potent to blight all the field of innocence with but one wicked look, and develop all its opposite with but a word. (207)

Despite the fact that, like everyone else, he secretly wears a scarlet letter, he pretends to be saintly and self-sacrificing and full of

Christian charity. He gives the community no hint that he is human, but fosters instead another, saintly role. He leads the community to think that he is too pure ever to consider a sexual union even in the bonds of matrimony: "he rejected all suggestions of the kind, as if priestly celibacy were one of his articles of church discipline" (124). The congregation considers him to be a man of "especial sanctity" (126). His diabolical constant companion, Chillingworth, ponders the public view of Dimmesdale and expresses his suspicion that Dimmesdale is cultivating an image that is far from the real truth: "pure as they deem him—all spiritual as he seems—[he] hath inherited a strong animal nature from his father or mother" (128). Furthermore, the narrator tells his readers that the community "deemed the young clergyman a miracle of holiness. . . . In their eyes, the very ground on which he trod was sanctified" (139). Just before he ascends the scaffold, seven years after his and Hester's adultery, he is still regarded by the people as saintly, wearing a halo rather than a scarlet letter: "Were there not the brilliant particles of a halo in the air about his head? So etherealized by spirit as he was, and so apotheosized by worshipping admirers, did his footsteps, in the procession, really tread upon the dust of earth?" (233). And after he has ascended the scaffold with Hester, the people, though somewhat puzzled, still view him as saintly: "nor would it have seemed a miracle too high to be wrought for one so holy, had he ascended before their eyes, waxing dimmer and brighter, and fading at last into the light of heaven" (235).

Though he never forgets that he has committed a great sin, even he himself seems to continue to believe that he is fundamentally saintly and pure.

In masking his true nature from the rest of the community—in effect, concealing the "A" that he wears—Dimmesdale also begins to delude himself. One instance is shown in a scene in "The Leech and His Patient," when it is ironically the liar, Chillingworth, who points out the truth to this man of God. Chillingworth asks him why anyone who harbored a heavy secret would not want to confess it and get it off his chest. Dimmesdale's self-deluded reply is that if a saintly man reveals that he has committed a sinful act, he loses all his influence to lead people to do good. Chillingworth's reply has a hard ring of truth in this instance.

Not only is he guilty of self-deception, but Dimmesdale harbors other darker aspects of human nature as represented by the scarlet "A" in his heart. Above all, he conceals an "A" for ambition to which he will sacrifice anything. In following his overweening desire to be a great and revered minister in the Puritan world, he is selfish and egocentric—the very opposite of love. From first to last, Dimmesdale is most concerned not with his own soul, not with Hester's pain, but with what other people think about him and how it will affect his career. When Pearl asks him to stand on the scaffold with them in the daylight, he panics; "all the dread of public exposure that had so long been the anguish of his life had returned upon him" (148). Even in the forest, when Hester reveals Chillingworth's identity to him, he can only think of being exposed and, as he puts it, of "the indelicacy" of the situation (185). He confesses to her that he has lived with the horror that someone might figure out that Pearl looks like him and reveal him to be her father. "O Hester, what a thought is that, and how terrible to dread it!—that my own features were partly repeated in her face, and so strikingly that the world might see them!" (195). In two other important scenes, the narrator shows his own judgment about the selfish depths of Dimmesdale's heart, with special reference to the scarlet letter. The first comes when the minister stands on the scaffold at night with Pearl and Hester and sees a display of phenomenal lights in the sky. Dimmesdale decides that it is God's sign sent to him personally:

But what shall we say when an individual discovers a revelation, addressed to himself alone, on the same vast sheet of record! In such a case, it could only be the symptom of a highly disordered mental state, when a man, rendered morbidly self-contemplative by long, intense, and secret pain, had extended his egotism over the whole expanse of nature, until the firmament itself should appear no more than a fitting page for his soul's history and fate!

• • •

We impute it, therefore, solely to the disease in his own eye and heart, that the minister, looking upward to the zenith, beheld there the appearance of an immense letter—the letter "A"—marked out in lines of dull red light.

Thus again as he returns to town from his meeting in the forest with Hester, as he thinks how relieved he is that she has not planned for the three of them to leave Boston immediately, we see once more the extent of his base ambition and egocentric drive. His reason here is largely the same one he gives for continuing to deny that he should also wear the scarlet letter—that it will interfere with his ambition to be a great ministerial leader of the community:

The minister had inquired of Hester, with no little interest, the precise time at which the vessel might be expected to depart. It would probably be on the fourth day from the present. "That is most fortunate!" he had then said to himself. Now, why the Reverend Mr. Dimmesdale considered it so very fortunate, we hesitate to reveal. Nevertheless—to hold nothing back from the reader—it was because on the third day from the present he was to preach the Election Sermon; and, as such an occasion formed an honorable epoch in the life of a New England clergyman, he could not have chanced upon a more suitable mode and time of terminating his professional career. . . . Sad, indeed, that an introspection so profound and acute as this poor minister's should be so miserably deceived! We have had, and may still have, worse things to tell of him; but none, we apprehend, so pitiably weak; no evidence, at once so slight and irrefragable, of a subtle disease that had long since begun to eat into the real substance of his character. No man for any considerable period can wear one face to himself and another to the multitude, without finally getting bewildered as to which may be the true. (203)

But still Dimmesdale's hidden scarlet letter represents more than passion, adultery, and concern for self. It also stands for artist and author, which words describe his profession as a writer of sermons. For just as Hester creates art with her needle and thread, Dimmesdale creates art with the words he delivers from the pulpit. His art is described as almost magical, hypnotic, reaching his parishioners "in gushes of sad, persuasive eloquence" (139). For this ambition in his vocation as an artful minister, he sacrifices his child and lover and the truth of his heart. One might even argue that for ambition he sacrifices love.

Dimmesdale's "A" at last represents "anguish" and "agony," words frequently used in describing him. He acknowledges these qualities to himself, believing that his own pain and suffering are in fact far greater than Hester's. Still, the question arises as to whether this also is a self-delusion, especially when the reader realizes that Hester's agony and anguish have caused her to contemplate murdering Pearl and committing suicide: "At times, a fearful doubt strove to possess her soul, whether it were not better to send Pearl at once to heaven, and go herself to such futurity as Eternal Justice should provide" (160). Yet despite all that, Dimmesdale's agony is still not enough to drive him to reveal the truth about himself.

CHILLINGWORTH

Chillingworth, in his connection with the scarlet letter, is the worst of the Puritan community. He is always identified as the devil or the devil's emissary (126), as an "archfiend" (151). Pearl, who sees through everyone, is the first to associate him with Satan. And by the time of Hester's last private interview with him, just before she reveals his identity to Dimmesdale, she also sees him as a satanic figure in the form of a bat (169).

He is the epitome of cold intellect and old age, without the full range of redeeming qualities generated by the heart and soul. He has been a scholar in Europe and passes for a medical scholar in the New World. In Hester's memory of him, even when they married, he was already old and wedded to his books. She remembers him as "a man well stricken in years, a pale, thin, scholar-like visage, with eyes dim and bleared by the lamplight that had served them to pore over many ponderous books" (65). In the jail after Hester has stood on the scaffold, Chillingworth describes himself as "a man of thought, the bookworm of great libraries—a man already in decay, having given my best years to feed the hungry dream of knowledge" (78). Then, seven years later, Chillingworth adds to this, remembering himself as a cold, old intellectual when he was married to Hester in Europe:

Even then I was in the autumn of my days, nor was it the early autumn. But all my life had been made up of earnest, studious, thoughtful, quiet years, bestowed faithfully for the increase of mine own knowledge. . . . Was I not, though you might deem me cold, nevertheless a man thoughtful for others . . . and of constant if not warm affections? (166).

Chillingworth's evil character—like something right out of melodrama—is also reflected in his physical appearance. As his human faculties become more and more out of balance—his intellect becoming overdeveloped at the expense of his heart—one side of his body becomes out of balance with the other. Even when he married Hester, this man of the study and laboratory already had a humped back. His deformity of body finally represents a deformity of character in which heart and soul play little part. As a result, he becomes at last bent over toward the ground, more like a snake than a human being. The contrast here is with Pearl, who, while she is thought by some in the community to be the child of Satan, is still strikingly beautiful, a perfect physical specimen.

In one aspect of human nature, however, Chillingworth is like no other. While not sharing in the full range of human warmth and emotions encompassed by the "A," he becomes monomaniacally supreme in one aspect alone, sacrificing all things good, even his own life and health, for that diabolical distortion of human character—revenge. He embodies the "A" for avenger. Torturing the man who has fathered a child with his wife becomes the sole purpose of Chillingworth's life. Then, through his determined searching, he discovers at last that Dimmesdale, too, has an "A" on his heart corresponding to Hester's.

Chillingworth's "A" may also stand for alchemist and artist, for he is both. While intent on probing into Dimmesdale's heart, he says that he is determined to continue, "were it only for the art's sake" (135). Later he tells Hester, "What art can do, I have exhausted on him" (165). Unlike Hester's creative art, however, his is a wholly destructive black art, clearly meaning black magic and witchcraft. Some in the community are suspicious of his connection with Dr. Forman, a man accused of witchcraft in England, and also suspect that among the Indians he may have picked up what is described as "their skill in the black art." This refers to the Puritans' early beliefs that God had prepared a way for them in the wilderness and that the native Indians were minions of the devil.

CONCLUSION

The close association of Chillingworth (who, as avenger, becomes the Black Man or devil) with the community creates a number of ironies. These affinities are established as soon as Chillingworth enters the community, when they rejoice that he, the old physician, can treat the ailing young minister Dimmesdale, who initially, and secretly, rejects this. Despite Dimmesdale's resistance, however, the community successfully elevates Chillingworth and presses Dimmesdale to move in with the "leech": "There was much joy throughout the town when this greatly desirable object was attained" (123). By this time, however, some of the community sense something unsavory about Chillingworth, one of them reporting that Chillingworth had been connected with "Doctor Forman, the famous old conjurer" (125). But the community leaders, of course, are the ones who prevail.

From this allegiance of Chillingworth and the community come several other ironies. While the community thinks that the Black Man abides in the forest, he actually abides among them in the form of their honored guest and "healer," Chillingworth. And while the community believes that witchcraft is practiced somewhere in the depths of the forest, the most heinous black magic is practiced with their approval and cooperation right under their noses in Chillingworth's laboratory.

The conclusion that the reader is given to draw, then, is that Hester and Pearl are not respectively, lover and daughter of a Black Man or Satan who inhabits the forest. Rather it is the community itself which has a close relationship to the Black Man, in the person of Chillingworth, and encourages his dark arts.

Finally, in exploring the meaning of the "A," the reader arrives at Hawthorne's stated moral: "Be true! Be true! Be true! Show freely to the world, if not your worst, yet some trait whereby the worst may be inferred!" (242). The true nature of every human is both sinful and angelic, somber and joyful, selfish and loving. To "be true" means to recognize that we all wear a scarlet letter.

TOPICS FOR WRITTEN OR ORAL EXPLORATION

1. The major project for this chapter is the writing (and, if possible, staging) of a production of *The Scarlet Letter*. Remember that you must choose which scenes to stage and which dialogue to move from the novel to the stage.

2. Whether or not the play is actually performed for an audience, another part of the project is to plan the details of staging. Will there be a conventional set, or just properties that give a suggestion of the scenes? Write and/or sketch the various sets to be used. Costuming here is also of utmost importance. Will you use the somber gray and black of the Puritan stereotype or the rich colors of the English Renaissance?

3. One alternative to a full-scale production is the construction of a reading theater production, choosing key dialogue from the novel for presentation. Listen to a variety of different interpretations of Chillingworth, Dimmesdale, and Hester; have students who read answer questions from the audience about their interpretations.

4. Compose an essay on the theme of revenge in the novel.

5. Compose an essay on the theme of growth (or lack of it) through trial in the novel.

6. Compose an essay on the theme of survival in the novel.

7. After a careful reading, paying attention to the words of the Reverend Wilson and reactions of others, write an analysis of Dimmesdale's behavior in the chapter entitled "The Recognition."

8. We are never told exactly why Hester agrees to keep Chillingworth's true identity secret. Write a short essay on her possible motives for doing so and for finally revealing his identity to Dimmesdale. At least one critic has argued that she may know from the start that she is not doing Dimmesdale a favor by keeping Chillingworth's identity secret.

9. On two occasions when Hester and Chillingworth speak together, he implies that some of the fault for the adultery lies with him. Examine these scenes and discuss his and her reasons for placing some of the blame on him.

10. Carefully analyze the way in which Pearl is characterized. How would you finally describe her? Is she a demon? a brat? an active all-American child? Support your conclusions carefully.

11. Frequently in *The Scarlet Letter* we see an interplay of the active and the passive, especially as it involves Hester and Dimmesdale. Examine

the scenes in which this interplay occurs and interpret how such scenes shed light on the characters and the novel as a whole.

12. Write an essay on Chillingworth's past before he comes to the New World. In a novel as tightly structured as this one, what are we to conclude about him from these details about his past life?

13. Write an essay on Pearl as truth-seer.

14. Hester despises wearing the scarlet letter; yet when Chillingworth tells her that the town has agreed that she can take it off, she refuses. Similarly, we are told that when members of the community begin speaking to her in the street, she refuses to return the greetings and points to the scarlet letter. Her motives here are open to question. Write an essay on why she behaves as she does.

15. The narrator suggests in rich detail how a number of the characters in the first marketplace scene looked. Draw an illustration of that scene for a hypothetical edition of *The Scarlet Letter*.

16. Illustrate scenes from the novel that you think are key visual opportunities.

17. Without ever providing a definitive answer, the narrator asks why Chillingworth came to the New World in the first place; using the text as a guide, what reasons might he have had for leaving what appears to have been a stable and respectable life in the Old World?

18. The narrator never explains why Chillingworth leaves a fortune to Pearl; is this a believable action? Why or why not? Explain what possible reasons he may have had for doing this, given what we know of his character.

19. Readers continue to disagree about whether the Reverend Dimmesdale has made up for the mistakes of his life by the time he dies. Stage a classroom debate on this question, one side arguing that he has made up for his mistakes and another that he has not.

20. A similar question can be raised about Hester: does she seem to see the truth of her heart and her situation when she meets Dimmesdale in the forest, or does this come only when she returns after many years?

21. In the chapter entitled "A Flood of Sunshine," the narrator writes: "Shame, Despair, Solitude! These had been her teachers—stern and wild ones—and they had made her strong, but taught her much amiss." Write a paper analyzing these lines.

22. Especially for the time, what is shocking about Hester's proposal to Dimmesdale in the forest? Why do you suppose she is capable of making such a proposal, whereas he is not?

23. Trace the references to death and cemeteries in the novel. Construct a thesis sentence involving these references and develop a theme from them.

24. Pearl is continually referred to as a symbol in the novel. Consider what she represents. What meaning is there in the fact that she leaves America, never to return?

25. Notice that the novel opens with the scaffold scene, is divided in half by a scaffold scene, and ends with a scaffold scene. Examine these scenes and the meaning of the scaffold as a symbol in the novel.

26. Why do you suppose the narrator never reveals whether or not Dimmesdale actually had a scarlet letter on his chest?

SUGGESTED READINGS

Abel, Darrel. *The Moral Picaresque: Studies in Hawthorne's Fiction*. West Lafayette, Ind.: Purdue University Press, 1988.

Baym, Nina. *The Scarlet Letter: A Reading*. Boston: Twayne, 1986.

———. *The Shape of Hawthorne's Career*. Ithaca: Cornell University Press, 1976.

Bell, Michael Davitt. *The Development of American Romance: The Sacrifice of Relation*. Chicago: University of Chicago Press, 1980.

———. *Hawthorne and the Historical Romance of New England*. Princeton: Princeton University Press, 1971.

Bercovitch, Sacvan. *The Office of the Scarlet Letter*. Baltimore: Johns Hopkins University Press, 1991.

Brodhead, Richard H. *Hawthorne, Melville, and the Novel*. Chicago: University of Chicago Press, 1982.

———. *The School of Hawthorne*. New York: Oxford University Press, 1986.

Coale, Samuel Chase. *In Hawthorne's Shadow*. Lexington: University of Kentucky Press, 1985.

Colacurcio, Michael. *The Province of Piety*. Cambridge, Mass.: Harvard University Press, 1984.

Crews, Frederick. *The Sins of the Fathers: Hawthorne's Psychological Themes*. New York: Oxford University Press, 1966.

Desalvo, Louise. *Nathaniel Hawthorne*. Atlantic Highlands, N.J.: Humanities Press International, 1987.

Dryden, Edgar. *Nathaniel Hawthorne: The Poetics of Enchantment*. Ithaca: Cornell University Press, 1977.

Erlich, Gloria. *Family Themes and Hawthorne's Fiction*. New Brunswick, N.J.: Rutgers University Press, 1984.

Fogle, Richard H. *Hawthorne's Fiction: The Light and the Dark*. Norman: University of Oklahoma Press, 1952; rev. ed., 1964.

Hall, Lawrence. *Hawthorne: Critic of Society.* New Haven: Yale University Press, 1944.

Jehlen, Myra. "Introduction: Beyond Transcendence." In *Ideology and Classic American Literature.* Ed. Sacvan Bercovitch and Myra Jehlen. Cambridge, England: Cambridge University Press, 1986: 1-- 18.

Johnson, Claudia. *The Productive Tension of Hawthorne's Art.* Tuscaloosa: University of Alabama Press, 1981.

Kaul, A. N., ed. *Hawthorne: A Collection of Critical Essays.* Englewood Cliffs, N.J.: Prentice-Hall, 1966.

Lawrence, D. H. *Studies in Classic American Literature.* New York: Thomas Seltzer, 1923.

Levin, Harry. *The Power of Blackness: Hawthorne, Poe, Melville.* New York: Knopf, 1958.

Male, Roy R. *Hawthorne's Tragic Vision.* Austin: University of Texas Press, 1957.

Martin, Terence. *Nathaniel Hawthorne.* Twayne's United States Authors Series, 75. New York: Twayne, 1965.

Matthiessen, F. O. *American Renaissance.* New York: Oxford University Press, 1941.

McPherson, Hugo. *Hawthorne as Myth-Maker: A Study in Imagination.* Toronto: University of Toronto Press, 1969.

McWilliams, John P. *Hawthorne, Melville, and the American Character.* Cambridge, England: Cambridge University Press, 1984.

Pearce, Roy Harvey, ed. *Hawthorne Centenary Essays.* Columbus: Ohio State University Press, 1964.

Person, Leland. *Aesthetic Headaches.* Athens: University of Georgia Press, 1988.

2

The Scarlet Letter and the Puritans

CHRONOLOGY

1565	Spanish settlement at St. Augustine, Florida
1588	John Winthrop born
1590	William Bradford, leader of Pilgrims, born in Yorkshire
1591	Organization of first Puritan church in England
	Anne Hutchinson born in England
1598	Edward Johnson, Puritan settler and historian, born
1603	Roger Williams born in London
1607	English settlement at Jamestown, Virginia
1608	Separatist Puritans reach Holland
1612	Poet Anne Bradstreet born in England
1620	Pilgrims (Puritan Separatists) settle Plymouth, Massachusetts
1624	Dutch settle New York
1625/26	Rev. William Blackston settles in Boston
1630	Puritans settle Massachusetts Bay with John Endicott as governor and CEO and John Wilson as minister of Boston church
	Among the first settlers are Anne and Simon Bradstreet, John Winthrop, John Wilson, Richard Bellingham
1631	Roger Williams arrives in Massachusetts Bay

1632	Michael Wigglesworth, Puritan minister and poet, born
1633	John Cotton moves to Massachusetts Bay
1634	Anne and William Hutchinson move to Massachusetts Bay
1635	Roger Williams banished from Massachusetts Bay for insisting on religious toleration; founds Providence, Rhode Island
	Henry Vane, eventually a governor, arrives in Massachusetts
1636	Founding of Harvard College
1636–38	Antinomian (Anne Hutchinson) controversy
1637	Henry Vane, former governor and Hutchinson supporter, returns to England; John Winthrop becomes governor, a post he holds for over ten years
1638	Hutchinson banished, moves to Rhode Island
1641	Massachusetts Body of Laws and Liberties, uniting church and state by making Old Testament part of civil code
1643	Hutchinson killed in Indian raid in New York
	By this time 20,000 people had immigrated to Boston area, making Boston the largest town in America
1644	Massachusetts Bay changed from trading company to commonwealth
	Roger Williams publishes his version of his disagreement with the Puritans
1642–48	Civil War in England; Puritans win
1649	John Winthrop dies
1651	First of obnoxious Navigation Acts hindering Massachusetts trade
1652	Samuel Sewall born in England
1653	Michael Wigglesworth begins his diary
1656	Quakers begin moving to New England
1659	William Bradford dies
	Two Quakers hanged on Boston Common
1660	Mary Dyer, Quaker, hanged on Boston Common
	King (Charles II) returned to English throne
	Rev. Hugh Peters, former Hutchinson enemy, executed
1661	William Leddra, Quaker, hanged on Boston Common
	King Charles orders execution of Quakers stopped
1662	On legislator William Hathorne's orders Ann Coleman, Quaker woman, is stripped and whipped through streets of Salem
	Henry Vane, former governor and Hutchinson supporter, executed
	Half-way covenant, which says children of "saints" are automatically church members
	Publication of best-selling poem, *The Day of Doom,* by Michael Wigglesworth

1663	Stamp Act passed
1665	After persecution, Baptists are allowed a church in Boston—the first church that is not Puritan
1672	Edward Johnson dies
	Anne Bradstreet dies
1673	Duty Act passed
	Samuel Sewall, businessman and legislator, begins his diary
1675	King Philip's War
1683	Roger Williams dies
1684	Crown revokes Massachusetts Bay's charter
1685	James II comes to the throne of England
	Colonies given governors appointed by king instead of elected
1686	Royal governor forces Massachusetts to accept an Anglican church, King's Chapel
1688	William and Mary come to the throne of England
1689	Bostonians overthrow Governor Andre (appointed by James)
1692	New charter, forcing separation of church and state and lessening power of the Puritan clergy
	Witch trials begin in Salem, Mass.; John Hathorne of Salem an active interrogator from the start
1697	Samuel Sewall publicly apologizes for his part in the witch trials, as do some others on the court
1711	General Court reverses bills of attainder against all condemned witches
1764	Governor Thomas Hutchinson's history of New England

CHARACTERS

William Bradford, leader and historian of Plymouth Plantation

William Blackston, first English resident of Boston. See *The Scarlet Letter*

John Endicott, first governor. See Hawthorne's "Endicott and the Red Cross"

John Winthrop, governor. See *The Scarlet Letter*

Richard Bellingham, governor. See *The Scarlet Letter*

John Wilson, first minister of Boston Church. See *The Scarlet Letter*

John Cotton, second pastor, Boston Church

Simon Bradstreet, governor

Anne Bradstreet, distinguished American poet

Thomas Dudley, deputy-governor

Hugh Peters, minister

Roger Williams, minister. See Hawthorne's "Endicott and the Red Cross"

Edward Johnson, merchant and historian

William Hathorne, legislator from Salem, involved in Quaker persecutions

Henry Vane, governor, supporter of Anne Hutchinson

Michael Wigglesworth, poet, Harvard professor, and minister at Malden, Mass.

Anne Hutchinson, banished from Massachusetts Bay for religious reasons

Mary Dyer, Quaker executed by the Puritans

Edmund Andros, royal governor deposed by coup

Increase Mather, Cotton Mather's father; opposed witch trials

Cotton Mather, second generation Puritan, minister, scholar, and historian; supporter of witch trials

John Hathorne, Salem legislator involved in witch trials

Samuel Sewall, businessman, diarist, and judge in witch trials

THE DEVELOPMENT OF PURITANISM

Having done a literary analysis of *The Scarlet Letter*, the reader who wants to master the novel should then look at the Puritan world in which it is set. The study of the Puritans, especially their bizarre system of crime and punishment, is essential for a full understanding of *The Scarlet Letter*. In the first place, of course, Puritan New England, Boston specifically, is the setting for Hawthorne's story, and the Puritan system of belief, which horrified and fascinated him, is intrinsic to the novel's meaning. Subjects relevant to Puritanism that arise in the course of *The Scarlet Letter* include:

• government by elderly men
• the wilderness
• human character, especially sexuality
• tolerance and freedom
• witchcraft
• Anne Hutchinson
• the Quakers
• view of women
• ornamentation and art

Each of these issues will be explored in the following chapters.

In his novel, Hawthorne, in effect, rewrites the history of the

Puritan colony in Massachusetts Bay. Of particular importance as a portrait of the community leadership are the initial chapters, "The Prison Door," "The Market Place," and "The Recognition"; the middle chapters, "The Governor's Hall" and "The Elf-Child and the Minister"; and the final chapters, "The New England Holiday" and "The Procession." In each of these chapters we see evidence of the old age that dominates the town and its accompanying sternness and narrowness in direct conflict with the nature, creativity, and passion associated with youth.

Even the preface to *The Scarlet Letter*, although set in the nineteenth century, is steeped in seventeenth-century Puritanism through its references to Hawthorne's Puritan ancestors, who were instrumental in torturing Quakers and hanging witches and now speak across time about their shameful descendent, who is no more than an "idler," writing books. Still, they are ancestors with whom, he says, he shares many traits. There is also the setting of "The Custom-House," Salem, which lives in the memory of U.S. citizens as the place where the infamous witch trials were held by Puritans.

Hawthorne used the Puritan past as a setting or subject in many other works of fiction, each of which sheds light on the complex use of Puritanism in *The Scarlet Letter*. The most prominent of these tales and sketches are:

- "Main Street," sketches of Salem throughout history, including a scene in which a Quaker woman is beaten
- "Endicott and the Red Cross," about Puritan cruelty; includes citizens with their ears cut off and cleft sticks on their tongues as well as one who wears an "A" for adultery
- "Young Goodman Brown," about a newlywed Puritan's meeting with witches
- "The Gentle Boy," about Puritans hanging Quakers
- *The House of the Seven Gables*, about the effects in nineteenth-century Salem of a curse uttered by a seventeenth-century witch who was hanged

BACKGROUND AND HISTORY

Before we can proceed to an analysis of the place of the Puritans in *The Scarlet Letter*, some fundamental definitions need to be established. Who exactly were the Puritans? When did their religion develop? What relationship do they have with other religious sects? Why did they come to the New World? What course did Puritanism follow in the New World? Why did Puritanism disappear?

> It was an age in which the human intellect, newly emancipated, had taken a more active and wider range than for centuries before.
> *The Scarlet Letter*, 158

To understand the origins of Puritanism and its position with regard to other Christian religions, let us look at a simple diagram:

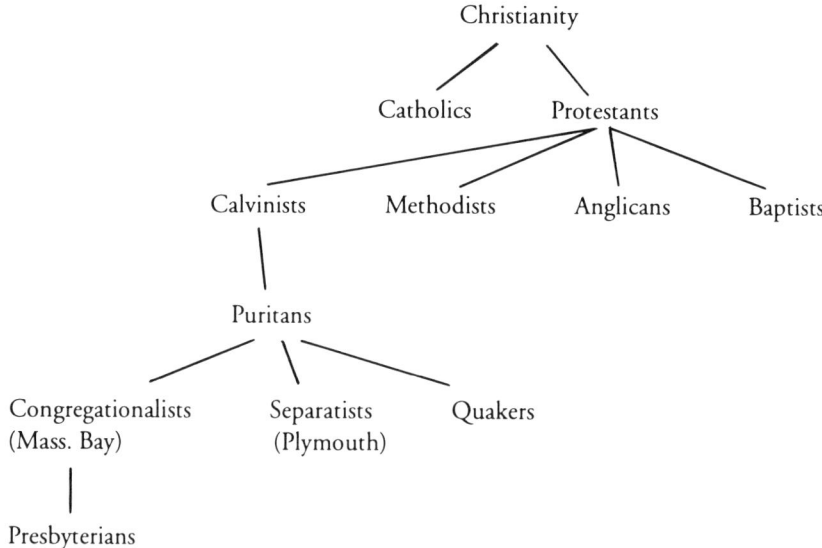

We see from this that the Puritans are classified in the larger sense as Christian, in a narrower sense as Protestant, and in a still more specialized sense as Calvinist. They regarded Catholics as their chief opponents, but also believed that high church Anglicans, Methodists (who did not come to the fore until late in the seventeenth century), Baptists, and Quakers were wrong in their religious beliefs. Their opposition to these last sects was so vehement that they persecuted them and refused to allow the establishment of their churches in Massachusetts Bay until 1665, when at last a Baptist congregation was tolerated—a full thirty-five years after the

Puritans came to Boston. Presbyterians and Congregationalists are likely the chief descendents of the old Puritanism, which had dissipated by the middle of the eighteenth century.

> Men of the sword had overthrown nobles and kings.
> *The Scarlet Letter*, 159

How did Puritanism develop? To answer this we need to look back many years before Puritanism appeared, to the fifteenth century, when most nations had *official* religions and tolerated no others. In the late Middle Ages, the Roman Catholic Church dominated all of western and northern Europe and most of the Christian world, seeing itself as the "one universal church." It was a tight but increasingly corrupt and vulnerable world, centered in Rome under the leadership of the pope, filled with conflict and seething with social, economic, and newly discovered national unrest.

Then, in 1517, a German monk, Martin Luther, nailed to the church door at the University of Wittenberg a list of ninety-five questions, or challenges—the famous ninety-five theses—which he intended only as subjects for debate (in accordance with the custom of the time). But so ripe were the times and so widespread the discontent that within months all of Europe was inflamed; soon it was in arms. Central to Luther's challenges (and to the entire Protestant Reformation) was the idea that every man was his own priest—a belief that, if followed to its logical conclusion, would render unnecessary priests, bishops, the papacy, and the entire church hierarchy. (Priests, in fact, according to Luther, should be spiritual guides to help show the way, not formal leaders or intercessors.) Key also for Luther was the idea that men should be, or are, justified before God by an inner faith—"justification by faith"—not by good works or any outward show of virtue.

At about the same time in Zurich, Switzerland, a reformer named Zwingli preached much the same reforms for the same reasons, until he was killed in one of the earliest bloody battles fought between Protestants and Catholics. In Geneva a third reformer, John Calvin, preached another form of Protestantism, which swept through Germany, France, and the Lowlands, and across the Channel to England.

In England the Reformation, fused with all these elements, took a very peculiar turn. The English king, Henry VIII (who in fact privately retained his basic Catholic beliefs to the very last), after winning the accolade "Defender of the Faith" from the pope for his vigorous attack on Luther, formally broke with the Roman Catholic Church in 1534 over the matter of divorce and thus formed the Church of England (or Anglican Church) with himself as head.

The growth of the many Christian denominations known as Protestants derives from this rebellion by Luther, through one route or another. These denominations include various "Reformed" churches; Presbyterians; Methodists; Baptists; Lutherans; Episcopalians; and others. The Puritans, Baptists, Methodists, and Quakers were all classified as "dissidents," rebels against the main Catholic, Lutheran, or Anglican churches.

Out of this mix of elements came the Puritans—one of a number of groups preaching reformation and opposing certain practices and beliefs of the Church of England. With the English government—and the English church—feeling harassed on all sides, and particularly sensing real danger from its chief rivals, France and Spain, and with the Puritans feeling seriously limited and threatened in a hostile environment, the situation became intense. English playwrights ridiculed, and the English government forcibly attempted to smother, the newly formed and strangely dressed sect. The Puritans, striving to be "pure" and pristine in their daily lives, became true social oddities.

In 1581 the first Congregational (Puritan) Church was established at Southwark in London, England. One branch of Puritans was called Separatists because they wanted to pull away from the established Anglican Church to form a separate church. Another branch of Puritans was comprised of non-Separatists who wanted to reform the Protestant church, not form a new sect.

Members of these two branches of Puritans and other dissident religious groups who rebelled against the official state religion were largely treated as outlaws in England, persecutions being particularly severe during the reign of the Stuart kings, James I and Charles I, from 1603 to 1642. To practice a religion other than Anglicanism was to defy the king of England, who was the official head of the church. The Puritans were not allowed to congregate freely as separate congregations; their ministers were often prohibited from preaching and imprisoned for disobedience; and members were sometimes subject to arrest if they were found even to be reading scripture; like the Catholics, the Anglican clergy believed that priests should be the official presenters and interpreters of scripture. (Another revolutionary act of Martin Luther had been to translate the Bible into vernacular German so that ordinary people could read it.) In 1608 some of the Separatist Puritans began moving to Holland, where they were not subject to persecution.

The Puritan Move to the New World

In 1620 the English monarchy, as eager to be rid of the Puritans as the Puritans were to be rid of the king, granted a group of Puritan Separatists a charter to make a settlement in the English colonies in the area that is now New Jersey and New York. There were economic incentives for the Puritan move to the New World, including economic upheaval in Europe and the prospect of making a profit in America, but their chief incentive was religious: they would be able to practice their religion without impediment. In late fall some 103 settlers, most of them Englishmen who had lived in the Netherlands for a time, sailed on the *Mayflower* and arrived in what is now Plymouth, Massachusetts, although they had been heading for an area a good deal south of New England. Unlike an earlier, purely commercial English venture in Virginia, the Plymouth Plantation group did survive, but by the end of the first year, the harsh conditions had taken the lives of over half of the people.

In 1628, provoked by King Charles I's increasing intolerance, a group of non-Separatist Puritans formed a business corporation, the Massachusetts Bay Company, for settlement of the New World. Their group arrived on Cape Ann, just north and east of what is now Boston, where the Reverend William Blackston (mentioned in *The Scarlet Letter*) had already settled in 1625 or 1626. Unlike the settlements financed by the Spanish crown in the New World, which were governed from Spain, the English colonies were largely run by the corporations that financed them. Most of these companies were located in Europe, but the founders of the Massachusetts Bay Company relocated the entire corporation from London to Massachusetts, giving it greater independence from the English crown. By 1630, 1,000 English settlers, largely Puritan and non-Separatist, had immigrated to the Boston area. By 1643 there were some 20,000 immigrants in the general area of the Massachusetts Bay Colony, making Boston the largest and most prosperous town in America.

The Struggle Against England

> After the kings of Great Britain had assumed the right of appointing
> the colonial governors, the measures of the latter seldom met with
> the ready and general approbation, which had been paid to those of
> their predecessors, under the original charters. . . . The annals of Mas-
> sachusetts Bay will inform us, that of six governors, in the space of
> about forty years from the surrender of the old charter, under James
> II., two were imprisoned by popular insurrection.
>
> Nathaniel Hawthorne, "My Kinsman, Major Molineux"

In 1642 the monarchy had been deposed by a Puritan commoner
named Oliver Cromwell who ruled England until his death in
1658. During this time, the English colonies in America governed
themselves without serious interference from the mother country.
By 1660 a king, Charles II, was restored to the English throne, and
the new royal government became acutely aware that the American
colonies, which had been allowed to develop pretty much on their
own, could be profitable to the mother country. In 1662, to protect
English trade, Parliament passed the Navigation Acts, which prevented the colonies from trading freely with Europe. These so-
called "abominable" acts remained in force until 1696. In 1685
King James II abolished self-government in the northern colonies,
appointing royal governors in place of the governors elected by
the people. Through his royal governors, the king had veto power
over the colonial legislature. He also enforced the Navigation Acts.
When James was deposed and William and Mary came to the
throne in 1688, the Bostonians in Massachusetts Bay arrested the
royal governor, Edmund Andros, and sent him packing back to
England. (See Hawthorne's short story based on this incident, "My
Kinsman, Major Molineux.")

For close to eighty years the Puritans held absolute power in
New England. They contributed positively to the eventual breaking
away from English control, the development of education, and the
development of sea trade, urban business, farming, and, eventually, manufacturing. Our present political system derives from the
legislative model they originally set up, which had fixed dates for
regular elections by the voting populace, and which disregarded
inherited status. Despite this, Puritan government was scarcely
what could be called democratic: only males who owned land
could vote; only members of the established church could vote. In

addition, religious doctrine became civil law, and the rule of the leaders was absolute. While the whole of New England was largely Puritan, it is those who settled in and around Boston who are credited with such great influence on American culture and of whom Nathaniel Hawthorne wrote.

The Demise of Puritanism

> And what hast thou to do with these iron men, and their opinions?
> They have kept thy better part in bondage too long already.
> *The Scarlet Letter*, 188

Toward the close of the seventeenth century, Puritanism, as it had been defined during the early days of settlement, began coming apart for a number of reasons. In 1692 a new charter, forced on Massachusetts Bay by the crown, lessened the political power of the clergy. Common citizens, previously accustomed merely to follow, began to see the clergy as overeducated, elitist, and out of touch with reality, as well as increasingly tyrannical. Moreover, the fierce cruelty and intolerance of the Puritan leaders in America caused them to lose the support of Puritans in England. At the same time, with New England merchants prospering from trade, congregations began to be more concerned with worldly matters than with the state of the soul and heaven and hell, thus lessening Puritanism's spiritual sway. Those who moved west, away from the New England Puritan community, enjoyed freedom from Puritan oppression, so converts were few and Puritanism remained confined to New England.

"A" IS FOR AUTHORITY

The conflict between youth and age, passion and authority, creativity and suppression, which has been discussed in the literary analysis of the novel, was developed by the author of *The Scarlet Letter* in his careful depiction of the Puritan leaders. The New World these settlers came to was an untainted place, untouched by the age-old wrongs of Old World Europe—"virgin soil," the author writes—a place where there could have been a truly new beginning—"a utopia." Instead, he notes, the community's leaders have brought much of the worst of the Old World's wrongs with them, symbolized by that ancient, ugly building—the prison. Massachusetts Bay allows religious persecution of Quakers and the "sainted Anne Hutchinson" and her followers, cruelty to the native Indians, barbaric punishments, and slavery (note Governor Bellingham's bond servant); its caste system allows those in high office the ornate dress and comfortable lifestyle that are forbidden the lower classes. The village of Boston, according to the author, "seemed never to have known a youthful era" (55). So even though the colony is only about fifteen years old, it has the aspect, as Hawthorne describes it, of the oldest town in the world. Note the descriptive words used in just the first two paragraphs: bearded men, sad-colored garments, gray hats, heavily timbered, iron spikes, sepulchres, old, weather-stains, age, darker, gloomy, rust, ponderous, iron-work, antique, crime, ugly, black flower, condemned, doom.

The leaders themselves are ancient men—authoritarian, stern, grim, hypocritical, overly intellectual, and unnecessarily intrusive in the minutest details of the lives of even the least influential members of the community. Old age has become the new aristocracy:

> In that old day, the English settler on these rude shores—having left kind, nobles, and all degrees of awful rank behind, while still the faculty and necessity of reverence were strong in him—bestowed it on the white hair and venerable brow of age . . . on endowments of that grave and weighty order which gives the idea of permanence and comes under the general definition of respectability. (222)

The important things to note are, first, that the Puritan government and Puritan religion were virtually inseparable, the clergy exercising tremendous political power as the chief advisors to the magistrates. The narrator describes them as "a people amongst whom religion and law were almost identical, and in whose character both were . . . thoroughly interfused" (57–58). Second, both magistrates and ministers held absolute authority. Of the group of men who sit above Hester on the balcony as she stands on the scaffold, the narrator notes that "the forms of authority were felt to possess the sacredness of Divine institutions" (70). At this moment, old Governor Bellingham speaks "in an authoritative voice" to force the reluctant young Dimmesdale to plead with Hester (72). The heavy hand of authority can be seen in the fact that the highest officials in the land—the governor, several legislators and judges in addition to all the town's ministers—take an interest in the birth of her child. Hester must also get permission from these same people to live just outside the town; and even then she finds that one of the most powerful men in New England is planning to see that her child is taken from her. When she visits the governor's hall to plead that the child not be taken from her, Bellingham speaks of himself and old Reverend Wilson as "we, that are of authority and influence" (110). The children are disciplined strictly by the authoritative parent, often being whipped even when they have done nothing wrong—"as a wholesome regimen for the growth and promotion of all childish virtues" (93) and just because, as the Bible says, if you spare the rod, you'll spoil the child. In the same spirit, the old men of the community treat the ordinary citizens as if they were children, meddling in their private lives, inflicting humiliating and cruel corporal punishments, and even prying into their thoughts.

These traits of intractable and severe old age bring the leaders of the community into direct conflict with Hester and Pearl and cause them to stamp out everything youthful, creative, and passionate.

THE PURITAN AS REBEL

Hawthorne's portrait of the Puritan leaders is consistent with the transformation that Puritanism actually underwent in history. The course of Puritanism can be compared to the stereotypical transformation that occurs so often in the lives of fractious individuals who, rebellious against authority in youth, gradually become staid, strict, and authoritarian in old age. For example, Protestants were initially the Christian *protest-ants* against the authority of the established Roman Catholic Church; and the sect called the Puritans were, when they first appeared, among the most radical and the most courageous of those in protest. Like many radicals, they fiercely defied authority—in this case both established Protestant and Catholic churches. Church officials, whether priests or ministers, were, in the beginning at least, believed to be no holier than ordinary people: "Every man his own priest" was, in effect, the battle cry of the Protestant Reformation. Therefore, they believed, it was necessary that every individual, not just priests, be allowed to read and interpret scripture. Similarly, they refused to recognize the sacredness of many church practices: they scorned adornments in church and holy statuary as deceptive idols that had no place in the sanctuary; they banished instrumental music; and they eliminated attendant rites such as mass and confession.

In their defiance of the authority of the state-supported church in England, Puritans suffered imprisonment and even death, like many other rebels throughout the ages. Like many others, too, they became what they had once condemned.

OLD WORLD CIVILIZATION AND NEW WORLD WILDERNESS IN *THE SCARLET LETTER*

> Here, on this wild outskirt of the earth, I shall pitch my tent.
>
> *The Scarlet Letter*, 80

Ironically, these Puritans, who were rebels in the old civilization, attempted to enforce that same civilization on the pristine new world to which they fled. Nature and the wilderness, which represented the dark evil in human life, became the transplanted Puritan's enemy, and *The Scarlet Letter* is in large measure the story of the Puritans' tragic struggle against nature. In a real sense, the novel's wilderness setting makes it one of our early "westerns." Outlaws (the pirates, for example) frequent the town. Indians live all around the town. And there is the ever-present dark forest out of which the Puritans have carved something like a frontier town. It is a place where Chillingworth and others, like the characters who fled to the American West, could possibly lose their old identities and take up new ones. So Chillingworth leaves behind his old identity as Mr. Prynne, Hester's husband and a prominent European scholar, and becomes Roger Chillingworth, who just appears in town from out of nowhere without a past.

The wilderness in the New World is synonymous with nature in the extreme, untouched by civilizing forms and institutions such as established churches and governments, creeds and laws, as Europe knew them. The wilderness of the New World has both literal and symbolic meaning critical to an understanding of the novel. Wild, untamed nature surrounds and permeates the little settlement of Boston in which Hester and Dimmesdale live, and untamed nature as a symbol of a side of human character that the Puritans fear and reject resides within.

The Physical Reality of the American Wilderness

Consider first the physical reality of the wilderness as Hawthorne portrayed it in *The Scarlet Letter*. Only a few years before the action of the novel the Boston community had been carved from total wilderness, as Hawthorne describes it in "Main Street." Hawthorne speculates in his short story that a Puritan arriving in Massachusetts for the first time would find it hard to believe that a town could ever grow from this wilderness:

Can it be that the thronged street of a city will ever pass into this twilight solitude,—over those soft heaps of the decaying tree-trunks,—and through the
swampy places, green with water-moss,—and penetrate that hopeless entangle-
ment of great trees, which have been uprooted and tossed together by a whirl-
wind! It has been a wilderness from the creation. Must it not be a wilderness for
ever?

In *The Scarlet Letter* he writes of the New World as a "forestland, still so uncongenial to every other pilgrim and wanderer" (84). The harshness of the surrounding area outside the town itself meant that the punishment of banishment was often a death sen-tence—survival was psychologically and physically impossible. The Puritans that Edward Johnson and William Bradford write about left an old and well-established civilization behind them when they set foot in Massachusetts. Hester feels this loss of a civilized home as well: "the village of rural England, where happy infancy and stainless maidenhood seemed yet to be in her mother's keeping" (84). When the Puritans first arrived, they had almost none of the material comforts of civilization: most had no shelters at all, no furniture, no church buildings, no roads or paths, no domestic animals, no familiar vegetation in this place largely untouched by European society. As historian and early settler Johnson describes it, they had to struggle with a state of nature so wild that they had difficulty even walking through the terrain. At times, Bradford re-ports, it appeared that the wilderness would swallow them up. Even at the time of the story, probably between 1640 and 1645, emigrants from England feel, as Chillingworth does, that the New World settlement is a "wild outskirt of the earth."

The Encircling Wilderness in *The Scarlet Letter*

By the time Hester's story takes place, some fifteen to twenty years after the first settlers arrived in the Massachusetts Bay Colony, the Puritans have cleared the wilderness away to make several towns, among them Boston and Salem, the home of Hawthorne's ancestors. The setting may be the town, but the reader is always made aware of the encircling wilderness in many ways. From the first we see that Hester has the option of leaving the community and living with the Indians in the wilderness, where she will be out of reach of Puritan punishment and humiliation: "having also the passes of the dark, inscrutable forest open to her, where the wildness of her nature might assimilate itself with a people whose customs and life were alien from the law that had condemned her" (83). That she resists the temptation to flee into the heart of the wilderness seems indicative of her determination not to give in to the wildness within herself. So instead she and Pearl are banished from the heart of the small village to a hut on *the edge* of the wilderness to signify that Hester has broken a law of civilization and is constantly in danger of becoming wild and one with the wilderness.

Characters Who Belong to the Wilderness

Under these circumstances, Pearl, who "could not be made amenable to rules" (93), thus grows up being more at home in the forest than in the town, where she and her mother are both considered to be freaks. Like the wilderness, she is uncontrollable.

The reader is reminded of the threatening presence of the frontier when occasionally Indians, those inhabitants of the wilderness, visit the town, as they do on the day Hester is made to stand on the scaffold. On this same day, Chillingworth emerges on the scene from the wilderness where he has lived with Indians. In the words of a townsman who speaks to Chillingworth on this occasion, we see a contrast between what was regarded as the lawless nature of the wilderness and the harsh and oppressive rules of civilization. The man assumes that Chillingworth, having been so long in the forest, will be reassured to know that in this civilized community harsh punishments are meted out for breaking the law:

"Truly, friend; and methinks it must gladden your heart, after your troubles and sojourn in the wilderness," said the townsman, "to find yourself, at length, in a land where iniquity is searched out, and punished in the sight of rulers and people; as here in our godly New England."

Chillingworth, the old alchemist, brings some of that wilderness with him into town, as he gathers noxious weeds to make medicines the way the Indians have taught him to. We see too that while the Indians in the frontier surrounding the town teach something of their wild culture to Chillingworth, another Puritan, the Reverend John Eliot, attempts to subdue their wildness by teaching them about the Christian religion.

Nature and Lawlessness

In addition to its existence as a physical and spiritual symbol, the wilderness assumes importance in the novel as the setting for Hester's private confrontation with Dimmesdale, who meets her on the way back from his visit with the missionary to the Indians, the Reverend Eliot. Before the meeting, Hester and Pearl follow a path that leads them out of Boston into deep wilderness: the path "straggled onward into the mystery of the primeval forest . . . black and dense on either side," so dense in fact that they can scarcely see the sky (175). When Dimmesdale appears, the three of them leave the path and glide "back into the shadow of the woods" (181). The implications of their meeting in the wilderness are numerous, but the chief one is perhaps the most obvious: that here they will be hidden and can say and do things that the Puritans would call lawless.

Hester's first suggestion to Dimmesdale at this meeting is that the three of them escape into the wilderness:

Does the universe lie within the compass of yonder town, which only a little time ago was but a leaf-strewn desert, as lonely as this around us? Whither leads yonder forest track? Backwards to the settlement, thou sayest! Yes; but onward, too! Deeper it goes, and deeper, into the wilderness, less plainly to be seen at every step! until, some few miles hence, the yellow leaves will show no vestige of the white man's tread. There thou art free! So brief a journey would bring thee from a world where thou hast been most wretched, to one where thou mayest still be happy! Is there not shade enough in all this boundless forest to hide thy heart from the gaze of Roger Chillingworth?

The forest inspires her to think that they can be free of both the Puritans and their moral code. She is suggesting the unthinkable: that they live together outside the bonds of matrimony.

The Wilderness as the Devil's Domain

The wilderness, however, is not just a secret meeting place for lovers, where they can dream of freedom from bondage; it is seen by the Puritans as the home of Satan and the meeting place of his disciples, the witches. When old Mistress Hibbins talks of the forest, it becomes synonymous with witches and Satan, who is called the Black Man. When she invites Hester to join with the witches, she makes this identification in saying, "There will be a merry company in the forest; and I well-nigh promised the Black Man that comely Hester Prynne should make one" (116). She makes the same connection in telling Dimmesdale when he returns from meeting Hester: "So, reverend Sir, you have made a visit into the forest," the place where, she assumes, he will eventually receive "a fair reception from yonder potentate," meaning the devil (208). And Pearl repeats the folk wisdom that connects the devil with the wilderness when she talks to her mother, who is waiting for Dimmesdale to appear on the path: she asks Hester to tell her a story of the Black Man—"how he haunts this forest" (177). Pearl also tells her mother that she heard an old woman of the town say that Hester meets the Black Man "here in the dark wood" (177).

The Wilderness as Symbolic

Obviously, the wilderness is more than an actual place; the narrator clearly invites the reader to view it as symbolic and pervasive. Even as Hester waits for Dimmesdale before the forest scene, the narrator says that the black and dense forest "imaged not amiss the moral wilderness in which she had so long been wandering" (175). Throughout *The Scarlet Letter*, the various references to the wilderness imbue it with distinct and consistent characteristics. It is a place of loneliness, terror, the unknown, rebellion, palpable evil, mystery, lawlessness, unbridled joy, pleasure, emotion, and sexuality. Here people like Dimmesdale and Hester can give way at least momentarily to the wilderness within themselves. Given these characteristics, it is appropriate that the evil man, Chillingworth, should emerge from the forest; that Hester, who has broken a divine law, should live on the edge of the wilderness; and that her child, who seems to know no bounds and is a child of nature, should feel so at home there.

The Puritans Battle the Wilderness

The Puritan response to the wilderness is actually at the heart of the tragedy of *The Scarlet Letter*. It is he.e that they have seen their future and their past, their strengths and their overwhelming weaknesses. They have not only carved a small civilized community out of the wilderness; they have been compelled to combat or convert all the wilderness and all it represents to them—persecuting those they see as witches, slaughtering the Indians or converting them, suppressing natural joys and pleasures, negating all passion and mirth. The Puritans pretend that their own civilization has not and should not have any of the elements of the wilderness in it. They are, in fact, the enemies of nature and pretend to embody everything that is the opposite of the wilderness and nature. To the author of *The Scarlet Letter*, however, this is a mistake and a delusion. A perfect example of this is Dimmesdale, a man who adopts the mantle of sainthood instead of admitting that he is a human being with all the characteristics of the wilderness as part of his human nature. The Puritans attempted to impose their civilization on all of nature, and it was done with a certain amount of violence. Instead of acknowledging the full range of their human nature, they stressed society and civilization to an exaggerated degree. All that they embrace is part of civilization: the church, religious education, intellect rather than emotion, rigid forms and rules rather than freedom. Old age, associated with civilization, rather than the youth of nature, rules in this Puritan society in *The Scarlet Letter*. Note, for example, that they have already built a prison, which the narrator labels "the black flower of civilized society" (57). All these characteristics of a civilization untaught by nature and supremely rigid in construction can be summed up in the character of the Reverend Wilson: "the eldest clergyman of Boston, a great scholar like most of his contemporaries in the profession," whose kind and genial spirit "had been less carefully developed than his intellectual gifts" (71). Of the Reverend Wilson the narrator writes: "He looked like the darkly engraved portraits which we see prefixed to old volumes of sermons; and had no more right than one of those portraits would have, to step forth, as he now did, and meddle with a question of human guilt, passion and anguish" (71).

At the same time, however, despite their pretense that as a community and as individuals they have conquered and are free of the wildness of nature and all the unchained passion and mystery it represents, the wilderness lies there always, suppressed beneath the veneer of their civilization. The licentiousness—the unchained sexuality—and destructiveness beneath the surface of the pious-appearing Dimmesdale come once more to the surface after his walk in the forest. By this time the reader already knows that in the past Dimmesdale has committed adultery with Hester, a fact he has hidden while trying successfully to cultivate an image of himself as saintly. Here the natural impulses, associated with the wilderness, come to the surface of his "civilized" character and become exaggerated, perhaps because they have for so long been suppressed: "At every step he was incited to do some strange, wild, wicked thing or other, with a sense that it would be at once in-voluntary and intentional" (205). He is tempted to say something blasphemous and terrifying to an old deacon and an old woman he meets on his way home from the forest. And when he encoun-ters a young girl who adores him, he is tempted to make an in-decent suggestion to her.

THE PURITAN REBEL TURNED CONSERVATIVE

> . . . a community which owed its origin and progress to its present state of development, not to the impulses of youth, but to the stern and tempered energies of manhood and to the sober sagacity of age . . . belonging to a period when the forms of authority were felt to possess the sacredness of divine institutions.
>
> *The Scarlet Letter*, 70

> She assumed a freedom of speculation, then common enough on the other side of the Atlantic, but which our forefathers, had they known it, would have held to be a deadlier crime than that stigmatized by the scarlet letter.
>
> *The Scarlet Letter*, 159

In conclusion, the Puritan attitude toward the wilderness and nature in the New World led them to take on the role of perse-cutors, asserting that their intention from the first was to tolerate only those who exactly agreed with them. They were, in fact, much more intolerant than the Puritans who remained in England, and were constantly having to justify their punishments to their English brethren. Some ministers in Boston even believed that religious toleration was ungodly.

Church and state in this new colony were one, so the authority of those who ruled was doubly strong, and it was comprehensive. And since the church in Massachusetts Bay was the ultimate authority in virtually all matters, the Puritan ministers had even more genuine power than the Protestant clergy whose authority they had once challenged in the Old World.

They were, as Hawthorne pictures them in reference to Hester, forever meddling in the private lives of their flock, exercising incredibly tight control over individuals, insisting that everyone conform in word and deed—even legislating how much finery someone of the lower classes could wear, outlawing the wearing of lace, and punishing those who celebrated Christmas or cursed at an animal. It was not a world of freedom that they created. It was a world of tyranny, oppression, and wrong.

TOPICS FOR WRITTEN OR ORAL EXPLORATION

1. Write a paper (or make a class presentation) on the development of any one religion in the United States. What country (primarily) did it come from? In what area of the United States did it first develop, and when? Who were its first leaders in the United States? How was it received? What effect did it have on the people already here?

2. Write a paper on *The Scarlet Letter* as a conflict of generations—the old versus the young.

3. Write an analysis of the role of the clergy in *The Scarlet Letter*.

4. The issue of separation of church and state comes before our courts consistently, with opposing sides often arguing that their position is supported by the Constitution. Write an essay or stage a debate on one such case. Do not use secondhand information about the Constitution. Quote it exactly. Some possibilities for exploration are prayer in schools, prayer at graduation, and allowing religious meetings on school property.

5. Certain religious sects today have practices that break the law: the use of illegal drugs or the use of animal sacrifice as part of the ritual, the nonpayment of taxes, and so on. Research some of these issues in newspaper files and stage a debate on whether the government should interfere in such practices. Where should the line be drawn?

6. Write a personal history of your own ancestors' move to the United States—whether it was in the seventeenth century or yesterday. In this history, compare the Puritans' motives for the move with those of your own family.

7. How is your life influenced by the situation and culture of your ancestors who first came to this country? Consider their culture, religion, and habits that may have affected you and your life.

8. A popular bumper sticker reads "Question Authority." What would a Puritan in seventeenth-century America respond to such a direction? Write an essay on the subject of authority in *The Scarlet Letter*.

9. Write an essay on the multiple authorities in "My Kinsman, Major Molineux," set in a period somewhat later than that of *The Scarlet Letter*.

10. Write an essay on your own relation to authority—whether it be people (like parents, teachers, and older friends) or institutions (like school, police, or church). Is your relationship with authority basically positive or negative?

11. Read some historical accounts of the Boston rebellion against Ed-

mund Andros and write a paper on the incident as a model for "My Kinsman, Major Molineux."

12. Try to imagine arriving on the New England coast back in 1620, carrying only the most limited provisions onto shore. Write a diary of the first day. What did you see? What frightened or confused you? What did you eat? How did you prepare your shelter? What plans did you make for the next day and the next month?

SUGGESTED READINGS

From Nathaniel Hawthorne's tales: "My Kinsman, Major Molineux," "The Grey Champion," "Endicott and the Red Cross," and "Main Street."

3

The Puritan Mind

By the sympathy of your human hearts for sin, ye shall scent out all the places—whether in church, bed-chamber, street, field or forest—where crime has been committed, and shall exist to behold the whole earth one stain of guilt, one mighty blood-spot. Far more than this! It shall be yours to penetrate, in every bosom, the deep mystery of sin, the fountain of all wicked arts, and which inexhaustibly supplies more evil impulses than human power . . . can make manifest in deeds. . . . Depending upon one another's hearts, ye had still hoped that virtue were not all a dream. Now are ye undeceived! Evil is the nature of mankind.

Nathaniel Hawthorne, "Young Goodman Brown"

THE RELIGIOUS BELIEFS

In "The Custom-House," Hawthorne's introduction to *The Scarlet Letter*, the narrator says of his Puritan ancestors, "Strong traits of their nature have intertwined themselves with mine" (21). Certainly the novel draws heavily on the Puritan view of the world, sometimes as a way of endorsing that view but often as a way of criticizing it. Especially pertinent to *The Scarlet Letter* are

• the Puritans' view of human nature
• their tendency to be self-righteous, self-deceptive, and hypocritical in light of their convictions about human nature
• a gloomy, guilty, morbid, and self-absorbed disposition

In an analysis of the novel in light of Puritanism, it will be apparent that their view of human nature is most apparent in the community's treatment of Hester; that all of the characters, Hester and Dimmesdale included, deceive themselves; and that Puritan gloom is not only officially endorsed by the elders, but is strikingly evident in the character of Dimmesdale.

Puritan View of Biblical History

The First Covenant

Before proceeding to this analysis of how Hawthorne dramatizes the Puritan mind in his characters, however, the reader should examine the fundamentals of Puritanism from which these beliefs and leanings originate. To begin with (always) there is the Garden of Eden. Puritan doctrine is rooted in a Calvinistic view of biblical history called covenant theology. According to the Puritans, the world began with a "covenant" or contract between God and Adam and Eve (humankind's representatives). God's part of the contract was to provide a paradise—the Garden of Eden—for Adam and Eve to live in, where nature was tranquil and harmonious and a reflection of the heavens. Adam and Eve's part of the contract was to give God their praise and obedience, and specifically to avoid eating fruit from the tree of knowledge of good and evil.

Humankind's Disobedience and the Fall

> . . . the outward guise of purity was but a lie . . . if truth were everywhere to be shown, a scarlet letter would blaze forth on many a bosom.
>
> *The Scarlet Letter*, 90

The most cataclysmic event of all time, in Puritan history, occurred when Adam and Eve, being tempted by the devil to break their part of the contract, disobeyed God and ate the fruit of the forbidden tree. God became so angry that his rage was all-absorbing and never-ending. From this moment on, the Puritans believed, though God encompassed all things, anger was his chief attribute. As a result of his wrath at the breaking of the first covenant, the whole world and the nature and fate of human beings radically changed. Nature would no longer reflect the heavens or

God and would no longer be good; instead, it would be cruel and discordant, the lion now lunging for the lamb's throat. Through nature God would continually punish humans with diseases and disasters. Even worse, the hearts and souls of all human beings were believed to be evil from the moment of conception, and their minds and wills were so flawed that they were forever helpless to unravel the great mysteries of God or to help themselves toward salvation. Reality—this hard reality of depraved human nature—according to the Puritans, lay hidden beneath the surface of human character. Therefore, no matter how good anyone appeared to be on the surface, no matter how kind or how pious they might act, the reality underneath was that they were capable of every sin. Because of the disobedience of Adam and Eve, which subsequently corrupted the nature of every human being, everyone, without exception, was damned to hell in the hereafter.

The Second Covenant and the Elect

The Puritans believed that this situation changed somewhat with the appearance of Jesus on earth. For God entered into a second covenant with Jesus on man's behalf by means of which a very, very few individuals would be saved from damnation. These few were called "the elect" because God had elected them to be saved. The basic nature of these few fortunate people never changed. In fact, in the Puritan view, even the elect deserved to be damned, but by God's grace they were saved despite their corrupt natures. In the strictest sense of doctrine, no one could be certain which people were elected and which were not, but gradually Puritans began to believe that there were signs of election—if a person was good, godly, and pious, and God seemed to be good to him or her, there was a strong suspicion that that person might be one of the elect. The Puritans as a whole believed themselves to be God's "Chosen People," so there was a sense that they, especially, were recipients of God's grace.

Good Deeds

Is there no reality in the penitence thus sealed and written by good works?

The Scarlet Letter, 183

Another curious thing about election is that there was almost nothing one could do to secure it. If God had not from the beginning of time elected a person, no amount of good deeds would change what God had decided. Giving to the poor, helping the sick, going to church, praying, being honest—none of these things helped one get into heaven, even though these acts were encouraged for other reasons.

The Religious Experience

There was only one thing elected persons could do to help themselves: they had to have a religious experience in order to make their election good—to make it stick. Even though those damned by God could not change their ultimate fate in the hereafter in any way, all people were encouraged by their ministers to prepare themselves for religious experiences for several reasons. First, they couldn't be *sure* that they weren't members of the elect and would need the religious experience in order to go to heaven. Second, even if they weren't members of the elect, if they had a true religious experience, God would be less angry with them in this life, and therefore would not bring as much suffering on them as he would otherwise.

Puritan Intolerance and God's Punishment of the Community

It is also important to emphasize the Puritans' belief that God punished the whole community on the slightest provocation, for example, for the misbehavior of any one of its members. If some members of the community refused to attend church, violated moral codes, or expressed false or impious beliefs (in their opinion), God might well punish the whole community with disease, famine, or other natural disasters. This explains why Puritans were so aggressive in punishing moral infractions; they wanted to show the Almighty that poor behavior was not tolerated in the community and that he need not continue to punish the whole group for the actions of one person.

THE DOCTRINE OF ORIGINAL SIN IN
THE SCARLET LETTER

The very fact that it is the pious Mr. Dimmesdale who has committed one of the worst of sins, according to the Puritans, underscores their tenet that every human being, whether pious or humanitarian, is depraved and corrupt. He himself struggles with the irony that he is considered to be a man of God, yet hides from them the fact that he is human, which is to say sinful. He pictures himself saying to them:

I, whom you behold in these black garments of the priesthood—I, who ascend the sacred desk, and turn my pale face heavenward, taking upon myself to hold communion, in your behalf, with the Most High Omniscience—I, in whose daily life you discern the sanctity of Enoch—I, whose footsteps, as you suppose, leave a gleam along my earthly track, whereby the pilgrims that shall come after me may be guided to the regions of the blest—I, who have laid the hand of baptism upon your children—I, who have breathed the parting prayer over your dying friends, to whom the Amen sounded faintly from a world which they had quitted—I, your pastor, whom you so reverence and trust, am utterly a pollution and a lie! (140)

Dimmesdale's sermons to his adoring congregation speak to the doctrine of natural depravity in a peculiar sort of way. He is trying to confess his own specific sin with Hester (without smearing himself), but his general way of putting his message makes the congregation think that they are hearing the usual message on the sinfulness of all human beings since the Fall:

More than once—nay, more than a hundred times—he had actually spoken! Spoken! But how? He had told his hearers that he was altogether vile, a viler companion of the vilest, the worst of sinners, an abomination, a thing of unimaginable iniquity; and that the only wonder was that they did not see his wretched body shrivelled up before their eyes by the burning wrath of the Almighty! (140)

As we have seen in Chapter 1, the scarlet "A" represents human nature, which Pearl sees as natural, or green, but which, by contrast, the Puritans see as seeming "to derive its scarlet hue from the flames of the infernal pit" (74). Throughout the novel, then, attitudes toward the "A" are almost identical with attitudes toward human nature itself. The sermons delivered in *The Scarlet Letter* give ample evidence of the Puritans' view of the natural depravity of human beings. The first sermon, preached by the Reverend John Wilson, which goes on "for an hour or more" while Hester is standing on the scaffold with her infant, is "a discourse on sin, in all its branches, but with continual reference to the ignominious letter" (74). Clergymen continue throughout her life to use her as a symbol of human depravity, stopping her on the street to make her the subject of impromptu sermons on sin and using her as an example of depravity when she attends church (88).

One passage in *The Scarlet Letter* speaks more strongly than any other of the universality of corruption of the human being since the Fall: the one in which Hester is able to see the scarlet letter, that is, sin of the heart, on every person she meets, even the pure virgin, the older maiden lady, the most sanctimonious minister. These revelations horrify her:

What were they? Could they be other than the insidious whispers of the bad angel, who would fain have persuaded the struggling woman, as yet only half his victim, that the outward guise of purity was but a lie, and that, if truth were everywhere to be shown, a scarlet letter would blaze forth on many a bosom besides Hester Prynne's? (90)

PURITAN SELF-RIGHTEOUSNESS IN
THE SCARLET LETTER

Despite the religious teaching that all people are basically corrupt, what we see in *The Scarlet Letter* is the tendency for everyone, but especially the Puritans, who saw themselves as God's Chosen People, to believe that they themselves are not really so bad at heart or that in some way they can overcome or cancel out their human nature. We see this in community leaders who deal with Hester's misbehavior very self-righteously, as if they are exempt from the feelings to which she and her lover gave in. There is even the assumption on their part that, because they are better than she, they have the right to take Pearl from her. Much of the community leaders' self-righteous attitude in treating her as a pariah, making her the subject of their sermons, and forcing her to wear a scarlet letter for life may come from their false assurance that they are among God's elect. But the narrator scarcely seems to think they have the wisdom and goodness to judge Hester as they do, remarking as he does on the distinguished group assembled on the balcony to observe Hester on the scaffold:

But, out of the whole human family, it would not have been easy to select the same number of wise and virtuous persons who should be less capable of sitting in judgment on an erring woman's heart, and disentangling its mesh of good and evil, than the sages of rigid aspect towards whom Hester Prynne now turned her face. (70)

HESTER'S DELUSION ABOUT GOOD WORKS AND SUFFERING

But Hester is as deluded about herself as the Puritans are about themselves. She thinks that she can redeem herself, can make up for what she is and has done, by becoming a martyr and a sister of charity. At first, she thinks that staying in Boston, where she would experience constant humiliation and shame, will eventually "purge her soul and work out another purity than that which she had lost; more saintlike, because the result of martyrdom." This the narrator calls "half a truth and half a self-delusion" (84). Her worst self-delusion, however, is in believing that the good works done by her and Dimmesdale will redeem them. While her good works help her to survive, they do not change her basic nature.

Dimmesdale, guilt-ridden though he is, is also deluded into believing that he can forever hide his true nature, pretend to be a saint, and still somehow make up for what he has done. He cultivates his piousness so carefully that the congregation "deemed the young clergyman a miracle of holiness. . . . The very ground on which he trod was sanctified" (139). Furthermore, he believes that he is really being good in not revealing that he is Pearl's father, that keeping this secret is really a great sacrifice on his part. Speaking of his own condition in the third person, he says that should good and godly persons reveal what they are really like, "no good can be achieved by them; no evil of the past be redeemed by better service. So, to their own unutterable torment, they go about among their fellow-creatures looking pure as new-fallen snow; while their hearts are all speckled and spotted with iniquity" (130).

In summary, while Hawthorne seems to agree with the Puritan view that human beings tend to be sinful and weak, he shows that individual Puritans, and especially their leaders, seem to think that they themselves are exceptions. The irony of the novel is that the Puritans have not learned compassion and brotherhood from this common curse; instead, despite their beliefs, they act as if only *other* people are weak and sinful. This is the essential message of

Hawthorne's "Young Goodman Brown," in which the young Puritan husband, seeing both bad and good in people, chooses, lovelessly, to believe the worst, and comes to see everyone as an agent of the devil, just because they are human, while he himself is the only good man.

PURITANS' GLOOMY SELF-ABSORPTION

Every aspect of Puritan thought encouraged a gloomy self-absorption: a sordid history of disobedience lay in the biblical past; a depraved nature capable of committing every sin and God's constant punishing wrath pressed the Puritan down in the present; and the prospect of everlasting hell lay in the future. Furthermore, the Puritans were taught that they had no hope of salvation, even if chosen by God, unless they had a full experience of the horror of their own hearts. In addition, they were constantly searching their souls for the reasons for their suffering in this life.

One of the best examples of Puritan gloom can be found in the person of the Reverend Michael Wigglesworth, the most famous Puritan poet of the time and a minister of some standing in the community. His intense and gloomy soul-searching and guilt are recorded in his diary. In reading the words of Wigglesworth, the student is reminded of Arthur Dimmesdale, who also was burdened with guilt and remorse. Included below are excerpts from Wigglesworth's diary while he was a teacher at Harvard College. This record of his thoughts shows the tortured frame of mind that the gloomy Puritan view of the world tended to foster.

WIGGLESWORTH AND DIMMESDALE

> He had told his hearers that he was altogether vile, a viler companion of the vilest, the worst of sinners, an abomination, a thing of unimaginable iniquity; and that the only wonder was that they did not see his wretched body shrivelled up before their eyes by the burning wrath of the Almighty! . . . He thus typified the constant introspection wherewith he tortured, but could not purify himself.
>
> *The Scarlet Letter*, 40, 41

Michael Wigglesworth, whom many have called the stereotypical Puritan, was born in England and immigrated to New England in 1638 when he was six years old. He went to Harvard College and then taught there for many years, during which time he continually worried about the morals of his students who, for example, without sober regard for their sins or respect for the Almighty, laughed on Saturday evening, shortly before the Christian Sabbath. At one time he was asked to serve as president of Harvard. (A building on the present Harvard University campus is named Wigglesworth Hall.) In 1655 he went to Malden, not far from Boston, to become the community's pastor and physician. Curiously enough, for twenty years he did no preaching, even at Malden, because of an illness that many of his friends suspected was all in his head.

History remembers Wigglesworth as a best-selling author of the religious poem *The Day of Doom*. Wigglesworth took almost a decade to put a dream he had (we might say nightmare!) into the form of a poem. *The Day of Doom*, published in 1662, graphically painted the horrors that would befall human beings on Judgment Day. In the poem, after a blinding light and a horrible scream announce that the end of the world is at hand, people go berserk, tearing their flesh and, ironically, trying to kill themselves to escape the awful scene. God subsequently divides humankind into the sheep, who will be saved, and the goats, who will be damned. These unfortunate goats are chained and dragged down to hell by monsters:

> Their pain and grief have no relief,
>   their anguish never endeth.
> There must they ly, and never dy,
>   though dying every day;

There must they dying ever ly,
  and not consume away.

The poem was immediately a best seller. By some estimates *The Day of Doom*, which was reprinted numerous times, was the most frequently read book in America for two centuries, rivalled only by the Bible and *Pilgrim's Progress*, an allegory by the English dissident John Bunyan. There were only 36,000 people in New England in 1662 when the poem was published, and by the end of the year 1,800 volumes were sold, an incredible number for the population.

The Day of Doom is, by modern standards, a strange and perhaps astonishing poem. Two famous scholars of Puritanism, Perry Miller and Thomas H. Johnson, have described it as "the embodiment of repulsive joylessness" and "a monstrous example of unrelieved horror."[1]

While *The Day of Doom* is useful as a clarification of Puritan doctrine, the diary of this exceptional poet is a window on the tortured Puritan mind. The Puritan in New England was characterized by his obsession with the state of his own soul and the souls of others. Note the appeal by Governor Bellingham and the Reverend Wilson trying to persuade Dimmesdale to get Hester to name her child's father. Bellingham says to Dimmesdale, "Good Master Dimmesdale . . . the responsibility of this woman's soul lies greatly with you" (72). The Reverend John Wilson seconds the sentiment, saying to Dimmesdale, "Speak to the woman, my brother. . . . It is of moment to her soul, and therefore, as the worshipful Governor says, momentous to thine own, in whose charge hers is" (72).

Ministers also believed that God had instructed them to be responsible for the behavior of other people and that the whole community would suffer from God's wrath if others did not behave properly or did not acknowledge their own moral weaknesses. It follows that the Puritans often concerned themselves with other people's lives in ways that we would consider nosey, or invasions of privacy, as, for example, when they try to find out the name of Pearl's father.

Almost every indulgence, every worldly pleasure, every act of mirth, and every independent thought were possible sins inviting the wrath of God; and thus halting indulgence in these things became everyone's business. It is no wonder, then, human weakness being what it is, that Puritans, including clerical leaders, gradually became more obsessed with the sins they could find in others than with the sinful tendencies of their own hearts. For one thing, of course, the sinful behavior of others is often easier to spot than one's own. Still, it is the devil and not God who tells Young Goodman Brown that, from now on, he will be more aware of the secret sins of others than of his own sin.

Michael Wigglesworth, author of *The Day of Doom*, spent his days agonizing over his own guilt, especially his pride and lust, and worrying about the moral character of his Harvard students—whom he had seen smiling on Sunday, playing music, and objecting to having to learn foreign languages. Wigglesworth's abiding interest in the immorality of his students even caused him to recognize on one occasion that he sometimes had "a greater desire of others finding Christ than of my own."

The excessive self-absorption and obsession with the morality of others that Hawthorne portrayed as being so distasteful in "Young Goodman Brown" is nowhere more apparent than in Wigglesworth's diary. (Notice that, like Hawthorne's Young Goodman Brown, Michael Wigglesworth is troubled by dreams, and that his fire-and-brimstone poem, *The Day of Doom*, which shows all people as vile and evil, was inspired by a dream.) Equally, there is a close resemblance here between Wigglesworth, who agonizes over his own health and lustfulness, and the sickly Dimmesdale, especially in the chapter entitled "The Interior of a Heart," where the lines could have come straight from Wigglesworth's diary:

His inward trouble drove him to practices more in accordance with the old, corrupted faith of Rome than with the better light of the church in which he had been born and bred. In Mr. Dimmesdale's secret closet, under lock and key, there was a bloody scourge. Oftentimes, this Protestant and Puritan divine had plied it on his own shoulders, laughing bitterly at himself the while, and smiting so much the more pitilessly because of that bitter laugh. It was his custom, too, as it has been that of many other pious Puritans, to fast—not, however, like them, in order to purify the body and render it the fitter medium of celestial illumination, but rigorously, and until his knees trembled beneath him, as an act of penance. He kept vigils, likewise, night after night, sometimes in utter darkness; sometimes with a glimmering lamp; and sometimes, viewing his own face in a looking glass, by the most powerful light which he could throw upon it. He thus typified the constant introspection wherewith he tortured, but could not purify himself. In these lengthened vigils, his brain often reeled and visions seemed to flit before him; perhaps seen doubtfully, and by a faint light of their own, in the remote dimness of the chamber, or more vividly, and close beside him, within the looking glass. Now it was a herd of diabolic shapes that grinned and mocked at the pale minister. (141)

In the following excerpts from Wigglesworth's diary, the italics are his own.

FROM *THE DIARY OF MICHAEL WIGGLESWORTH* (1631)

If the unloving carriages of my pupils can goe so to my heart as they doe; how then do my vain thoughts, my detestable pride, my *unnatural filthy lust that* are so oft and even this day in some measure stirring in me how do these griev my lord Jesus that loves me infinitely more then I do them? . . .

Pride and vain thoughts again prevail over me to the grief of my god, cleanse me, o lord, when shall it once be? I had opportunity (purposely, takeing of it) to discourse with one of my pupils much of the things of god; as also with another out of the college whom I went to visit, who spake something to me about his spiritual condition, the lord helping me to speak much to him again with some affection. . . .

Peevishness vain thoughts and especially pride still prevails in me. I cannot think one good thought, I cannot do any thing for god but presently pride gets hould of me. . . . I find my heart prone to take secret pleasure in thinking how much I do for others' good. . . .

Sabbath 13
    . . . Innumerable vain thoughts crowded in upon me this day, and I find it utterly impossible to overcome them my self, I cannot for my life withdraw my mind from an unsuitable object it is so forced upon me: but ah! I am oft slouthful and lay down the weapons of my warfare and do not fight, cry strive as I should against them, the dispensation of so waighty a truth as that, he that beleiv's not is condemn'd already seem'd to me too scholastically exprest and not with vehemency sufficiently prest, so that I could not but undervalue. . . . I neglected also to speak to some whom I heard profanely laughing aloud Lord forgive this neglect.

• • •

15
    Pride I feel still again and again abounding, self-admiration, though destroying my self daly. . . . Ah Lord I am vile, I desire to abhor my self (or that I could!) for these things. I *find such unresistable torments of carnal lusts or provocation unto the ejection of seed that I find myself unable to read anything to inform me about my distemper because of the prevailing or rising of my lusts. This I have procured to myself. God*

hath brought this to my eye this day Thou hast destroyed thy self but in me is thy help. Lord let me find help in thee though I have destroyed my self by my iniquity.

4th day. 3 speciall times pride remarkably prevailing in me. besides passionate distempers inwardly prevail. vain thoughts *carnal lusts some also. . . .*

I took a good deal of time this day to look thorowly into the vilest of that sin of pride. . . . yet so sensual and mind so full of vain thoughts, as I could not get my heart into a praying frame. . . .

The last night a filthy dream and so pollution escaped me in my sleep for which I desire to hang down my head with shame and beseech the Lord not to make me possess the sin of my youth and give me into the hands of my abominations. I find both pride in speciall so monstrous prevalent again and again this day, and vain thoughts together with weariness of the length of dutys in the morning, also sensuall outgoings of heart or proneness thereto, and so to crossness and peevishness, slighting of others, lashing out in too much eagerness of spirit in discours, dishonouring god and shaming my self thereby. . . . I loath my self, and could even take vengeance of my self for these abominations. . . .

. . . *Behold I am vile* behold I am vile *what shall I say* to the preserver of men why hidest thou thy face from me. . . .

• • •

Feb. 25

    26

Deal not with me according to the pride this day exceedingly again prevailing over me. *Some filthiness escaped me in a filthy dream. The Lord notwithstanding,* enlarged my heart in prayer in the morning in private. . . . ah sensuall spirit, that art so avers from savouring the things of god, his grace his will, his ordinances,! that cannot feed upon the heavenly manna and be satisf'd, but when creatures fail thy heart fails: when creatures smile god is undervalew'd. . . .

I found god in the forenoon mightily affecting my heart in publick prayer in the assembly. . . . yet in the fore part of the sermon I found my spirit so distracted *with* vain thoughts and so disquited within me, because one of my pupils was ill and absent from the ordinances, that I could not attend to the word. . . .

• • •

[June] 24

John Haines one of my pupils having formerly desired liberty to go toward Ibswich and being denied by me (for I was afraid of him and of that degeneracy which I to my grief saw in him since my return) I say he went away on the 2d day to salem without my leave or either the President's knowledge or mine and stayed out until the 5th day and night and then came not to give any account of his journey nor to obey their commendation to me that sent them to him. The thing was very exercising and grievous to me from the fact that I had been of such hopes did now quite fail my expectation in such wise. Upon his return this 6th day I took occasion to speak to him though having premeditated a convicting discourse and having set myself to find out arguments to wrestle with the Lord for him and others and having besought the Lord seriously before hand and desired him not for my sins to withhold his blessing from others and from this whole society. I told him not only of his evil carriages in this business (which indeed be too apparent) and of his breach of his own engagement at his admission and his endeavoring to disable me from rending an account of him either to god or man as I accounted myself solemnly charged to do but also of the great grief he put both me and others of his friends to in seeing our expectations and high hopes so strangely failed and he so suddenly altered from what he sometimes seemed at least to be. I told him that danger of backsliding from former attainments how Satan enters in with no spirits worse than himself and the latter end of that may become worse than his beginning. . . . I asked him further if himself did not see that to be true that I had spoken to him that his heart was gone after pleasure and off from those good ways he had sometimes walked in and he answered somewhat in way of assent thereto fearing that it was so. I told him also of the dangers of pleasure and how they had like to have been my ruin Knowing the danger of them therefore I dissuade both myself and others. And so I bade him farewell. But that very evening he was again at play I think among the students and when he saw me coming he slinked home. . . .

I set my self again this day to wrestle with the Lord for my self and then for my pupils and the Lord did pretty much inlarge my heart in crying to him. But still I see the Lord shutting out my prayers and refusing to hear for he whom in special I pray'd for, I heard in the forenoon with ill company playing music, though I had so solemnly warn'd him but yesterday of letting his spirit go after pleasures. And again I see light and vain carriage in him just at night on this last day at even.[2]

June 26

. . . yet after this a munday my spirit was almost quite discouraged and soul and body both ready to quail, because of my sorrows for what mine eyes daly behould in others sins and mispence of their precious hours. . . . Lord I am vile, but thou are gracious, turn to me rather in meercy than in displeasure. ah let not my sins fall upon others of thy people. . . .

Sabbath
July 3

I am still afraid that my sorrow for sin should not be true because I find such vehement and unappeasable affections toward others longing, striving, raging for their good; and yet so little mourning and fighting against and restless striving for deliverance from my owne prevailing iniquitys. . . . God let me see in the forenoon that two violent impetuous desiring of lawful things and unseasonable desireing them becomes a lust when the soul is even ready to dy away if it have them not presently, both these I am guilty of in reference to my pupils good. The latter of them to my shame this day. . . . O confounding vileness of an unthankful, impenitent heart! . . .

4–5

In the next day I found so much of a spirit of pride and secret joying in some conceived excellence in my self which is too hard for me and I cant prevail over and also so much secret vice and vain thoughts in holy duties and thereby weariness of them and such filthy lust also flowing from my fond affection to my pupils whiles in their presence on the third day after noon that I confess myself an object of God's loathing as my sin is of my own and pray God make it so more to me.

• • •

9

. . . Blind mind! Carnal heart! I am affraid, ashamed, heavy laden under such cursed frames of heart, as ever and anon beset me. My soul groans   my body faints   o Lord whilest I pray and cry to thee for pardon and redemption. Is there no baulm in Gilead? no physician there? Look down and see my plague sores which I spread before thee my saviour; wounds and old putrifyd sores which provoke the Lord, stink in his nosthrils, and poison the peace and comfort of my own soul. Behold I am vile, when thou showest me my face I abhor my self. who can bring a clean thing out of filthiness, I was conceived bred brought up in sin. . . . I deserve to be the stepping-stone of thy wrath. . . .

• • •

March 5

I have been much troubled with the spleen these divers days   And all I can do wil not get it remov'd. This hath exposed me to temptations of 3 sorts. 1 Too much frothyness and unsavoury discours, finding a necessity of some mirth; readiness to be too much addicted thereto. so that I find no power to attend or love serious and savoury discours. 2ly. To weariness of religious dutys, and negligent performance of them at some times. 3ly To Carnal lusts, by reason of the abundance of flatulent vapours that annoy me. . . .

Edited by Edmund Sears Morgan. New York: Harper & Row, 1946.

NOTES

1. *The Puritans* (New York: American Book Co., 1938), p. 548.
2. The Puritan Sabbath began at sundown on Saturday night, thus the "light and vain carriage" that Wigglesworth detects was a breach of the Sabbath.

TOPICS FOR WRITTEN OR ORAL EXPLORATION

1. The Puritans believed that human nature was basically evil. People needed society or civilization to make them better. After all, they argued, even a so-called innocent baby had the vices of anger, greed, and selfishness. But the great philosophers of Hawthorne's day believed just the opposite, that human beings were basically good and learned bad habits from society. Stage a major debate on this topic. Marshal your arguments with examples.

2. To approach the problem another way, list the arguments that support the contention that humans are "naturally" good, and list the arguments that support the contention that humans are basically evil.

3. Do a "campy" stage production of *The Day of Doom*. Use your imagination along with hints from Wigglesworth to specify sets, costumes, properties, lighting, and sounds.

4. As an exercise to see what little children went through, and just how easy it is to master Wigglesworth's rhythms, see how long it takes you to memorize the first four stanzas.

5. (a) The comment has been made that Hawthorne is both Puritan-like and a critic of Puritanism in *The Scarlet Letter*. From what you have learned of Puritan doctrine or the Puritan view of human character, what in the narrator's views of Hester's and Dimmesdale's character seems consistent with the Puritan view of original sin? of good works? of hypocrisy? (b) In *The Scarlet Letter*, how does Hawthorne seem to be criticizing the Puritans' excessive guilt and preoccupation with sin and excessive self-involvement? What other aspects of Puritanism does he criticize in the novel?

6. Using Wigglesworth's diary, make a comparison between Wigglesworth and Dimmesdale.

7. Write an essay on children in Puritan times as they and their parents, teachers, and ministers are revealed in the diary and *The Scarlet Letter*. Notice the impact of Puritan religious doctrine in their lives.

8. Compare Young Goodman Brown with Michael Wigglesworth.

9. Would you argue that Brown actually comes upon a witches' meeting? Or would you say that it is all in his head, a dream, in short? Have a class debate on this question.

10. Write a paper on the symbolic use of colors in "Young Goodman Brown" and *The Scarlet Letter*.

11. Make the argument that Brown never emerges from the forest, symbolically speaking, using as well the images of the forest in *The Scarlet Letter*. Does the forest mean different things in these two works?

12. Does it appear to you that Brown is more alarmed that Faith is at the witches' meeting than that he is there himself? How do you interpret this? Is there any similarity between his attitude and Dimmesdale's view of Hester, or are their attitudes quite different?

13. For a class debate: Is Brown the only "good" man in a society of hypocrites? Or is he a "bad" man who lovelessly suspects the worst of neighbors?

SUGGESTED READINGS

From Nathaniel Hawthorne's tales: "Young Goodman Brown" and "The Minister's Black Veil."

Michael Wigglesworth's *The Day of Doom*.

4

Crime and Punishment in Massachusetts Bay

> . . . among the crowd were several, whose punishment would be life-
> long; some, whose ears had been cropt, like those of puppy dogs;
> others, whose cheeks had been branded with the initials of their mis-
> demeanors; one with his nostrils slit and seared; and another, with
> halter about his neck, which he was forbidden ever to take off, or to
> conceal beneath his garments.
>
> Nathaniel Hawthorne, "Endicott and the Red Cross," 543

Unfortunately, the most striking accounts in Puritan history—and
the ones their nineteenth-century descendent, Nathaniel Hawthorne, remembered so vividly in his fiction, like the lines quoted
above from one of his stories—are of notorious events in which
their religious fervor led them to cruel intolerance. The major
events include their criminalization of and harsh punishments for
"victimless crimes" like cursing cattle; their banishment of the Reverend Roger Williams in 1635; their banishment of Anne Hutchinson in 1637; their persecution of Quakers; and their persecution
of "witches" in 1692.

Nathaniel Hawthorne reveals that he is riveted by the idea of Puritan crime and punishment, not only in *The Scarlet Letter*, but in
other works as well: extreme and cruel punishments for a variety of
misdemeanors in "Endicott and the Red Cross," the persecution of

Quakers in "Main Street" and "The Gentle Boy," the banishment of Anne Hutchinson in his sketch of her, the persecution of a band of merry hedonists in "The Maypole of Merrymount," and the persecution of witches in "Alice Doane's Appeal," among others. In *The Scarlet Letter*, in particular, he is especially interested in the psychological effects of Puritan punishment and in how the Puritan fabric of crime and punishment is both cause and effect of an unhealthy crippling of the community by its elders. Useful divisions for examining crime and punishment in Puritan times can be developed from Hawthorne's portrayal of the whole pattern of atrocities and humiliations that form the backdrop of religious life in *The Scarlet Letter*: (1) the types of behavior considered criminal in Massachusetts Bay; (2) the types of punishments in Massachusetts Bay; (3) the punishment of adultery in relation to the novel; (4) the element of public humiliation in punishment levied by Puritans; and, finally, (5) the effect of the Puritan system of crime and punishment on the community of *The Scarlet Letter*.

> The founders of a new colony . . . have invariably recognized it among their earliest practical necessities to allot a portion of the virgin soil as a cemetery, and another as the site of a prison.
>
> *The Scarlet Letter*, 55

WHAT WAS CRIMINAL IN MASSACHUSETTS BAY?

The narrator of *The Scarlet Letter* makes a number of observations about the different crimes for which punishment was levied in Puritan times. The major one on which the novel focuses is, of course, adultery, which will be discussed at greater length below. But he also mentions as crimes sluggishness on the part of a servant, lack of dutiful behavior in a child, being a Quaker (or, indeed, holding any religious beliefs considered false by the Puritans), being a witch, wearing ornate dress (if you weren't high society or wealthy), being an idle Indian, joking, laughing, and putting on dramas or singing in public, to name a few. So many pleasurable and joyful activities were criminal acts that, according to the narrator, this "blackest shade of Puritanism . . . so darkened the national visage with it, that all the subsequent years have not sufficed to clear it up. We have yet to learn again the forgotten art of gayety" (218). This criminalization of essentially harmless human actions seemed to go against nature in a very destructive way. In his introductory sketch, "The Custom-House," the narrator states that happiness depends on living throughout the whole range of one's human faculties, but the novel Hawthorne writes shows a gloomy community in which exercising those faculties—just being human—is a crime.

Look at some actions the Puritans in the seventeenth century made into criminal acts punishable by law, usually with public whippings, but sometimes worse:

• disobedience on the part of children or servants
• speaking ill of the court or judge
• speaking ill of a magistrate or minister
• playing with cards or dice
• denying the divinity of any part of the Bible
• professing to be a Quaker
• befriending a Quaker
• telling lies
• acting unruly aboard a ship
• doing anything that could be interpreted as defiling the Sabbath (like laughing)
• drinking in a tavern on the Sabbath
• swearing at people or animals
• wandering around
• being idle
• being disorderly or rude
• marrying your brother's widow
• wearing the clothes of the opposite sex

THE DEATH SENTENCE IN MASSACHUSETTS BAY

Consistent with the events in *The Scarlet Letter* is the fact that by far the greatest number of crimes for which Puritans were brought to justice were sexual in nature. Scholars have discovered from looking at old records that almost half the crimes of which Puritans were convicted were sexual crimes between consenting partners. These included adultery, bigamy, sex between single partners (which was labeled fornication), and lewd behavior. Actual cases of sexual misconduct, other than rape and adultery, recorded by the Puritans in *The Records of the Massachusetts Bay Colony* include the following:

- John Bickerstaffe was censured to bee severely whiped for committing fornication with Ales Burwoode . . . Ales Burwoode was censured to bee whipt for yielding to Bickerstaffe without crying out, & concealing it 9 or 10 dayes. [Boston, 1638]
- John Kempe for filthy uncleane attempts with 3 young girles was censured to bee whipt both heare, at Roxberry & at Salem very severly & was committed for a slave to Lt. Davenport. [Boston, 1639]
- Dorothy Temple, for uncleanes and bringing forth a male bastard, is censured to be whipt twice; but shee fainting in the execution of the first, the other was not executed. [Plymouth, 1639]
- John Pope, for his unchaste attempt upon a girle, & dalliance with maydes, & rebellios or stubborne carriage against his master, was censured to bee severly whiped. [Boston, 1640]

Examples of actual court cases of a nonsexual nature include the following:

- John Baker shalbe whipted for shooteing att fowle on the Sabboth day Etc. [Boston, 1630]
- Roberte Shawe shalbe severely whipt, for wicked curseing; sweareing, justifyeing the same, & gloryeing in it, as hath been proved by oath. [Boston, 1632]
- John Lee shalbe whipt and Fined for calling Master Ludlowe false-hearted knave & hard-hearted knave heavy Friend, etc. [Boston, 1634]
- John Lee shalbe whipt and Fyned 40 pounds for speaking reproachfully of the Gouvenor sayeing hee was but a Lawyer's clerke, & what under-standing had hee more then himselfe, also taxeing the Court for mak-eing lawes to picke mens purses, as also for abuseing a mayde of the Governours pretending love in the way of marriage, when himselfe pro-fesses hee intended none, as also for intiseing her to goe with him into the cornfield, etc. [Boston, 1634]
- George Barlow for his idleness was censured to bee whipt. [Boston, 1637][1]

VIOLENT PUNISHMENTS IN MASSACHUSETTS BAY

> At the very least, they would have put the brand of a hot iron on Hester Prynne's forehead.
>
> *The Scarlet Letter*, 59

Drawing from history, *The Scarlet Letter* mentions an array of excessive and violent punishments: little Puritan children, in imitation of their elders, play at common punishments like "scourging Quakers" or "taking scalps in a sham fight with Indians." The "whipping post" was standard equipment for punishment by law, not to mention the gallows for public hangings, and the pillory, which the narrator describes as being similar in nature to the French guillotine:

In fact, this scaffold constituted a portion of a penal machine, which now, for two or three generations past, has been merely historical and traditionary among us, but was held, in the old time, to be as effectual an agent in the promotion of good citizenship as ever was the guillotine among the terrorists of France. It was, in short, the platform of the pillory; and above it rose the framework of that instrument of discipline, so fashioned as to confine the human head in its tight grasp, and thus hold it up to the public gaze. The very ideal of ignominy was embodied and made manifest in this contrivance of wood and iron. . . . In Hester Prynne's instance, however, as not unfrequently in other cases, her sentence bore, that she should stand a certain time upon the platform but without undergoing that gripe about the neck and confinement of the head, the proness to which was the most devilish characteristic of this ugly engine. (63)

The coarse women in the opening scene want Hester to go through another frequent mode of punishment—branding.

Again, these details in the novel are drawn from history. Punishments for crimes were actually what we would classify as inhumane. Public beatings were frequent. In extreme cases, victims (both male and female) would be stripped to the waist, dragged through the streets behind a cart, and whipped, a horror described by Hawthorne in "Main Street."

In some cases the prisoner would be physically mutilated. Prisoners' ears might be cut off, or they would be burned or branded like cattle: a "B" for burglar; an "F" for forgerer; an "I" for incest (which usually meant marrying the widow of a brother); a "T" for theft. The records show, for example, that in 1677 one George Majorin was branded on the forehead with the letter "B" for stealing pork and beef from John Knight. In 1631 Phillip Ratliffe was to be "whipped, have his eares cutt off, fined 40 pounds, and banished out of the limits of this jurisdiction for uttering malitious and scandalous speeches against the government and church of Salem, Etc." Another punishment received by a Joseph Gatchell for uttering blasphemy was to "have his tongue drawn forth out of his mouth and pierced through with a hot iron." More often, as Hawthorne describes in "Endicott and the Red Cross," the tongue would be pulled out and tied into a split stick for a given period of time.

The death sentence was given for the crimes of murder, rape, and treason. Death was also the sentence for adultery involving a married woman. If only the man in the adulterous relationship was married, it was not considered a capital crime. Death was also the penalty for sodomy (sex between two people of the same sex) and bestiality (sex between a human and an animal). Heresy, as in the case of Quakers, was in certain cases punishable by death.

THE CRIME OF ADULTERY IN MASSACHUSETTS BAY

> This woman has brought shame upon us all, and ought to die. Is there no law for it? Truly there is, both in the Scripture and the statute-book.
>
> *The Scarlet Letter*, 59

The crime of adultery is at the heart of *The Scarlet Letter*, and the punishment for adultery there creates an interesting puzzle for the reader. For Hawthorne departs from history in deciding the punishment to which his fictional Puritans condemn his main character. It is clear that the legally mandated penalty for adultery in the Massachusetts Bay Colony was death. Still, the Puritan court exercised great discretion in cases of adultery, and though it was committed frequently, perhaps only on one occasion were a pair of adulterers put to death. More often than not, the court would declare that there were not two witnesses to the crime, as required by law, or that there were other extenuating circumstances. Governor John Winthrop, it seems, was particularly uneasy about carrying out the death penalty. Nevertheless, adulterers were, at the very least, beaten, branded, imprisoned, fined, and banished from Massachusetts Bay.

The question many scholars have asked is this: Given the general historical accuracy of the story told in *The Scarlet Letter*, why does Hester escape the death sentence? One scholar, Hugh Dawson, has discovered that the failure to exact the death sentence was a matter of controversy in the colony. A few of the legislators became annoyed that the death sentence was rarely imposed for the crime of adultery. The reader of *The Scarlet Letter* sees these sentiments reflected in the words of the older women, one declaring: "If the hussy stood up for judgment before us five, that are now here in a knot together, would she come off with such a sentence as the worshipful magistrates have awarded? Marry, I trow not!" Another complains: "The magistrates are God-fearing gentlemen, but merciful overmuch—that is a truth" (59). Still another refers to the controversy over failure to pass the death sentence for adultery:

This woman has brought shame upon us all, and ought to die. Is there no law for it? Truly there is, both in the Scripture and the statute-book. Then let the magistrates, who have made it of no effect, thank themselves if their own wives and daughters go astray! (59)

Against Governor Winthrop's wishes, in 1641, the colony's hard-liners pushed through a "fixed" penalty for several crimes, including adultery. This was supposed to mean that under the New Code of 1641 the death penalty would be mandatory for adultery. The language is: "the adulterer and adulteresse shall surely be put to death." Two facts are especially interesting for the reader of *The Scarlet Letter* in this regard. One is that Hester, who is tried in June, after the mandatory death sentence is in place, is not executed.

The second interesting point, argued by Dawson, is that the Puritan legislator most bound and determined to make death the fixed penalty for adultery was Nathaniel Hawthorne's ancestor William Hathorne.[2]

The final question on the matter of Hester's punishment in *The Scarlet Letter* is why Hawthorne lets her escape the usual punishments for adultery—branding, a public beating, and banishment. Is it because Hawthorne wants to present his own Puritan ancestors as less cruel than they actually were? Or did he balk at putting a character he liked through the physical indignities of a public beating? Or did he believe, for various reasons, that such harsh punishments would interfere with his plot and character development?

There can be no outrage, methinks, against our common nature—whatever be the delinquencies of the individual—no outrage more flagrant than to forbid the culprit to hide his face for shame.

The Scarlet Letter, 63

HUMILIATION AS PUNISHMENT

Despite the horror of these corporal punishments inflicted by the Puritans, the punishment that receives the narrator's most consistent attention is more psychological than physical. What made many of the corporal punishments so horrible was the public arena in which they occurred—in the stocks or the pillory, at the whipping post, in the streets, and, in Hester's case, on the scaffold.

The narrator describes in detail the psychological terrors Hester feels in being publicly humiliated, writing of her walk to the scaffold:

Haughty as her demeanor was, she perchance underwent an agony from every footstep of those that thronged to see her, as if her heart had been flung into the street for them all to spurn and trample upon.

• • •

There can be no outrage, methinks, against our common nature—whatever be the delinquencies of the individual—no outrage more flagrant than to forbid the culprit to hide his face for shame; as it was the essence of this punishment to do. (62, 63)

The length of punishment for her crime is also cruel and unusual, for she must wear the scarlet letter for her entire life, to feel the stares and scorn all her life.

BANISHMENT

The psychological focus of the novel can be seen in the narrator's treatment of the punishment of banishment. Historically, the Puritans of Massachusetts Bay frequently condemned "criminals" to be banished, a sentence often tantamount to death, for to be banished from the colony would mean having to survive alone in utter wilderness unless one could find the way to Rhode Island, as Roger Williams did, or to Maine, New York, or Pennsylvania, not easily done without assistance. How could one person, utterly alone, find enough food or adequate shelter? The other alternative, which the narrator mentions as an option for Hester, was to find and join the native American Indians. But Hester is not actually banished, even though she is forced to move to the outskirts of

Boston. Yet her punishment is a form of psychological banishment from the heart and sympathy and activities of the community. She is in the community but not of it. The narrator details the effect on her life: ceaseless curiosity of others, who regard her as a freak, the circle of isolation that always surrounds her, the friendlessness of her life. The narrator writes of her banishment from the sympathy of the community, even after seven years, as if it had been a death sentence:

Her face, so long familiar to the townspeople, showed the marble quietude which they were accustomed to behold there. It was like a mask; or, rather, like the frozen calmness of a dead woman's features, owing this dreary resemblance to the fact that Hester was actually dead, in respect to any claim of sympathy, and had departed out of the world with which she still seemed to mingle. (213)

And her banishment from the sympathy of the community does not end at last with finding another community in Rhode Island or some other more tolerant place; it appears as if it will continue for the remainder of her life.

ELDERS' TREATMENT OF CITIZENS AS CHILDREN

The whole pattern of crime and punishment in New England seems posited on the leaders' authoritarian treatment of adult members of their community as children who lack the maturity to manage their personal lives privately, who must seek permission from the elders for every step they take, whose behavior needs to be monitored for their own safety.

And certainly the ordinary citizens in *The Scarlet Letter* are more like children than adults. Note how a man in the town quiets the old gossips in the marketplace, how old Bellingham and Wilson scold and order the young Dimmesdale, how the town elders force Dimmesdale, against his wishes, to share a house with Chillingworth, how young and old women idolize Dimmesdale and turn to him for advice about how to conduct their lives. And the members of the community are kept in intellectual dependency by the elders, who tell them what to believe and punish severely any religious speculation. Furthermore, rules and laws so minutely control the details of their lives that they are allowed little latitude to make independent choices.

OUTLAWING NATURE

Puritan laws, the breaking of which resulted in such harsh punishments, inevitably reined in human nature, in that the people were denied the mirth and imaginative play so essential to the development of a young child as well as the independent thinking and sexuality essential to adulthood. The result was a crippled community whose members' development was arrested. Pearl, in this as in most matters, is a contrast to the Puritans: she is not severely punished by Hester and is allowed the latitude and mirth and freedom so natural to childhood. Look for a moment at how the narrator sets up that contrast:

> The discipline of the family, in those days, was of a far more rigid kind than now. The frown, the harsh rebuke, the frequent application of the rod, enjoined by Scriptural authority, were used, not merely in the way of punishment for actual offences, but as a wholesome regimen for the growth and promotion of all childish virtues. Hester Prynne, nevertheless, the lonely mother of this one child, ran little risk of erring on the side of undue severity. (93)

And the narrator supposes that Pearl's freedom allows her to develop more fully as a sensitive human being:

> In the chaos of Pearl's character, there might be seen emerging—and could have been, from the first—the steadfast principles of an unflinching courage—an uncontrollable will—a sturdy pride, which might be disciplined into self-respect—and a bitter scorn of many things, which, when examined, might be found to have the taint of falsehood in them. (172)

FAILURE OF A SENSE OF PROPORTION

Puritan crimes and punishment underscore another negative aspect of life in Massachusetts Bay, that is, an essential loss of proportion and a hypocrisy at the core of society. For example, many crimes that are not cruel and that have little impact on the life of the community receive the same grim attention as murder, rape, and torture. So all the highest officials in the town, including the colony's major and some of its legislature, have come to observe and supervise not, as one might expect, an execution, but the public display of a woman being punished for adultery. The narrator makes a similar observation about the elders' concern with whether Hester should be allowed to keep her child. Here, again, those in high positions should scarcely have been involved with the disposition of a seamstress's child. But, as the narrator writes, "At that epoch of pristine simplicity, however, matters of even slighter public interest, and of far less intrinsic weight, than the welfare of Hester and her child were strangely mixed up with the deliberations of legislators and acts of state" (102). That lack of proportion, by which heinous crimes like murder are treated with the same attention as adultery, promiscuity, and insubordination, as well as certain inconsistencies in how the law is applied, lead to what the narrator calls "incomplete morality." A striking example is found in the chapter entitled "The New England Holiday," where one finds Hester still branded with the "A," still feeling a circle of isolation around her because of her sin of adultery seven years earlier. At the same time, pirates who made their livings by murder and theft are made to feel a welcome part of the group, and, furthermore, are allowed to break laws for which members of the community would be severely punished:

They were rough-looking desperadoes with sun-blackened faces and an immensity of beard. . . . They transgressed, without fear or scruple, the rules of behavior that were binding on all others; smoking tobacco under the beadle's very nose, although each whiff would have cost a townsman a shilling; and quaffing, at their pleasure, draughts of wine or aquavitae from pocket flasks, which they freely tendered to the gaping crowd around them. It remarkably characterized the incomplete morality of the age, rigid as we call it, that a license was allowed the seafaring class, not merely for their freaks on shore, but for far more desperate deeds on their proper element. The sailor of that day would go near to be arraigned as a pirate in our own. There could be little doubt, for instance, that this very ship's crew, though no unfavorable specimens of the nautical brotherhood, had been guilty, as we should phrase it, of depredations of the Spanish commerce such as would have perilled all their necks in a modern court of justice. (218–219)

In relating the Puritans' reaction to the commander of the seafaring men, we see something further of crime and punishment in Boston, and the hypocrisy with which the law is applied:

The latter was by far the most showy and gallant figure, so far as apparel went, anywhere to be seen among the multitude. . . . A landsman could hardly have worn this garb and shown his face, and worn and shown them both with such a galliard air, without undergoing stern question, before a magistrate, and probably incurring fine or imprisonment, or perhaps an exhibition in the stocks. (219)

Such was the state of crime and punishment in *The Scarlet Letter*.

NOTES

1. *Records of the Massachusetts Bay in New England* (Boston: William White, 1853).

2. Hugh H. Dawson, "Hester Prynne, William Hathorne, and the Bay Colony Adultery Laws of 1641–42," *ESQ* 32 (4th Quarter, 1986): 225–231.

TOPICS FOR WRITTEN OR ORAL EXPLORATION

1. Consider a question that has puzzled scholars for decades: Why, knowing history as thoroughly as he did, did Hawthorne refrain from having Hester publicly whipped, which would have invariably been the punishment for adultery in reality?

2. Corporal punishment, more specifically, spanking and whipping, has been a controversial issue for many years, even though it has not been used in this century by the government as a penalty for law-breaking. The issue took on currency in the 1990s, however, after an American teenager in Singapore was sentenced to be caned for acts of vandalism. Research and write on the following related topics:

   • When did it become illegal to use corporal punishment?

   • When did it become illegal to physically punish servants?

   • What were the arguments against corporal punishment of adults?

   • Is corporal punishment still used in schools, public or private?

   • What are the arguments for and against the use of corporal punishment in schools? by parents?

   • Are other forms of physical punishment (other than prison) used in the military?

   • To what extent is the Rodney King case relevant to the issue of official use of corporal punishment?

SUGGESTED READINGS

From Nathaniel Hawthorne's tales: "Main Street" and "Endicott and the Red Cross."

5

Anne Hutchinson and Hester Prynne

> This rosebush, by a strange chance, has been kept alive in history; but whether it had merely survived out of the stern old wilderness . . . or whether, as there is fair authority for believing, it had sprung up under the footsteps of the sainted Ann Hutchinson, as she entered the prison door—we shall not take upon us to determine.
>
> *The Scarlet Letter*, 56

> Then she might have come down to us in history, hand in hand with Ann Hutchinson, as the foundress of a religious sect.
>
> *The Scarlet Letter*, 159

> Hester had vainly imagined that she herself might be the destined prophetess.
>
> *The Scarlet Letter*, 245

CHRONOLOGY

1613	John Cotton becomes pastor in Anne Hutchinson's hometown in England
1628	Colony of Massachusetts Bay is founded
1633	John Cotton leaves England (under threat of death) for Boston
1634	Anne Hutchinson and husband William follow John Cotton to Boston; both become members of the only church in Boston, a Puritan congregation

1636	Anne's brother-in-law, the Rev. John Wheelwright, arrives in Boston and is admitted to church membership
1636	Open conflict erupts, with Anne and her brother-in-law being questioned by other clergy about their criticism of local sermons and religious teachings
1637	Anne is tried and banished; is placed under house arrest until her church hearing.
1638	Her husband leaves Massachusetts Bay to look for another place to settle
1638	Anne is tried by the church and excommunicated; leaves for Rhode Island, where her husband is located
1642	Anne moves to New York after her husband's death
1643	Anne and the family remaining with her are massacred by Indians
1652	John Cotton dies
1658	Katherine Scott, Anne's sister, is publicly whipped in Boston for religious beliefs
1660	Anne's friend Mary Dyer is executed in Boston for her religious beliefs
	Hugh Peters, one of Anne's primary attackers in Boston, is hanged in London for treason against the king
1662	Former governor of Massachusetts and Anne's friend, Henry Vane, is hanged in London for treason against the king

CHARACTERS

Leaders of the Puritan establishment in the Massachusetts Bay Colony:

John Winthrop—succeeded Henry Vane as governor

John Wilson—minister of the Boston church

Joseph Welde—the man in whose house Anne was imprisoned between trials

Hugh Peters—a minister, later important in the Cromwell government in England

Thomas Dudley—Deputy Governor

John Endicott—magistrate

The Antinomian Group:

Anne Hutchinson

John Cotton—minister of the Boston church

John Wheelwright—Anne's brother-in-law, a minister

Henry Vane—resigned as governor over this issue; later became important in the Cromwell government in England and was eventually hanged when monarchy returned

Mary Dyer—friend of Anne's; a Quaker, later hanged on Boston Common by the Puritan establishment

Most of the members of the Boston church

One of the most shameful chapters in the history of the American Puritans and one that captivated Hawthorne, who wrote about it in 1830, some twenty years before the appearance of *The Scarlet Letter*, involved a Boston resident named Anne Hutchinson, who inspired a large following as a religious teacher and was subsequently tormented and then banished from the Massachusetts Bay Colony, ostensibly for her religious beliefs, which in fact differed from those of the Puritan elders only slightly in emphasis.

Hawthorne sets Hester Prynne's life in the same place (Boston) within fifteen or twenty years of Anne Hutchinson's. The importance of the figure of Anne Hutchinson to *The Scarlet Letter* is reflected in the comparisons of the two women that frame the novel: at the beginning, Hester is seen walking in the footsteps of Anne Hutchinson outside Boston's prison; in the chapter entitled "Another View of Hester," the narrator speculates that under different circumstances, Hester, like Hutchinson, might have founded a religious sect; and at the end, with the reference to Hester's early desire to be a prophetess, a word Hawthorne often used to describe Hutchinson.

ANNE HUTCHINSON AND *THE SCARLET LETTER*

The reference to Anne Hutchinson in the first chapter, "The Prison Door," signals the importance of this historical figure to Hawthorne's tale. The rose outside the prison door, he writes, symbolizes "some sweet moral blossom that may be found along the track, or relieve the darkening close of a tale of human frailty and sorrow." This rose, the moral symbol, comes from a bush he describes as springing up from "under the footsteps of the sainted Ann Hutchinson" (56). Is the narrator trying to tell the reader that the story of Anne Hutchinson is a key to the meaning of his tale?

Parallels between the lives of the historical figure and the fictional character will become clear after an examination of Anne

Hutchinson's life and of identical circumstances in the life of Hester, as Hawthorne chose to portray her.

The Historical Hutchinson

Anne Hutchinson, born in Lincolnshire, England, in 1591, was the daughter of a minister. All of her life she was intensely interested in matters concerning God and the church. After her marriage to William Hutchinson, her interest continued to grow, along with her friendship with a minister named John Cotton, who had come to her hometown in England as a pastor and who came to be threatened because of his Puritan beliefs. In 1633 Cotton felt compelled to flee England—to join the Massachusetts Bay Colony, which had been set up as a haven for Puritan dissidents. Anne, her husband William, and their children followed Cotton to Boston the next year. Anne was forty-two. In the New World, the Hutchinsons immediately became prominent members of the community. William held several important positions there, including the high office of deputy to the Massachusetts General Court. Anne, who was known to be highly learned in religious matters, became a self-appointed sister of charity and especially a comforter and advisor to women in the community. Eventually she began holding religious meetings for women to discuss passages from scripture. The sessions became so popular that she agreed to hold some for men as well, so that in a given week she might be meeting with sixty or more people in various groups. The groups often discussed sermons that they had heard, with Anne Hutchinson generally following John Cotton's line.

Conflict with the Puritan Elders

The Hutchinson family prospered. But within two years of their arrival in Boston, a conflict between Anne Hutchinson and the Puritan clergy in Massachusetts Bay began because it was reported that Anne was praising the Reverend John Cotton's sermons over those of other ministers in the colony, even over those of John Wilson, who was the senior pastor. The clerical establishment, she maintained, was placing too much stress on the "works" or deeds of human beings, and not enough on God's gifts or grace. Anne and her followers were labeled "Antinomians" by the Puritan

Painting of Anne Hutchinson preaching. Courtesy of Picture Collection, The Branch Libraries, The New York Public Library.

clergy, meaning that their beliefs were contrary to law, or to the scripture, that is, opposed to the beliefs of established Puritan clergy. Antinomians placed little importance on *outward signs* of living a godly life or on adherence to ritual as an indication that one was going to heaven; instead they stressed other signs, such as religious experiences and meekness. Unlike mainstream Puritans, they did not believe that one had to go through a long period of being "prepared"—by the clergy—in order to have a religious experience.

To the modern reader, these may seem to be nit-picking quarrels. And perhaps they were. But remember that this new belief *bypassed the clergy*. Modern students of the Puritan period have argued that the quarrel arose not so much because of disagreements over points of doctrine as from the "disrespect" Hutchinson and her followers showed for the established clergy. In short, it was a *power struggle*—between the young John Cotton (and Anne Hutchinson and their followers) on one side and the older established Puritans on the other. It was a belief—and a battle—that challenged the power of ministers in general, by declaring that a person could experience a religious conversion without the help of ministers.

Even though Anne was teaching little else than what she gleaned from John Cotton, he had been welcomed into the community as a minister and had all along (with little or no objection) been preaching his special brand of Puritanism. As the other clergy began to object to Hutchinson's meetings, John Cotton began doing all he could to make peace, even to the extent of reversing or modifying some of his former statements.

Nevertheless, the trouble continued. In fact, it worsened. The problem seems to have escalated not principally because of the Antinomians' emphasis on God's grace over mankind's deeds, but over their reported criticism of ministers other than Cotton at Hutchinson's meetings. To add further to the bad feelings, it soon became clear, too, that the Anne Hutchinson/John Cotton group included most of the members of the Boston church. And then rumors began circulating that these Antinomians wanted to replace the Reverend John Wilson with Anne's brother-in-law, the Reverend John Wheelwright. (Recall that the Reverend Wilson is the character in *The Scarlet Letter* who instructs Dimmesdale to ask Hester to name the father of her child.)

The Puritan Ministers Strike Back

In October 1636, the conflict within the community came out into the open as a meeting was set up to include Anne Hutchinson, John Cotton, and the area ministers. At this confrontation the Antinomians formally requested that John Wilson, who bitterly opposed Cotton, be replaced. The response by the established Puritan clergy was outrage, and John Winthrop blocked any change.

Other meetings between opposing groups occurred in December 1636, with both sides blaming the other. Henry Vane, the governor of Massachusetts, who strongly sympathized with the Hutchinson/Cotton faction, resigned as a result, saying that he was going to move out of the Massachusetts Bay Colony before God punished the Puritans for having so many fights among themselves. Hutchinson's supporters, however, persuaded him to withdraw his resignation.

After many meetings and much controversy, the General Court met on May 17, 1637, to consider the Antinomian threat. Remember that state and church were essentially one in those days, and that though a legislative body was elected by the people, these men were also controlled by the church elders and made laws and determinations affecting religious matters such as this one. Clergymen participated actively in hearings, as the Reverends John Wilson and Hugh Peters both took part in this one. An attack on the clergy was considered an attack on the state, just as it had been in England. The court convened in Newtowne instead of Boston because Hutchinson had too many supporters in Boston, where virtually the entire church, except for its senior pastor, Wilson, was sympathetic with her. Governor Vane, a Hutchinson supporter, and John Winthrop, the old respected leader and friend of the Reverend Wilson, quarrelled bitterly, and publicly. At the end of the meeting, the anti-Hutchinson group had triumphed, and John Winthrop was elected governor to replace Vane, who immediately left for England, turning his house and land in Boston over to John Cotton. Laws were passed to keep any further Antinomians from even coming to Massachusetts Bay.

By the end of summer, some three months later, the already overheated passions of this peculiar power struggle had risen dramatically. On August 30, 1637, the General Court, instructed by the ruling clerical leaders, announced their conclusions: because they had found more than ninety "errors" in the thinking of the Hutchinson/Cotton faction, Antinomians were forbidden to hold any further meetings in Massachusetts Bay; they were in addition ordered to stop questioning and criticizing the established clergy immediately. They could only sit and listen, and obey.

It was at this meeting, officially, that John Cotton gave in, declaring himself to be in complete harmony with the older ministers.

The Civil Trial for Treason

In November the General Court decreed that the leaders of the Hutchinson group were no longer to be allowed to vote in elections, and all weapons were to be taken from Hutchinson sympathizers. In March of the following year, 1638, William Hutchinson, Anne's husband, left the colony to find a safe home for his extended family and friends.

Unlike John Cotton, the man who had inspired her, Anne Hutchinson refused to denounce her beliefs or to obey the court. So it was decided that she would be tried in civil court for seditious and disruptive behavior to be followed by a church trial for heresy. Consequently, on November 2, 1637, she was officially brought to a civil trial in which clerical leaders actively participated. Her most relentless questioner was the Reverend John Wilson, who had worked feverishly behind the scenes to see that she, personally, was brought to "justice." As a result of this two-day trial, she was sentenced to be banished from Massachusetts Bay; but for four months she was placed under house arrest in Roxbury, in the house of her bitter enemy, to await her church trial. In Roxbury, she was out of reach of her supporters, continually living among and being spied upon by enemies. Hostile members of the clergy came to her "prison" repeatedly to quiz her on minute matters of doctrine, often, she and her friends claimed, confusing and exhausting her until she said things she did not intend to say. All this was taken down in writing, to be used at her second trial in her church in Boston.

Her Imprisonment and Illness

In August 1638, after a long illness, a tumor was expelled from her uterus. Her enemies, hearing of it, declared it to be a monster fathered by the devil. Puritan histories of what came to be called the Antinomian Crisis made extensive use of this incident. After Hutchinson's friend Mary Dyer experienced a similar medical phenomenon the year before, the same rumors had circulated about Dyer's relationship with the devil.

The Church Trial for Heresy

On March 15, 1638, in a Boston church packed with unsympathetic outsiders who were not members of her church, Anne Hutchinson was subjected to a gruelling daylong inquisition, much of it conducted by her once adored minister, John Cotton, and closely observed by the Reverend Wilson. The transcript might well remind the reader of the early scenes of *The Scarlet Letter* when the Reverend Dimmesdale questions his former lover at the order of the same John Wilson.

Banishment

Immediately after this inquisition at the Boston church, Anne Hutchinson left for Rhode Island, where her husband had found sanctuary; but even here she still did not feel safe from the zealous leaders of the Massachusetts Bay Colony, despite the presence of many friends and supporters. She in fact had good reason to worry. Her sons' property in Massachusetts was seized; spies were sent to Rhode Island to report on her activities; and Massachusetts authorities continually threatened to try to take over Rhode Island, with the intent of bringing Anne Hutchinson back to Boston for retrial and further punishment. Whether she was actually in danger is not clear, but she did fear for her own and her family's lives. Several years later, she and what was left of her family (her husband had died) moved to what they thought would be a safer place: Rye, New York. In August 1643, Anne Hutchinson and all but one member of her extended family were killed in an Indian raid on the settlement where she lived.

HUTCHINSON AND HESTER

That Hutchinson may well have been one of Hawthorne's several inspirations for the character of Hester is strongly supported by several interesting parallels, in addition to the framing references:

(1) the strong, independent personalities of both women; (2) their independent thinking; (3) their conflict with and defiance of Puritan elders; (4) the proud, seemingly confident and dignified manner in which they underwent their public trials; (5) their strong personal connections to (and betrayal by) a well-respected Puritan clergyman; (6) the rumors that each had had a child by the devil; (7) their punishments of imprisonment and banishment—one actual, one psychological; and (8) their roles as advisors to other women.

Strength of Character

That Hester Prynne, like Anne Hutchinson, is a woman of strength and independence, uncommon for her time, is depicted by Hawthorne in a number of ways after her ordeal on the scaffold. First is her decision to remain in Boston to suffer whatever humiliations the community has in store for her. Her strength is seen in her rearing of her child alone, without family or friends, and her move to work out her penance by becoming a sister of charity for the very community that scorns her. Though her true charity is weak, she endures silently and with immense fortitude the humiliations visited upon her by the people she serves. She supports herself and her child as a seamstress. And she is undaunted in her willingness to stand up to the most powerful men in the colony in her determination to keep her child. When the elders in all their generosity tell her she can remove the scarlet letter, her refusal tells them, in effect, "*You* may have told me I had to wear this badge, but *I* will decide when I want to take it off." Similarly, when townspeople who have snubbed her and derided her for years remember her kindnesses as a nurse and begin speaking to her in public, her response of silently pointing to the scarlet letter is an act of pride and independence. Her strength is shown in the forest scene when she justifies their sin for Dimmesdale and makes decisions for him because she thinks he seems ready to "die for very weakness" (187). Dimmesdale, in contrast to her, says, "Think for me, Hester! Thou art strong. Resolve for me!" (187). So it is the independent woman who makes plans for the three of them to leave for Europe. Not less strong and independent, she returns alone to Boston to take up the scarlet letter again.

Independent Thinkers

She is also, like Anne Hutchinson, an independent thinker. One finds in "Another View of Hester" that she has turned from a person of intense feeling into one of deep thought, and, whether or not her ideas were wise, they were certainly ones she had formed independent of anyone in the community. The narrator indicates that she was "standing alone in the world" and that "the world's law was no law for her mind" (158). She has the spirit, he says, of an intellectual revolutionary who had "overthrown and rearranged—not actually, but within the sphere of theory . . . the whole system of ancient prejudice, wherewith was linked much of ancient principle" (159). Had Hester revealed her thoughts, as Anne Hutchinson did, she might, the narrator stresses, have received a much more severe punishment than she suffered for adultery: "She might, and not improbably would, have suffered death from the stern tribunals of the period for attempting to undermine the foundations of the Puritan establishment" (159). Remember that the accusation against Hutchinson was that she was attempting to disrupt the establishment.

Defiance of Old Age and Authority

In the struggle of youth against age and establishment, both Hester and Hutchinson find themselves in conflict with the elderly men who form the power base of the community. Hester defies them by refusing to name the father of the child, even when she is ordered to do so. She defies them when they try to take her child from her, "confronting the old Puritan magistrate with almost a fierce expression" (112). She tells them, "God gave her into my keeping. . . . I will not give her up!" (112, 113). Furthermore, she refuses to accept with gratitude their offer to remove the letter and forms her own religious opinions in defiance of them. She defies the very morality they stand for by trying to persuade Dimmesdale to run away with her, showing her true thoughts about them when she tells him, "And what hast thou to do with all these iron men, and their opinions?" (188). Her defiance parallels Hutchinson's, who refuses to obey the orders of the court to cease holding her meetings and, when she is tried, insults the clergy by insisting that they swear to their testimony under oath.

Proud Demeanor During Trials

Both Hutchinson's and Hester's defiant pride cause them to be seen as haughty and arrogant during their trials—Hutchinson in the courtroom and church, Hester on the scaffold. Pride, considered to be the greatest of sins by the Puritans, was what made it possible for Hester to endure her ordeal on the scaffold. Note Hawthorne's depiction: as the town beadle tries to guide her to the scaffold, "she repelled him, by an action marked with natural dignity and force of character" (60). She is a figure of "perfect elegance" (60), "characterized by a certain state and dignity" (61). She looks directly into the crowd, not shamefully down. Her demeanor is "haughty," and she has "a sense of deportment" (62). The women in the community interpret her as "brazen" and making "a pride" out of her punishment (61). A similar deportment is in evidence in Hutchinson's self-assured answers to her questioners in both her trials.

Hutchinson and Hester, Cotton and Dimmesdale

The women have other points in common. Each had a close relationship with a Puritan clergyman who abandoned her at some point. While Hester's relationship with Dimmesdale is sexual, Hutchinson's relationship with John Cotton is intimately religious. Hutchinson and her family followed John Cotton all the way from England, and it was his thinking she embraced and his preaching she so fervently advocated in her Boston meetings. She was, without question, his disciple. As Dimmesdale is instructed by Bellingham and Wilson to get Hester to name the father of her child, so Cotton is instructed by some of the clergy to deal with Hutchinson. He does this by taking her to his house before the last day of her church hearing to reason with her. He also becomes, at their request, the chief officiating officer at her church hearing. Just as Dimmesdale is as guilty of adultery as Hester, so John Cotton is as guilty as Anne Hutchinson of heresy (by Puritan standards), for their beliefs were identical. Hutchinson had only been advocating what he preached. That this is apparent to the other ministers becomes clear in the transcript of the trial. It is also clear in the transcripts that Cotton is trying to separate himself from her. So, like Dimmesdale, Cotton attempts to evade the very close connection between himself and a woman who holds him in high esteem, and for the same reason—in order to save his own career. In both cases, the women refuse to help themselves by capitalizing on their connections with the men. Hester refuses to name Dimmesdale as Pearl's father, and Hutchinson refuses to protest that her ideas came from John Cotton.

Children by the Devil

As a result of their "unnatural" defiance, both women are accused of delivering children fathered by the devil. Pearl is believed by many people in the community to be the child of the devil. Mistress Hibbins, for example, tells her in the scene in "The Procession": "They say, child, thou art of the lineage of the Prince of the Air! Wilt thou ride with me, some fine night, to see thy father?" (227). Similarly, when what modern science would recognize as a tumor is expelled from Anne Hutchinson's uterus, it is thought to be the result of her coupling with the devil. Hawthorne refers darkly and mysteriously to this event in his sketch "Mrs. Hutchinson." For many decades, however, learned historians, writing of the Antinomian Crisis, placed great stress on what they called Hutchinson's "monstrous birth" as proof of her witchcraft.

Advisors to Women

One role that singled out Hutchinson in Boston and Hester when she returned to Boston as an old woman was their activity as advisors to women. Hutchinson's trial, as well as various histories, fault her for "corrupting" women in the meetings she held to discuss the Bible. Although a few months later she was also asked to conduct meetings for men, and had many male supporters, her primary audience seemed to have been women, and it was this audience that was the main concern of the elders who tried her. Similarly, at the end of her life Hester ministers primarily to women:

And, as Hester Prynne had no selfish ends, nor lived in any measure for her own profit and enjoyment, people brought all their sorrows and perplexities and besought her counsel, as one who had herself gone through a mighty trouble. Women, more especially—in the continually recurring trials of wounded, wasted, wronged, misplaced, or erring and sinful passion—or with the dreary burden of a heart unyielded, because unvalued and unsought—came to Hester's cottage, demanding why they were so wretched, and what the remedy! Hester comforted and counselled them, as best she might. (245)

Imprisonment and Banishment

Finally, of course, both women were imprisoned, Hutchinson being placed under house arrest for four months. Then both were taken out of the circle of Boston life—Hester living on the western edge of the Trimontan Peninsula (what was then Boston), more a part of the wilderness beyond than the village behind her, and Hutchinson being altogether banished from the colony.

The following excerpts, which clarify the Hutchinson–Hester connection, include:

• Accounts of the Antinomian Crisis and Anne Hutchinson by two Puritans, one of whom, John Winthrop, was directly involved in the trials
• Excerpts from Anne Hutchinson's church trial

THE FIRST-HAND ACCOUNT OF GOVERNOR JOHN WINTHROP

John Winthrop's history of the Antinomian Crisis is a first-hand account. He was one of the most active participants in the affair, so it is not surprising that he makes no attempt at objectivity. Winthrop had a reputation for being more compassionate than other elders in most matters of religious tolerance. However, in defense of his clerical friends and in the interest of maintaining harmony in the colony, all of which he believed were threatened by the widespread popularity of Anne Hutchinson and her close supporters (including Henry Vane, governor of the colony), Winthrop was more severe in his judgment of the Hutchinson case.

In reviewing Winthrop's account, note the following things, which are relevant to *The Scarlet Letter*:

• His depiction of her character
• The early involvement of John Cotton as an Antinomian
• Winthrop's depiction of her defiance at trial
• Cotton's betrayal of her

FROM JOHN WINTHROP, *HISTORY OF NEW ENGLAND FROM 1630–1649* (1853)

(October 21, 1636)
One Mrs. Hutchinson, a member of the church of Boston, a woman of a ready wit and bold spirit, brought over with her two dangerous errors. . . . There joined with her in these opinions a brother of hers, one Mr. Wheelwright, a silenced minister sometimes in England. . . .

Mr. Wilson made a very sad speech of the conditions of our churches, and the inevitable danger of separation, if these differences and alienations among brethren were not speedily remedied; and laid the blame upon these new opinions risen up amongst us, which all the magistrates, except the governor and two others, did confirm, and all the ministers but two. . . .

The speech of Mr. Wilson was taken very ill by Mr. Cotton and others of the same church. . . . It was strange to see, how the common people were led, by example, to condemn him in that, which (it was very probable) divers of them did not understand . . . and that such as had known him so long, and what good he had done for that church, should fall upon him with such bitterness for justifying himself in a good cause; for he was a very holy, upright man, and for faith and love inferior to none in the country, and most dear to all men. . . .

(January 20, 1637) The differences in the said points of religion increased more and more, and the ministers of both sides (there being only Mr. Cotton of one party) did publicly declare their judgements in some of them, so as all men's mouths were full of them. . . .

(November 1) There was great hope that the lay general assembly would have had some good effect in pacifying the trouble and dissensions about matters of religion; but it fell out otherwise.

The court also sent for Mrs. Hutchinson, and charged her with divers matters, as her keeping two public lectures every week in her house, where to sixty or eighty persons did usually resort, and for reproaching most of the ministers (viz., all except Mr. Cotton) for not preaching a covenant of free grace, and that they had not the seal of the spirit, nor were able ministers of the New Testament; which were clearly proved against her, though she sought to shift it off. And, after many speeches to and fro, at last she was so full as she could not contain, but vented her revelations; amongst which this was one, that she had it revealed to her, that she should come into New England, and should here be persecuted, and that God would ruin us and our posterity, and the whole state, for the same. So the court proceeded and banished her; but, because it was winter, they committed her to a private house, where she was well provided, and her own friends and the elders permitted to go to her but none else. . . .

(March 1, 1638) While Mrs. Hutchinson continued at Roxbury, divers of the elders and others resorted to her, and finding her to persist in maintaining those gross errors beforementioned, and many others, to the number of thirty or thereabout, some of them wrote to the church at Boston, offering to make proof of the same before the church, etc., [March] 15; whereupon she was called. . . . When she appeared, the errors were read to her. . . . These were also clearly confuted, but yet she held her own; so as the church (all but two of her sons) agreed she should be admonished, and because her sons would not agree to it, they were admonished also.

Mr. Cotton pronounced the sentence of admonition with great solemnity, and with much zeal and detestation of her errors and pride of spirit. The assembly continued till eight at night. . . .

(March 22) . . . but when she was examined about some particulars, as that she had denied inherent righteousness, etc., she affirmed that it was never her judgement; . . . yet she impudently persisted in her affirmation, to the astonishment of all the assembly. So that, after much time and many arguments had been spent to bring her to see her sin, but all in vain, the church, with one consent, cast her out.

Boston: Little Brown, 1853.

COTTON MATHER'S ACCOUNT

Another Puritan, Cotton Mather, also gives his account, written from material received from others after the fact. Several matters in his record are pertinent to Hester Prynne and *The Scarlet Letter*: one relates to the relationship, similar to that of Hester and Dimmesdale, between Anne Hutchinson and John Cotton. Mather seems to have an interest in exonerating John Cotton from any damaging connection with Anne Hutchinson and the Antinomians. Mather represents John Cotton as something of an innocent bystander, implicated by the Antinomians as one of their own without his permission.

Another interesting point is Mather's presentation of Hutchinson as a siren who tempted other women, and who, in turn, like Eve, then tempted their husbands into these dangerous beliefs.

Mather also made a point of presenting Hutchinson as essentially being in conflict with the clerical elders, a stance that reminds us of Hester's defiance of the old men in *The Scarlet Letter*.

A third matter of importance to *The Scarlet Letter* in the Mather history is his lurid emphasis on the tumors of Anne Hutchinson and her friend Mary Dyer, which were mistakenly called still-births. These tales he offers as proof of their fiendishness.

FROM COTTON MATHER, *MAGNALIA CHRISTI
AMERICANA* (1698)

*Hydra Decapitata: Or, The First Synod of New-England, Quelling
a Storm of Antinomian Opinions, And Many Remarkable Events
Relating Thereunto.*

1. The church of God had not long been in this wilderness, before the dragon cast forth several *floods* to devour it; but not the least of those floods was one of Antinomian and familistical heresies, with which the country began betimes to be infested . . . but it may not be amiss to describe a little more particularly the *methods* whereof the devil therein served his interests. The sectaries acquainted themselves with as many as possibly they could, and carried on their acquaintance with all the courtesies and kindnesses that they could contrive to ingratiate themselves in the hearts of others, especially of *new comers* into the place. They here-

withal appeared wondrous holy, humble, self-denying, and spiritual, and full of the most charming expressions imaginable. . . . They began usually to seduce *women* into their notions, and by these women, like their first mother, they soon hook'd in the *husbands* also. Having wrought themselves any where into a good esteem, they set themselves with a manifold subtilty to undermine the esteem of the ministers, and intimate that their *teachers* themselves, never having been "taught of God," had mis-taught and mis-led the people; whence it came to pass, that even some who had followed these ministers three thousand miles, thro' ten thousand deaths, yet now took up such prejudices, not only against their *doctrines*, but against their *persons* also, that they did never care to hear them, or to see them any more. . . .

5. The Synod then thought it *convenient*—nay necessary—for them to come into a good understanding with Mr. Cotton, who was himself not the *least part* of the country; the rather, because the sectaries, through the country, had basely made use of his name to patronize their opinions; and indeed, his *charity*, wherein he was known to be truly eminent, inclining him to suspect no more *evil* of *them*, than what they would profess or confess to him in their personal conversation with him, exposed him the more to their pretences of his patronage.

. . . Mr. Cotton came to such an amiable and amicable correspondence with the rest of the ministers, that although in this "time of temptation," he had throughout these churches laboured under the hard character of being the chief *abettor* to the errors whereby the tranquillity of the churches had been disturbed, yet he now most effectually joined with the other ministers in witnessing against those errors. . . .

. . . It is the *mark of seducers* that *they lead captive silly women*; but what will you say, when you hear of *subtile women* becoming the most *remarkable* of the seducers? 'Tis noted of seducers that, like their father the devil, the old, the first seducer, they usually have a special design upon the *weaker sex*, who are more easily *gained* themselves, and then are fit instruments for the *gaining* of their husbands unto such *errors* as will cause them to *lose* their souls at last. . . . Wherein the prime seducer of the whole faction which now began to threaten the country . . . was a woman, a gentlewoman, of "an haughty carriage, busies spirit, competent with, and a voluble tongue" . . .

8. This our erroneous gentlewoman, at her coming out of Lincolnshire in England unto New-England, upon pretence of religion, was well respected among the professors of *this* religion; and this the more, because at the meetings of the women, which used to be called *gossipings*, it was her manner to carry on very pious discourses, and so put the neighbourhood upon examining their spiritual estates. . . . [Thus] many of them were convinced of a very great defect in the settlement of their

everlasting peace, and acquainted more with the "Spirit of the gospel," than ever they were before. This mighty *show* and *noise* of devotion, procured unto our dame, the NON-SUCH, the reputation of Hutchinson a *non-such* among the people; until at length, under the pretence of that warrant, "that the elder women are to teach the younger," she set up weekly meetings at her house, where to threescore or fourscore people would resort, that they might hear the sermons of Mr. Cotton repeated, but in such a sort, that after the repetition, she would make . . . applicatory declamations. . . .

It was not long before 'twas found that most of the errors, then crawling like vipers about the countrey, were hatched at these meetings. . . .

. . . Nevertheless, under such an infatuation of *pride* she was, that whilst the church was debating about this recantation, she did with a strange confidence and impudence assert, "that she never was really of any opinion contrary to the declaration she had now made." However, some of her expressions had been misconstrued: whereupon many witnesses arose, which demonstrated her guilty of gross *lying* in that assertion: and that caused Mr. Cotton to say, that her case was now altered: for being now convicted of lying, he thought she was to be *cast out* with them that "love and make a lie." So, with the full consent of the church, the sentence of *excommunication* was passed upon her.

11. While these things were managing, there happened some very surprizing *prodigies*, which were lookt upon as testimonies from Heaven, against the ways of those greater prodigies, the sectaries. The *erroneous gentlewoman* her self, convicted of holding about *thirty* monstrous opinions, growing big with child, and at length coming to her time of travail, was delivered of about *thirty* monstrous births at once; whereof some were bigger, some were lesser; of several figures; few of any perfect, none of any *humane* shape. This was a thing generally then asserted and believed; whereas, by some that were eye-witnesses, it is affirmed that these were no more *monstrous births*, than what it is frequent for women, labouring with *false conceptions*, to produce. Moreover, one very nearly related unto this gentlewoman, and infected with her heresies, was on October 17, 1637, delivered of as hideous a *monster* as perhaps the sun ever lookt upon. It had no head: the face was below upon the breast: the ears were like an ape's, and grew upon the shoulders; the eyes and mouth stood far out; the nose was hooking upwards; the breast and back were full of short prickles, like a thorn-back; the navel, belly, and the distinction of sex, which was female, were in the place of the hips; and those back-parts were on the same side with the face; the arms, hands, thighs and legs, were as other childrens; but instead of toes, it had on each foot three claws, with taleons like a fowl: upon the back above the belly it had a couple of great holes like mouths; and in each of them

stood out a couple of pieces of flesh; it had no forehead, but above the eyes it had four horns; two of above an inch long, hard and sharp; and the other two somewhat less. The midwife was one strongly suspected of witchcraft; . . . thro' whose witchcrafts probably it came to pass that most of the women present at the travel were suddenly taken with such a violent vomiting and purging, tho' they had neither eaten nor drunken any thing to occasion it, that they were forced immediately to go home: others had their children so taken with *convulsions*, which they never had before or after, that *they* also were sent for home immediately; whence none were left at the time of the monster's birth, but the midwife and *two* more, whereof one was fallen asleep: and about the time of the monster's death, which was two hours before his birth, such an odd *shake* was by invisible hands given to the bed as terrify'd the standers-by. It was buried without noise of its *monstrosity*. . . .

If I should now launch forth into a narrative of the marvelous *lewd things* which have been done and said by the giddy sectaries of this island, I confess the *matter* would be agreeable enough to the nature and the design of a church history, and for a warning unto all to take heed how they forsake the word of God and his ordinances in the societies of the faithful, and follow the conduct of *new lights*, that are no more than so many *fool's fires* in the issue; but the *merriment* arising from the ridiculous and extravagant occurrences therein, would not be agreeable to the *gravity* of such an history. Wherefore I forbear it. . . .

London: T. Pankhurst, 1702.

THE TRIALS OF ANNE HUTCHINSON

Anne Hutchinson was first tried by the court and then by the church. In her civil trial in 1837, her accusers claimed that Hutchinson said that her minister, John Cotton, was preaching the truth (what they called the covenant of grace) and that what the other ministers were preaching was false. Several ministers testified that this was indeed what she had said. But Hutchinson herself, and the men who spoke in her behalf—including Cotton—reported that she merely said that John Cotton preached these doctrines *better than* the others. There was an undercurrent here also: a claim that she had destroyed the peace of the community by undermining the church elders. In reality, they saw themselves as her parents, whom she had dishonored. She really infuriated them (and caused a flurry of confusion) by insisting that the clergy who testified against her be put under oath. They regarded this as the supreme insult. Finally, when all the evidence presented by her accusers at the civil trial seemed to be falling apart, they brushed all objections aside, saying merely that they now had sufficient grounds, or enough evidence, to convict her. So in 1837, at the end of her first trial, she was found guilty of treason and sentenced to be banished from the Massachusetts Bay Colony.

THE EVENTS OF HUTCHINSON'S CHURCH TRIAL

The First Day

The second trial—the church trial for heresy—took place four months later. The ministers first went over the "errors" they saw in her thinking. On the first day, the Reverend Wilson decided that he had the votes to throw her out of the church—to excommunicate her—but he asked her pastor, John Cotton, to speak to her: to "admonish" or officially scold her by telling her what she had done wrong.

In the first part of this excerpt, which occurred on the first day, Cotton spoke to the women of the church who had been especially helped by Anne Hutchinson. He told them that Hutchinson had misled them and that they should not pity or support her.

Next he told Hutchinson, in brutal language, what she had done wrong. He even told her that in holding meetings in her house, to which men and women were invited, she was paving the way for sexual immorality and would inevitably become an adulteress herself. Hutchinson denied all of his accusations.

The Second Day

At the end of the first day of the trial, and before she was to appear for sentencing, she was taken to John Cotton's house. He tried to get her to alter her testimony to suit the ministers and, thereby, to save herself. Since the majority of the people in the church were sympathetic to her, the accusing ministers were evidently fearful of acting with too great haste. They did not want a full-scale revolution on their hands.

On the second day of the trial, Hutchinson seemed to apologize—to say she was wrong; but the ministers refused to let the apology stand and continued to insist that she had to pay for her past criticism of them. As a result, she made a hasty and unwise move; in effect, she said: I *believe* in my heart what I always believed, but I am now *saying* something different.

That did it. With these words she gave the ministers a reason to condemn her by admitting that her repentance was not real. The ministers seized upon this with zeal. John Cotton, who had been trying to help her as much as he could, now felt himself threatened again, and so he also turned against her. Finally, the Reverend Wilson pronounced her sentence of excommunication and she was thrown out of the church.

In studying Anne Hutchinson's trial by the Massachusetts Bay Colony for heresy and disruptive behavior, note a number of parallels pertinent to Hester Prynne in *The Scarlet Letter*:

- the stress on her defiance of the elders in refusing to stop her meetings. Note also that the trial is being held to examine her, but she "impudently" examines them.

- the sentiment that her teaching and criticizing of the elders is behavior unbecoming to a woman.

- the involvement of John Cotton, the way the trial threatens to turn on him, and his attempt to distance himself from her.

The trial, in a nutshell, shows a woman who could well have been a model for Hester Prynne: proud and feisty, Hutchinson is not reluctant to defy the clerical elders; like Hester, she has an independent mind but has been inspired by a man she admires tremendously and who eventually abandons her. Her fate is wrapped up in the fact that she has stepped out of her rightful place as a woman to teach and question, as Hester somewhat more quietly did at the end of her life.

FROM *A REPORT ON THE TRIAL OF MRS. ANNE HUTCHINSON BEFORE THE CHURCH IN BOSTON* (March, 1638)

By My Brother Wilson. (Before Mrs. Hutchinson's Examination and her Answer in the Meetinghouse at Boston in New England on the Lecture Day March 15, 1638 when she was accused of divers Errors and unsound Opinions which she held; as was taken from her owne Mouth by Mr. Shephard and Mr. Wells Ministers and proved by further Witnesses.)

The First Day of the Trial

Mr. Cotton: . . . let me say somewhat to the Sisters of our owne Congregation, many of whom I fear have bine too much seduced and led aside by her; therefore *I admonish you* in the Lord to looke to yourselves and to take heed that you receive nothing for Truth which hath not the stamp of the Word of God from it. I doubt not but some of you have also received much good from the Conference of this our Sister and by your Converse with her. . . . But let me say this to you all, and to all the Sisters of other Congregations. *Let not the good you have received from her, make you to receive all for good that comes from her;* for you see she is but a Woman and *many unsound and dangerous principles are held by her*, therefor whatsoever good you have received own it and keepe it carefully, but if you have drunke in with this good any Evell or Poyson, make speed to vomit it up again and to repent of it and take [care] that you do not harden her in her Way by pittying of her or confirming her in her opinions, but pray to God for her and deale faythfully with her as you should in bearing Witnesse agaynst any unsound Thinge that at any Time she hath held forth to you.

And now, Sister, let me adresse myself to you. The Lord put Words into my Mouth, and carry them home to your Soule for good. . . . I would speake it to Gods Glory you have bine an Instrument of doing some good amongst us. You have bine helpfull to many to bringe them from thear unsound Grounds and Principles and from buildinge thear good Estate upon thear owne duties and performances or upon any Righteousness of the Law. And the Lord hath inbued you with good parts and gifts fit to instruct your Children and Servants and to be helpfull to your husband in the Government of the famely. He hath given you a sharpe apprehension, a ready utterance and abilitie to exprese yourselfe in the Cause of God. I would deal with you as Christ Jesus deales with his churches whan he goes to admonish them to take a Vow and to call to your mind the good Thinges that he hath bestowed upon you. Yet Notwithstanding: we have a few Thinges agaynst you and in some sense not a few but such as are of great Wayte and of a heavy Nature and dayngerous Consequences. Therefore let me warne you and admonish you in the Name of Jesus Christ to consider of it seriously, how the Dishonour you have brought unto God by thease unsound Tenets of yours, is far greater than all the honor you have brought to him. And the Evell of your Opinions doth outway all the good of your Doinges. Consider how many poore soules you have mislead, and how you have convayed the poyson of your unsound principles into the harts of many which it may be will never be reduced again. Consider in the fear of God that by this one Error of yours . . . that sinne of the community of Woemen and all promiscuous and filthie cominge togeather of men and Woemen without Distinction or Relation of Marriage, will necessarily follow. And though I have not here, nayther do I thinke, you have bine unfaythfull to your Husband in his Marriage Covenant, *yet that will follow upon it. . . .*

And soe your opinions frett like a Gangrene and spread like a Leprosie, and infect farr and near, and will eate out the very Bowells of Religion, and hath soe infected the Churches that God knowes when they will be cured. Therfor that I may draw to an End; I doe Admonishe you and alsoe charge you in the Name of Christ Jesus in whose place I stand and in the Name of the Church who hath put me upon this service, that you would sadly consider the just hand of God agaynst you, *the greate hurt you have done to the Churches, the great Dishonour you have brought to Jesus Christ* and the Evell that you have done to many a poore soul, and *seeke unto him to give you Repentance for it*, and a hart to give satisfaction to the Churches you have offended hereby; and bewayle your Weaknes in the Sight of the Lord, that you may be pardoned, and consider the great Dishonor and Reproch that hereby you have brought upon this Church of ours whereof you are a Member, how you have laid us all under a Suspition, yea, and a Censure of houldinge and mayntayninge Errors. Therfor thinke of it and be jealous of your owne Spirit in the rest and take heed how you Leven the hartes of younge Woemen with such unsound and dayngerous principles, but Labor rather to recover them out of the snaers as opertunetie shall serve; which you have drawen them to, and soe the Lord carry home to your Soule what I have spoken to you in his Name.

The Second Day of the Trial

[On the second day of the trial, she and Cotton claim that she meant no disrespect or criticism of her elders.]

Brother Wilson: Thear is one Thinge that will be necessary for you Sister to answer which was objected to you the last meetinge, but it being soe late we could

not take your Answer. And that was that you denied you held none of those
Things but since . . . you expressed contrary.

Mrs. Hutchinson: As my mind hath bine open, soe I thinke it needfull to acknowledge how I came first to fall into thease Errors. Instead of Lookinge upon
myself I looked at Men, I know my Dissemblinge will doe no good. I spake
rashly and unadvisedly. *I doe not allow the slightinge of Ministers nor of the
Scriptures* nor any Thinge that is set up by God. If Mr. Shephard doth con-
ceave that I had any of these Thinges in my Minde, than he is deceaved. It
was never in my hart to slight any man but only that man should be kept in
his owne place and not set in the Roome of God.

• • •

Mr. Cotton: The Sume of what she sayd is this, that she did not fall into thease
groce and fundamentall Errors till she came to Roxbury [after her civil trial].
And the Ground was this her Miscarriage and disrespect that she showed to
the Magistrates whan she was before them . . . she confesseth the Roote of
all was the hight and Pride of her Spirit. Soe for her slighting the Ministers
she is hartely sorry for it. For her particular Relation in her Speech to the
Disgrace of him She is sorry for it and desires all that she hath offended to
pray to God for her to give her a hart to be more truly humbled.

• • •

[The Ministers refuse to accept her apology so she changes her story.]

Mrs. Hutchinson: My Judgement is not altered though my Expression alters.

Brother Wilson: This you say is most dayngerous, for if your Judgement all this
while be not altered but only your Expressions, then your Expressions are
soe contrary to the Truth.

Mr. Simes: I should be glad to see any Humiliation in Mrs. Hutchinson. I am
afrayd that she looks but to Spriges [wizards], for I fear thease are no new
Thinges but she hath anciently held them and had need to be humbled for
her former Doctrines and for her abuse of divers Scriptures.

Mr. Peters: We did thinke she would have humbled herselfe for denyinge Graces
this day, for her opinions are dayngerous and fundamentall and such as takes
downe the Articles of Religion. . . .

Deputie [Deputy-Governor Thomas Dudley]: . . . sure *her Repentance is not in
her Countenance*, none cane see it thear I thinke.

• • •

Brother Wilson: I must needs say this and if I did not say soe much I could not
satisfie my owne Conscience herin, for wheras you say that the Cause or Root
of thease your Errors, was your slightinge and Disrespect of the Magistrates
and your unreverent Carriage to them; which though I thinke that was a
greate Sine, and it may be one Cause why God should thus leave you, but
that is not all, for I fear and beleve thar was another and a greater cause, and
that is the *slighting of Gods faythfull Ministers and contemninge and cryinge
downe them as Nobodies*. . . .

• • •

Deputie: I doe remember, that whan she was examined, about the six Questions or Articles, about Revelations etc., that she held nothinge but what Mr. Cotton held.

Mr. Wells: I cane affirme the same too, for whan I spake with heer she tould me that Mr. Cotton and she was both of one minde and she held no more than Mr. Cotton did in thease Things. And whan I told her that then she was lately chaynged in her Opinion, and I urged her with some Things that Mr. Cotton had left, some Things in Writinge expressly agaynst some of the opinions she held; *she affirmed still that thear was no difference betwene Mr. Cotton and She.*

• • •

Brother Wilson: I know she hath sayd it and affirmed it dogmatically, *that the Graces of God is not in us* and we have no Graces in us but only the Righteousnes of Christ Imputed to us, and if thear be any Actinge in us it is Christ only that acts. 53 Isaiah. Galatians 2.

• • •

Mr. Peters: I would desire Mrs. Hutchinson in the name of the Lord that she would search in to her hart farther to helpe on her Repentance. For though she hath confessed some Things yet it is far short of what it should be. . . . We are not satisfied in her Repentance, in that she hath expressed.

• • •

Brother Wilson: I cannot but reverence and adore the wise hand of God in this thinge, and cannot but acknowledge that the Lord is just in leavinge our Sister to pride and Lyinge, and out of the Spirit to al into Errors and divers unsound Judgments. And I looke at *her as a dayngerus Instrument of the Divell* raysed up by Sathan amongst us to rayse up Divissions and Contentions and to take away harts and affections one from another. Wheras before there was much Love and Union and sweet agreement amongst us before she came, yet since all Union and Love hath bine broken and thear hath bine Censurings and Judgings and Condemnings one of another. And I doe conceve all these wofull Opinions doe come from this Bottom, for if the Bottom hath bine unsound and corrupt, than must the Buildinge be such, and the Misgovernment of this Woman's Tounge hath bine a greate Cause of this Disorder, which hath not bine to set up the Ministry of the Word hear or else whear, but to set up her selfe and to draw disciples after her, and therfor she sayth one Thinge to day and another thinge tomorrow: and to speake falsely and doubtfully and dully wheras we should speake the Truth plainly one to another. . . . Therefor we should sine agaynst God if we should not put away from us soe Evell a Woman, guiltie of such Foule Evells. Therfor if the church be of an other minde let them express themselves, if he may not be separated from the Congregation of the Lord.

• • •

Mr. Eliot: . . . she hath carried on all her Errors by Lies, as that she held nothinge but what Mr. Cotton did, and that he and she was all one in Judgment. . . .

Mr. Cotton: . . . though she have confessed that she sees many of the Thinges which she held to be Errors and that it proceded from the Roote Pride of Spirit, yet I see this pride of Harte is not healed but is working still, and therfor to keep secret some unsound Opinions. God hath lett her fall into a manifest Lye, yea to make a Lye and therfor as we receaved her in amongst us I thinke we are bound upon this Ground to remove her from us and not to retayne her any longer, seeinge she doth prevaricate in her Words, as that her Judgment is one Thinge and her Expression is another.

• • •

Brother Wilson: For my part, if the Church proceds I thinke it is and it should be for her Errors in Opinion as well as poynt of Practise, for though she hath made some showe of Repentance yet it doth not seme to be cordial and sincere. . . .

• • •

Brother Wilson: The Church consenting to it we will proced to Excommunication. Forasmuch as you, Mrs. Hutchinson, have highly transgressed and offended and forasmuch as you have soe many ways *troubled the Church with your Errors* and have drawn away many a poor soul and have *upheld your Revelations:* and forasmuch as *you have made a Lye*, etc. Therefor in the name of our Lord Jesus Christ and in the name of the Church I do not only pronounce you worthy to be cast out, but I *doe cast you out* and in the name of Christ I *do deliver you up to Sathan* that you may learne no more to blaspheme to seduce and to lye. And I doe account you from this time forth to be a Heathen and a Publican and soe to be held of all the Bretheren and Sisters of this Congregation, and of others. Therfor *I command you* in the name of Christ Jesus and of this Church *as a leper to withdraw your selfe out of the congregation*; that as formerly you have despised and contemned the Holy Ordinances of God and turned your Backe on them, soe you may now have no part in them nor benefit by them.

Communicated by Franklin Bowditch Dexter to the Massachusetts Historical Society, October 11, 1888.

TOPICS FOR WRITTEN OR ORAL EXPLORATION

1. Write a paper on what Anne Hutchinson seems to represent to the Puritans. Consider that by this time the supreme values to the Puritans were order and obedience to authority in a place where wildness was always threatening to invade. Also consider that, to them, order was godly.

2. The figure of John Cotton is essential here and seems to reverberate in the character of Dimmesdale, who is so willing to sacrifice Hester to keep his good name in the community. Using various Puritan accounts, write a research paper on the different historical views of John Cotton.

3. Hawthorne was obviously a master of this history. Do you see any of John Cotton in the character of Arthur Dimmesdale—for example, isn't the good name they carry in the community more important to them than being loyal to someone they were close to, someone with whom they may have been "partners in crime"?

4. Write accounts of the trial as if you were an objective news reporter trying to get word of what was happening back to England.

5. Have a roundtable discussion of the trial in the manner of *Washington Week in Review*.

6. Outline, as if for a legal brief, the various charges presented against Hutchinson. Then stage a drama in which one person formulates and delivers to the class (as a jury) a "closing statement" in support of Hutchinson's conviction and another person speaks in her defense. Let the class deliberate aloud and decide whether or not to convict.

7. Secure a copy of the U.S. Bill of Rights (which, of course, was not in effect at this time). How many of these rights did the Puritans violate over the course of the Antinomian Crisis?

8. Turn the trial into a performance in which actors interpret the characters by examining their recorded words.

9. In the church trial, why do you suppose John Cotton addresses the women of the church before the trial begins? Remember, the women probably had no vote in this matter.

10. Analyze John Cotton's beginning speeches in the church trial carefully. What do his motives appear to be? Is he trying to save Hutchinson at first? Is he trying to save himself, since he has been associated with her? Make an argument reasoned from what he says in this early address.

11. Study the excerpts from the trial against an early history of the trial.

Does the trial give you any reason to doubt the accuracy of the history? Explain.

12. Hawthorne uses the idea of the prophet or prophecy in speaking of both Anne Hutchinson and Hester Prynne, in effect connecting the two. By analyzing the first paragraph in his sketch of Anne Hutchinson, what does he appear to be saying about woman as prophet?

13. There is ample evidence in the trial and Hawthorne's fiction that this event was about women and women's proper "place." Hutchinson's "dangerousness" comes from her assumption of attitudes and activities that do not belong to women, according to the Puritans. Her "poison" comes from "poisoning" the minds of other women to criticize male clergy. Analyze this in any early historical account, the trial, Hawthorne's sketch, and the novel itself. What exactly have Hester and Hutchinson done to cause the Puritans to view woman as a threat?

14. What does Hawthorne equate in the first paragraph of "Mrs. Hutchinson" with Hutchinson's teaching and speaking? How does this connect with Hester the seamstress?

SUGGESTED READING

Nathaniel Hawthorne's sketch, "Mrs. Hutchinson."

6

Witchcraft and *The Scarlet Letter*

CHRONOLOGY

Late 1691	Girls and Tituba in Rev. Parris's house play at "little sorceries"
Feb. 1692	Girls' odd behavior comes to attention of the community
	Parris consults physician
	It is suggested that "witch cake" of suspects' urine be fed to a dog to determine source of trouble
Feb. 29	Warrants issued for arrest of Sarah Good, Sarah Osborne, and Tituba
Feb. 30	Legislators Jonathan Corwin and John Hathorne aggressively begin interrogation of suspects
Early March	Additional suspects begin to be jailed
March 11	Girls' continued affliction prompts day of prayer
March 20	Rev. Deodat Lawson arrives in Salem to observe and join Rev. Parris in a sermon which stirs up populace against suspects
March 21	Martha Corey arrested
March 23	Mother of one of afflicted girls gets ill, and hysteria spreads

	Dorcas Good, four-year-old daughter of Sarah Good, is placed in jail, in irons, for nine months
March 24	Rebecca Nurse examined and jailed
April 21	Rev. George Burroughs arrested in Maine
	Jails packed with suspects
May 10	Sarah Osborne dies in jail
May 14	William Phips, new governor, arrives
May 17/18	Phips appoints panel of judges to hear cases
June 10	Bridget Bishop hanged
June 15	A group of ministers, including Increase Mather and Samuel Willard, convey their concern and misgivings about the trials to Gov. Phips
June 29	5 cases tried; all sentenced to death
Aug. 5	6 more trials and convictions
Aug. 19	5 executed, including Rev. George Burroughs
Early Sept.	6 more condemned, two of whom escape being hanged
Sept. 17	9 more condemned
Sept. 19	Giles Corey pressed to death
Sept. 22	8 executed (These are the last executions.)
Oct. 3	Increase Mather challenges court on grounds that evidence was inadmissible and that it is better that ten witches escape than that one innocent person be hanged
Oct. 12	Gov. Phips forbids any further arrests
	Remaining prisoners gradually tried and released (By spring 1693 all had been released.)
Dec. 17, 1696	Legislature commands day of fasting as atonement for the hangings
Jan. 14, 1697	Fast day in penance for witch trials
	Samuel Sewall's apology read in church by Rev. Samuel Willard
1703	Legislation passed removing the criminal convictions and establishing compensation

CHARACTERS

Executed by hanging:

June 10, 1692	Bridget Bishop
July 19, 1692	Sarah Good
	Sarah Wildes

	Elizabeth How
	Susanna Martin
	Rebecca Nurse
August 19, 1692	George Burroughs
	John Proctor
	George Jacobs
	John Willard
	Martha Carrier
Sept. 22, 1692	Martha Corey
	Martha Esty
	Alice Parker
	Ann Pudeator
	Margaret Scott
	Wilmot Reed
	Samuel Warwell
	Mary Parker

Giles Corey was pressed to death on September 19, 1692, after refusing to enter a plea. Ten other women were condemned but not executed. Another 150 women were accused and arrested.

Panel of Judges:

William Stoughton, Chief Justice
Samuel Sewall
John Hathorne
Jonathan Corwin
Bartholomew Sergeant

First Accusers:

Elizabeth Parris, 11-year-old daughter of Rev. Parris
Abigail Williams, her cousin
Ann Putnam, their teenage friend

Other Important Participants:

Rev. Samuel Parris, in whose house "afflicted" girls met
Tituba, Parris's servant, who confessed to witchcraft

Gov. Phips, who appointed a court to hear the trial and later disbanded it

Rev. Deodat Lawson, who returned to Salem to encourage arrests

Rev. Cotton Mather, of Boston, who supported the trials

Rev. Increase Mather, Cotton's father, who worked to end the trials

Rev. Samuel Willard, of Boston, who disapproved of the trials and helped some of the accused escape

Thomas Brattle, Boston businessman who wrote against the trials

Rev. John Hale, who supported the trials until his wife was arrested

> . . . a physical curse may be said to have blasted the spot, where guilt and phrenzy consummated the most execrable scene, that our history blushes to record. For this was the field where superstition won her darkest triumph; the high place where our fathers set up their shame, to the mournful gaze of generations far remote. The dust of martyrs was beneath our feet. We stood on Gallows Hill.
>
> Nathaniel Hawthorne, "Alice Doane's Appeal"

> "The little baggage hath witchcraft in her, I profess," said he to Mr. Dimmesdale. "She needs no old woman's broomstick to fly withal!"
>
> *The Scarlet Letter*, 115

> At the moment when the Reverend Mr. Dimmesdale thus communed with himself, and struck his forehead with his hand, old Mistress Hibbins, the reputed witch-lady, is said to have been passing by. . . .
>
> "So, reverend, Sir, you have made a visit into the forest," observed the witch-lady, nodding her high headdress at him.
>
> *The Scarlet Letter*, 208

HAWTHORNE AND WITCHCRAFT

Not only does Hawthorne refer to witchcraft in Puritan times in *The Scarlet Letter* and related short stories, witchcraft is important in unraveling the meaning of the novel. It is mentioned specifically in *The Scarlet Letter* in any number of ways: Governor Bellingham's sister, Mistress Hibbins, who was a historical character hanged on Boston Common for witchcraft, serves as a symbol of uncontrollable darkness running throughout the novel. Hibbins, who in the novel has learned her craft from an English "witch" named Ann Turner, seems to have a special insight into the other characters, instinctively knowing that Dimmesdale has some particular connection with Hester and Pearl and that he could well commit some evil deed and easily be persuaded to meet with the devil in a witches' meeting in the forest. Hearing Dimmesdale's outburst on the scaffold at midnight, she "interpret[s] it, with its multitudinous echoes and reverberations, as the clamor of the fiends and night-hags, with whom she was well known to make excursions into the forest" (145). She is Hester's temptress, knowing when Hester might be most vulnerable to throw off the bonds of Puritan morality and authority and give herself up totally to passion in the wilds of the forest where the witches supposedly meet:

"Hist, hist!" said she, while her ill-omened physiognomy seemed to cast a shadow over the cheerful newness of the house. "Wilt thou go with us tonight? There will be a merry company in the forest; and I well-nigh promised the Black Man that comely Hester Prynne should make one."

"Make my excuse to him, so please you!" answered Hester, with a triumphant smile. "I must tarry at home and keep watch over my little Pearl. Had they taken her from me, I would willingly have gone with thee into the forest, and signed my name in the Black Man's book too, and that with mine own blood!"

"We shall have thee there anon!" said the witch-lady, frowning, as she drew back her head.(116)

Witchcraft and Chillingworth

Each of the four main characters has a distinct connection with witchcraft. Chillingworth, like Hibbins, has been involved with English witches or "conjurers," and there seems to be little question that he himself is a witch because of his magical potions and his friendship with Indian sorcerers. The narrator says of him:

There was something ugly and evil in his face. . . . According to the vulgar idea, the fire in his laboratory had been brought from the lower regions, and was fed with infernal fuel. . . . It grew to be a widely diffused opinion that the Reverend Arthur Dimmesdale . . . was haunted either by Satan himself, or Satan's emissary, in the guise of old Roger Chillingworth. (126)

Witchcraft and Hester

Hester herself is treated by the townspeople, not just Mistress Hibbins, as if she is already a witch. Children who don't know the meaning of the scarlet "A" spy on her as if she were a witch and then "scamper off with a strange, contagious fear" (85). Rather than tell Pearl the truth about the scarlet letter, Hester, in effect, tells her that she played the witch on at least one occasion, that is, that she met the Black Man in the forest once and that the "A" is his mark. She is also often paired, as in the final marketplace scene, with the supposed witch, Mistress Hibbins:

> a person whose eccentricities—or insanity, as we should term it—led her to do what few of the townspeople would have ventured on; to begin a conversation with the wearer of the scarlet letter in public. . . . Seen in conjunction with Hester Prynne—kindly as so many now felt towards the latter—the dread inspired by Mistress Hibbins was doubled, and caused a general movement from that part of the market place in which the two women stood. (225)

Witchcraft and Dimmesdale

Similarly, Dimmesdale seems to be bewitched by Chillingworth. Moreover, by his behavior after meeting with Hester in the forest, Dimmesdale is close to yielding himself to witchcraft. His dark side is so obvious to Mistress Hibbins that she is sure that he is now a witch: "You carry it off like an old hand! But at midnight, and in the forest, we shall have other talk together!" (209). He thinks, after Mistress Hibbins accuses him of having met with the devil: "Have I then sold myself . . . to the fiend whom, if men say true, this yellow-starched and velveted old hag has chosen for her prince and master!" (209). She continues to believe that Dimmesdale is a witch, even as he is passing by in all his ministerial and righteous pomp in the procession on Election Day, and needles Hester with her suspicions:

> "Now, what moral imagination could conceive it!" whispered the old lady con- fidentially to Hester. "Yonder divine man! That saint on earth, as the people uphold him to be, and as—I must needs say—he really looks! Who, now, that saw him pass in the procession, would think how little while it is since he went forth out of his study—chewing a Hebrew text of Scripture in his mouth, I war- rant—to take an airing in the forest! Aha! we know what that means, Hester Prynne! But truly, forsooth, I find it hard to believe him the same man. . . . Dost thou think I have been to the forest so many times, and have yet no skill to judge who else has been there? . . . But this minister! Let me tell thee, in thine ear! When the Black Man sees one of his own servants, signed and sealed, so shy of owning to the bond as is the Reverend Mr. Dimmesdale, he hath a way of ordering matters so that the mark shall be disclosed in open daylight to the eyes of all the world! (225, 226)

HISTORY AND BACKGROUND OF THE 1692 WITCH TRIALS

The historical background of Hawthorne's commentary on witches and Puritans dates to 1692 when, in his hometown of Salem, his ancestor, John Hathorne, sat on the board of judges that condemned and executed twenty people for witchcraft and imprisoned hundreds of citizens.

It was a shameful episode in American history, a frenzy that swept many people into its path and horrified as many others. What made so many people in Puritan times susceptible to this hysteria? How did the witch trials unfold? What caused them to come to a halt?

Reasons for the 1692 Hysteria

Scholars have given many reasons to explain the rise of this hysteria. First, one has to realize that this was a superstitious age, one in which even the most scientific persons, like Cotton Mather, genuinely believed in the power of spirits and demons. In every small occurrence the Puritans saw the direct hand of God, or of Satan, operating. When the wind blew a copy of Cotton Mather's sermon out of his hand, he was not exceptional in believing, without question, that this was caused by Satan, who did not want people to hear Mather's godly message. Nor, for that matter, was the practice of trying witches limited to America. In this, at least, the Puritans were typical of the world they left behind. Puritans had been accusing and hanging so-called witches in the New World ever since they arrived. However, Salem stands out as a time of mass hysteria in which almost anyone was in danger of being accused of witchcraft.

Furthermore, the Puritan creed especially fostered belief in witchcraft. They believed in natural depravity, and that only God's gift of grace kept anyone from becoming a witch—that is, a plaything of the devil. In short, people had a natural tendency to be witches, and since such evil was likely to spread, it had to be stamped out without mercy lest it infect all.

Because of this, it was necessary to constantly combat the devil in others, otherwise witches would help the devil to take over the whole of society. Furthermore, the Puritans believed that God punished the whole community because of the sins of a few people in it. So it followed that if even one witch was allowed to operate, the whole community would be in danger of suffering—from disease, natural disasters, Indian attacks, or political oppression by the English.

Puritans also believed that the devil was working especially hard in this place and at this time to convert them to witchcraft—which was, in effect, the devil's religion. This, they felt, was true because the devil was most active where he was most feared, which was in the Puritan community of God-fearing souls. They also believed that the end of the world was very near, and that for this reason the devil was especially active in converting souls to himself, as witches.

But why did mass hysteria erupt? This was a particularly traumatic period for the Massachusetts Bay community. There were, for example, persistent clashes with Indians, who were seen by the Puritans as witches or demons. There were clashes with the Quakers as well as great public sympathy for both Quakers and Antinomians, which the Puritan leaders found to be very unsettling. Throughout the 1670s there were severe and troubling disputes among the clergy, and in the 1680s the Puritans labored under threats from England, which instituted policies to undermine their mission. The Puritans felt a constant threat that the forces of darkness, irreligion, and disorder were going to win out. Some scholars argue that in light of all these challenges to clerical authority, certain members of the clergy excited the populace against witches in order to give themselves more importance as they took active roles, with great pomp and display, in rooting them out.

There is also evidence that the Salem witch hunt grew because of rivalries within the community, so that some families or members of one faction would accuse a person with whom they were feuding of being a witch. Often, those accused of witchcraft were ornery people who had been in some kind of legal controversy with members of the community. There is further evidence that many accusations of witchcraft arose from the accuser's desire to acquire another's land. If accused, whether one pled innocent or guilty, one's property was put up for grabs.

Chronology of Events

The first case of witchcraft madness occurred in the household of a clergyman named Samuel Parris, who, with his friends, was involved in a heated feud with another faction in 1690 over who should be minister of one of the churches and other matters. In 1691 several young girls associated with the Parris household, including his own eleven-year-old daughter and his niece, began behaving strangely and seemed to be subject to some strange nervous disorders, somewhat like convulsions. Upon seeing this, in February of 1692 Parris sought the help of a physician and some of his friends, but nothing seemed to alleviate the girls' condition.

In the course of this investigation of their maladies, it was discovered that the girls had spent a good deal of time with a maid in the Parris house named Tituba, who had grown up in Barbados. She and the girls had been amusing themselves with palm-readings and other games—similar to Ouija board games, one suspects. Parris and the local magistrates decided that the girls had been bewitched, and measures were taken to find out how this had happened.

Before the end of February, 1692, the girls, supposedly under the direction of the Reverend Parris and his friends, had accused three women of bewitching them. Warrants were issued for the arrest of the women, and they were interrogated and imprisoned. The three women were Tituba, who confessed to being a witch; Sarah Good, who was considered cantankerous; and Sarah Osborne, who had lived in the same house with a man before marrying him and who had not been attending church regularly (churchgoing was compulsory). It was not only the actions and character of the accused that made them candidates for accusations of witchery. From the first, greed for land and bitter local feuds played a distinct if shadowy part in the accusation of the two Sarahs.

In the superheated atmosphere, the charges and the arrests were like sparks to powder. Three powerful Puritan figures immediately rose to the fore. First was Cotton Mather, a prominent Boston clergyman, perhaps the most powerful and the most learned man of his time. A regular and intense observer, he had already tried to "cure" young so-called witches by moving them into his own house so that he could observe and pray for them; and he had written a book on witches in New England, which many believed helped create the hysteria.

The second was Jonathan Corwin, one of the original interrogators and ultimately one of the judges appointed to try the "witches" in Salem. The third was John Hathorne, a Massachusetts

Bay legislator, ancestor of Nathaniel Hawthorne and son of the William Hathorne who had fiercely persecuted Quakers. Like Corwin, John Hathorne was in the forefront of the early investigations and was named to the panel of judges. The zeal of all three was intense, and, in fact, John Hathorne never expressed remorse for his part in the executions that followed.

The arrest of Tituba and the two Sarahs was only the beginning. The ailments of the "bewitched" girls—always under the spotlight now and the center of attention—continued unabated, as did their accusations. In an atmosphere of mounting hysteria, Tituba, under fear of death or torture, confessed her own guilt and implicated others. Suddenly all of New England was in a state of satanic siege. Witches appeared behind every bush; accusations followed every faltering step, dead cow, or failed crop. The hysteria continued like wildfire into the fall of 1692. Those accused of witchcraft would, in the terror of the moment, confess and name other "witches" in order to escape the hangman. Those newly accused would be arrested, and the cycle would continue. In that intense spotlight, the young girls, who continued as the prime movers in this frenzied episode, would claim to have been bitten or burned or in some other way attacked by whoever was accused, and would almost in unison begin screaming, rolling their eyes, and babbling whenever they saw an accused person. Eventually, the accusations by the girls were reinforced by the testimony of others who claimed suddenly to have seen the accused fly through the air, or to have had his or her "specter" or spirit lie on top of them like a demon.

A little more than a month after the young girls were first found to be afflicted, on March 1, 1692, the Reverend Parris held a day of prayer to combat the evil; and another minister, Parris's friend Deodat Lawson, came to town to add his support (some would say to "excite").

On March 21, Martha Corey, who had publicly ridiculed the procedures, was arrested and interrogated by Corwin and Hathorne, and immediately jailed as a witch. When her husband, Giles, a cantankerous, hard-bitten man in his eighties, strenuously objected, he too was accused of witchcraft and arrested. Now, in an atmosphere of terror, any misfortune, minor clash, harsh word could be attributed to witchcraft, as could illnesses, accidents, deaths, or even animals' ailments—anything that could not easily be explained.

On March 23, Sarah Good's four-year-old daughter, Dorcas, was arrested. She was imprisoned and held in chains for nine months before being released. An old woman much respected in the community, Rebecca Nurse, was arrested on March 24. When her sisters, Mary Esty and Sarah Cloyse, objected to Rebecca's arrest, they too were accused and hauled off to jail. Interrogations, usually led with great pomp and zeal by John Hathorne, were outrageous attempts to entrap, threaten, and terrify the accused; the questioners simply assumed the truth of charges made with no evidence.

In April the jails in Salem and Boston were literally packed with those accused of witchcraft. On April 21 many of the Boston clergy were stunned when the Reverend George Burroughs of Maine was arrested and brought to the Salem prison to await trial on charges that he too was a witch. In this atmosphere of terror, many people, including Boston area clergymen Samuel Willard and Increase Mather, Cotton Mather's father, began speaking out against the trials, complaining that the situation was getting out of control, and that, at the very least, the cases should be processed in a regular, lawful way through genuine, legitimate trials. Four days after his arrival from England, the new governor, William Phips, appointed a council to hear the witchcraft cases in Salem. And so began perhaps the most incredible trials in American history.

Two kinds of "evidence" assumed great importance in these trials. One was the presence on the body of what the examiner called "a witch's teat." Often a mole, a wart, an old scar, or a fold of skin would be reported to the court as a witch's teat—clear proof that the defendant was a witch. In addition, the court readily admitted what was called spectral evidence. It was well known, of course, that witches could be in several places at the same time, that your neighbor, for example, might be in his kitchen eating dinner while his specter or another embodiment of his evil spirit was out riding a broom. And so "alibi" had no meaning at all. Accusers often reported that they had seen the specter of the accused do witchcraft, and the court admitted this as evidence.

On June 2 the official hearings before the court began. The panel of judges included Chief Justice William Stoughton and Associate Judges Samuel Sewall, John Hathorne, Bartholomew Sergeant, and Nathaniel Saltonstall, who resigned after the first trial and was replaced by Jonathan Corwin. At the first trial, the panel pronounced Bridget Bishop guilty. She was hanged on June 10.

Painting of George Jacob's 1692 trial for witchcraft in Salem, Massachusetts, by T. H. Matteson, 1855. Courtesy, Peabody Essex Museum, Salem, Massachusetts.

On June 15 a group of citizens from the Boston area, including businessman Thomas Brattle and ministers Increase Mather and Samuel Willard, conveyed their alarm to Governor Phips.

On June 29, despite all protests, five more cases were tried, and wild arrests continued. On July 19 Sarah Good, Sarah Wildes, Elizabeth How, Susanna Martin, and Rebecca Nurse were hanged, on what came to be called Gallows Hill, on the outskirts of Salem. Their bodies were dumped without ceremony into unmarked graves there.

The trials continued throughout the summer. On August 19 the next executions occurred, when the Reverend George Burroughs, John Proctor, George Jacobs, John Willard, and Martha Carrier were all hanged on Gallows Hill.

Giles Corey, the old man who had objected to his wife's arrest, could not officially be tried because he refused to enter a plea. Had he been tried and convicted, his property would have been taken from his family; but with no plea that could not be done. And so Giles Corey suffered the worst horror of all: without benefit even of trial or evidence, on September 19 he was slowly pressed to death, as one heavy stone after another was placed upon his prone body in a vain effort to make him plea; but the old man remained silent, until at last he was pronounced dead.

Three days later, on September 22, eight more of the accused were hanged including Martha Corey (Giles's wife) and the sister of Rebecca Nurse, Mary Esty. These eight were the last to be executed, although the accusations and the arrests continued.

On October 3, Increase Mather made another public objection, directly challenging the court on the grounds that the evidence it accepted was inadmissible and that it was better for ten witches to go free than for one innocent person to be punished. On October 12, Governor Phips at last issued an order forbidding any further arrests. The official court and the enquiries, and maybe even the official witch hunts, ended; but the memories did not, nor did the moral sting of their existence—beyond a doubt one of the darkest periods in American history.

A REVERSAL OF OPINION

Many people, caught up in the hysteria, began to lose sympathy with the witch hunt only when accusations began to hit home. In the very beginning the accused had been mostly lower-class people who somehow were suspect anyway; but as arrests began to penetrate the homes of the pious, to invade their own families, the upper classes began to turn hostile. When they saw one of their own, the Reverend George Burroughs, led to execution, at last some ministers began to speak openly against the entire process. When the Reverend John Hale (involved personally at the beginning, and wholly sympathetic to the witch hunt), saw his wife among the accused, he too became an opponent.

Over the next four years, several of those involved in the trials expressed public remorse for what they had done as judges. In November 1694, Governor Phips pardoned all who had been condemned. On December 17, 1696, a proclamation written by Samuel Sewall, but expressing the sentiments of most of the members of the government, was issued asking God's help and forgiveness for anything they might have done wrong with regard to the trials and ordering a day of fasting and prayer.

As time passed, other jurors involved in the Salem trials also expressed remorse for their part in the terrible tragedy in written statements. However, John Hathorne, Nathaniel's ancestor, was not among them. Even Cotton Mather—not a jurist but surely one of the chief instigators of witch hysteria and the chief apologist of the "wonders of the invisible world"—in the wake of public realization of the true horror involved in the entire episode, came at last to cast (or to admit) doubt as to the reliability of spectral evidence, for the devil (as he noted some time later) could not be relied upon to act as expected in such cases. That was about as close as he came to admitting fault or to apologizing. The general public, many of whom had been wary of the trials from the beginning, were openly critical of the judges by the end of the year. And so witchcraft, and the hanging of witches, vanished from the scene—except as material for the artist and for the historian studying mass hysteria or the tragic aberrations of a terrible, dark period in American history.

THE MEANING OF WITCHCRAFT IN THE NOVEL

In *The Scarlet Letter*, the idea of witchcraft assumes several distinct functions. First of all, it is a genuine presence as well as a symbol, represented concretely by the dark forest, the regular appearance of Mistress Hibbins, and the sinister machinations of Chillingworth. In addition, it is a pervasive dark element in human nature—a facet seen by the Puritans as the unchanging fate of Fallen Man after the expulsion from Eden; and it is concretely the supernatural element of the devil. Thus, the passion and rebellion that Hester feels and that Dimmesdale tries to hide, the passion that has created Pearl and that she displays as part of her nature— all these are viewed as witchcraft, as palpably satanic, by the community.

There are several essential aspects of the history and documents of the 1692 hysteria to consider in studying *The Scarlet Letter*:

1. The attribution of specific characteristics to witches: note the defiance and independence shown in the testimony of the women, the characteristics attributed to them by their accusers, and the parallel view the community has of Hester Prynne.

2. The failure of the accused women to be respectfully subservient to the judges and magistrates: this trait, which is apparent in the testimony of those accused of witchcraft, is also to be noted in Hester, who challenged the community leaders in the matter of her child and refuses to obey their order to name the father of her child.

3. The refusal of the magistrates to consider the innocence of anyone once they have been accused: like the "witches," for whom mere accusation is a death sentence, Hester automatically is regarded as a symbol of depravity for seven years.

4. The supposed power of the witch, like the artist, to effect transformations: like the witches who make a cow sick or a young girl have fits, Hester can transform the "A" on her dress and use the magic of her needle to transform simple, honest cloth into objects of vanity.

5. The connection between witches and Satan parallels Hester's admission to Pearl that she once met the Black Man.

6. The admission of "spectral" evidence that contradicts physical evidence parallels the community's view of Hester: they see her as evil even while she is serving as a sister of mercy.

7. The backlash that occurred, whereby the accusers became the villains, parallels Hester's case, in which the Black Man is seen as dwelling not in the forest so much as in the village, in the person of Roger Chillingworth.

Defiance and Witchcraft

In the historical community of 1692, many traits, as the records demonstrate, were attributed to witches: they were defiant, contentious, eccentric, poor, solitary, litigious (they tended to file lawsuits), and so on. In *The Scarlet Letter*, as well, the community attributes particular qualities to witches. The three most prominent for our understanding of the novel are rebelliousness against ancient authority, sexuality, and creativity. We have observed in the previous chapter the defiance of old age and authority on the part of both Anne Hutchinson and Hester. Such defiance, also observable in cases of women and men who refused to confess to witchcraft in 1692, had the taint of witchcraft in the public mind. Hawthorne underscores how the community equates witchcraft with lack of respect in the character of the "witch-baby," Pearl. When she charges at the "civilized" Puritan children of the village, she sounds as if she is delivering witches' curses. When she flees the grasp of the old men in Governor Bellingham's mansion, Wilson declares that she has witchcraft in her; her uncontrollable nature even makes her mother wonder if she isn't a little witch.

Creativity and Witchcraft

The second characteristic the community views as witchlike is creativity, whether it be sexual or artistic; both kinds are associated with Hester in the public mind. She is the woman whom all know to have defied the community's moral code. Because of her child, her sexuality cannot be hidden. When Hester guardedly explains the scarlet letter to Pearl, she identifies herself as a witch because of her adultery, by telling Pearl that the scarlet letter signifies her one meeting with the Black Man. And, of course, all views of Pearl herself as the devil's child reinforce the identification of her mother's sexuality as witchery. Hester's act of forbidden sex causes Mistress Hibbins, the old woman hanged as a witch, to believe that Hester is a candidate for her witches' coven.

Hibbins also recognizes witchcraft in Dimmesdale at a particularly sexually charged moment—when he returns from the forest after meeting his former lover and finds himself tempted to make indecent and immoral suggestions to several of the parishioners he meets along the way.

Hester's creative sexuality and creative art meet in the scarlet letter she has so richly embroidered, and like Pearl, the creation of her act of illicit sex, her artistic creations are connected with witchcraft and suspiciously immoral, as are Hawthorne's fictions, as we shall see in the analysis of "The Custom-House." Like a witch, Hester can transform things. With her skills, she transforms her punishment into "a pride," as one old woman says. She feels that there is something wrong with her art—she has "rejected it as a sin"—a perception reinforced by the Puritans' outlawing of ornate decoration for everyone but those of importance.

Spectral Evidence and Point of View

The pervasiveness of witchcraft in *The Scarlet Letter* is no accident, for, as in Hawthorne's story "Young Goodman Brown," it is the vehicle for examining point of view—the way we see other people. The result is a reversal of categories of good and evil, very like the reversal that occurred after the hysteria of 1692 whereby the "witches" were perceived as martyrs and the accusers and condemners were seen as persecutors. Hawthorne is interested in what people's points of view and judgment tell us about them, so the focus in the discussion of witchcraft is primarily on those who see witchcraft in others. What can we deduce about a person who constantly sees others as witches, demons, or consorters with the devil? Hawthorne's "Young Goodman Brown" is a key to this aspect of witchcraft in *The Scarlet Letter*. Here is a young man, just married, who, it can be argued, has a dream in which he sees all the best people in the village, including his wife, as witches. Presumably, in his experience with sex in his newly married state, the sexuality—the human quality—of everyone, including his wife, his parents, his minister, and his teachers, dawns on him in a traumatic way in that he has always been taught by his Puritan teachers that the flesh is sinful. Faith, his wife, while also "troubled" by the sinfulness she sees in even the best of people, can still love them. Goodman Brown, however, in seeing both the best and the worst in human nature, loses his "faith" and his love, and chooses to believe the worst. People, just by being human, are, in his loveless eyes, witches. Those who have this loveless view of others have already, ironically, partaken of the devil's baptism. Like Brown they forever after will be "more conscious of the secret guilt of others,

both in deed and thought, than they could now be of their own"
(287). Brown's view of his fellow human beings is shared by the
characters in *The Scarlet Letter*. Sexuality, mirth, and creative art
are seen not as human, but as witchlike. Brown *represents* Puritanism in a very real sense. In *The Scarlet Letter*, Hester, for example, despite all evidence to the contrary—her upright life and
her charity to the sick and dying—is viewed as witchlike, a consort
of the devil. The letter, which Pearl rightly sees as green and natural, has the lurid red light of hell as far as the community is
concerned.

Reversals

As a consequence, a reversal occurs. By another criterion based
on love, the whole community of *The Scarlet Letter*, at least in the
early days of Hester's punishment, becomes a witches' coven—not
because its members are sexual, but because they are loveless. In
this novel, the Black Man (or Satan) dwells not in the forest, but
in the village in the form of Chillingworth, who is embraced by the
leaders as a man of importance and authority. The community is
witchlike because it has a loveless view of others and kills the love
in other people, like Dimmesdale, who is determined to turn cold
and saintly, and Hester, whose only love is for her child.

This reversal in ideas of who the witches are parallels the progress of the 1692 trials which, by the end of the year, came to be
viewed by most of the people in Massachusetts Bay as an inquisition of innocents by misguided people of ill will. In a real sense,
then, in both cases, the witch-hunters became the witches.

THE DOCUMENTS

The documents that follow tell something of the story of witchcraft in Salem, Massachusetts, which since the 1640s had been the
home of Hathornes/Hawthornes and which both fascinated and
repelled Nathaniel Hawthorne.

The first group of documents are records of the 1692 investigations and trials as the events unfolded. Included are the interrogation of and testimony against one of the first women arrested,
Sarah Good, who was subsequently executed. The excerpts of Susanna Martin's trial are recorded by Cotton Mather, an enthusiastic

supporter of the trials. These excerpts are followed by a detailed legal analysis by a businessman, Thomas Brattle, who objected to the trials from the first.

The final document is Samuel Sewall's public apology for his part as a judge who condemned the witches; it was read in the Old South Church in 1696.

THE 1692 WITCH TRIALS AND HESTER PRYNNE

The actual records of the 1692 trials have the capacity to take the student back in history as if he or she were sitting in the Salem courtroom or reading about the happenings in the next day's newspaper.

The trials of Sarah Good and Susanna Martin present us with vivid pictures of the kind of women who were first accused of witchcraft. Though they are poor and seemingly uneducated, they have essential traits in common with Hester. Many women, under the badgering of magistrates who were convinced of their guilt upon accusation and arrest, pled guilty and expressed remorse, and therefore escaped execution. But Sarah Good and Susanna Martin were among those who refused to be bullied into a confession by the magistrates, even though it would mean sure death.

The parallel with Hester is clear. She too could have made her life easier had she given in to the orders of the Reverend Wilson and Governor Bellingham and named Dimmesdale as the father of her child. At least she would have forced him to shoulder the *public* guilt and burden with her. This she refused to do.

These two women, like Hester, reveal that, despite their poverty, they are proud, quick-tongued, independent in their thinking, and rebellious—certainly not humbled by those in authority. They stand up to the magistrates in their trials and even dare to imply that the authorities have been gullible in believing the antics of the young "afflicted" women.

Note the quality of the evidence as well, especially (1) the tendency of the magistrates to accept the validity of the fits of the afflicted and their testimony that the accused (who are sitting still in the witness chair) are "hurting" them; and (2) the magistrates' acceptance of a kind of scapegoating testimony: any bad happening for which no ready explanation could be found (like a cow dying suddenly) was interpreted as a result of witchcraft.

The most controversial element of the trials, discussed in some depth by Thomas Brattle, was the wholesale and unquestioned admission of "spectral" evidence. A witness could testify that he or she had seen the *illusion* of a particular person doing something horrible, and this was accepted as eyewitness evidence. You could be seen by a hundred people on a stage making a speech at 2 P.M., but a witness could still accuse you of coming to his house in the form of a specter or illusion, to bite and pinch him, on the same day at the same time. In a novel filled with references to witchcraft, the idea of spectral evidence is relevant to the discussion of point of view—how a community and its leaders view certain people, and how a person's point of view and judgment of other people usually say more about the judge than about the person being judged. In short, witchery, like beauty, is often in the eye of the beholder.

FROM WILLIAM E. WOODARD, ED., *RECORDS OF SALEM WITCHCRAFT* (1864)

Warrant vs. Sarah Good

Salem February the 29th 1691–92

   Whereas Messrs. Joseph Hutchinson, Thomas Putnam, Edward Putnam, and Thomas Preston, Yeomen of Salem village in the County of Essex, personally appeared before us and made complaint on Behalf of their Majesties against Sarah Good the wife of William Good of Salem Village above said for suspicion of Witchcraft by her committed, and thereby much Injury done by Eliz. Parris, Abigail Williams, Ann Putnam and Elizabeth Hubbard all of Salem Village aforesaid sundry times within this two months and Lately also don, at Salem village Contrary to the peace of our Sovereign Lord and Lady William and Mary, King and Queen of England etc.—You are therefore in their Majesties' names hereby required to apprehend & bring before us, the said Sarah Good tomorrow about ten of the clock in the forenoon at the house of Lt Nathaniel Ingersoll in Salem Village or as soon as may be then and there to be examined Relating to the above said premises and hereof you are not to fail at your peril.

   Dated. Salem, February 29th 1691–92

John Hawthorne ⎫ Jonathan Corwin ⎭	Assistants.

To Constable George Locker.

Officer's Return.

   I brought the person of Sarah Good the wife of William Good according to the tenor of the within warrant, as is Attest by me

George Locker—Constable

1 March 1691–92

• • •

Examination of Sarah Good

The examination of Sarah Good before the worshipful Assistants John Hathorne and Jonathan Corwin

Q: Sarah Good what evil Spirit have you familiarity with?

A: None.

Q: Have you had no contract with the devil?

Good answered no.

Q: Why do you hurt these children?

A: I do not hurt them. I scorn it.

Q: Who do you employ then to do it?

A: I employ nobody.

Q: What creature do you employ then?

A: No creature but I am falsely accused.

Q: Why did you go away muttering from Mr. Parris his house?

A: I did not mutter but I thanked him for what he gave my child.

Q: Have you made no contract with the devil?

A: No.

H[athorne] desired the children all of them to look upon her and see if this were the person that had hurt them and so they all did look upon her, and said this was one of the persons that did torment them—presently they were all tormented.

Q: Sarah Good do you not see now what you have done, why do you not tell us the truth, why do you thus torment these poor children?

A: I do not torment them.

Q: Who do you employ then?

A: I employ nobody I scorn it.

Q: How came they thus tormented?

A: What do I know you bring others here and now you charge me with it.

Q: Why who was it?

A: I do not know but it was some you brought into the meeting house with you.

Q: We brought you into the meeting house.

A: But you brought in two more.

Q: Who was it then that tormented the children.

A: It was Osborne.

Q: What is it you say when you go muttering away from a person's house?

A: If I must tell I will tell.

Q: Do tell us then.

A: If I must tell, I will tell, it is the commandments. I may say my commandments I hope.

Q: What commandment is it.

A: If I must tell I will tell, it is a psalm.

Q: What psalm?

After a time she muttered over some part of a psalm.

Q: Who do you serve?

A: I serve God.

Q: What God do you serve?

A: The God that made heaven and earth.

Though she was not willing to mention God, her answers were in a very wicked spiteful manner, reflecting and retorting against the authority with base and abusive words and many lies she was taken in. It was here said that her husband had said that he was afraid that she either was a witch or would be one very quickly. The worshipful Mr. Hathorne asked him his reason why he said so of her, whether he had ever seen anything by her, he answered no, not in this nature, but it was her bad carriage to him, and indeed said he I may say with tears that she is an enemy to all good.

Ann Putnam Jr. vs. Sarah Good.

The Deposition of Ann Putnam Junior who testifieth and saith, that on the 25th of February 1691–92 I saw the Apparition of Sarah Good which did torture me most grievously, but I did not know her name till the 27th of February and then she told me her name was Sarah Good and then she did price me and pinch me most grievously, and also since several times urging me vehemently to writ[e] in her book and also on the first day of March being the day of her Examination Sarah Good did most grievously torture me and also several times since, and also on the first day of March 1692. I saw the Apparition of Sarah Good go and afflict and torture the bodies of Elizabeth Parris, Abigail Williams and Elizabeth Hubbard also I have seen the Apparition of Sarah Good afflicting the body of Sarah Vibber.

(mark)
Ann Putnam

Ann Putnam owned this her testimony to be the truth on her oath; before the Jurors of Inquest this 28: of June 1692.

And further says that she verily believes that Sarah Good doth bewitch and afflict her.

Sworn before the Court

Sarah Vibber vs. Sarah Good.

The Deposition of Sarah Vibber aged 36 years, testifieth and saith that the Saturday night before Goody Dustin of Reading was examined I saw the apparition of Sarah Good standing by my bedside and she pulled aside the curtain and turned down the sheet and looked upon my child about 4 years old and presently upon it the child was struck into a great fit that my husband and I could hardly hold it.

Sarah Vibber on her oath did own this her testimony before the Jurors for Inquest this 28: of June 1692

Jurat Sarah Vibber

Roxbury, Mass.: Privately Printed, 1864

FROM COTTON MATHER,
THE WONDERS OF THE INVISIBLE WORLD (1693)

The Tryal of Susanna Martin, at the Court of Oyer and Terminer, Held by Adjournment at Salem, June 29, 1692

Susanna Martin, pleading *Not Guilty* to the Indictment of *Witchcraft*, brought in against her, there were produced the Evidences of many Persons very sensibly and grievously Bewitched; who all complained of the Prisoner at the Bar, as the Person whom they believed the cause of their Miseries. And now, as well as in the other Trials, there was an extraordinary Endeavor by *Witchcrafts*, with Cruel and frequent Fits, to hinder the poor Sufferers from giving in their Complaints, which the Court was forced with much Patience to obtain, by much waiting and watching for it.

II. There was now also an account given of what passed at her first Examination before the Magistrates. The Cast of her *eye*, then striking the afflicted People to the Ground, whether they saw that Cast or no; there were these among other Passages between the Magistrates and the Examinate.

Magistrate: Pray, what ails these People?

Martin: I don't know.

Magistrate: But what do you think ails them?

Martin: I don't desire to spend my Judgment upon it.

Magistrate: Don't you think they are bewitched?

Martin: No, I do not think they are.

Magistrate: Tell us your thoughts about them then.

Martin: No, my thoughts are my own, when they are in, but when they are out they are anothers. Their Master ———

Magistrate: Their Master? Who do you think is their Master?

Martin: If they be dealing in the Black Art, you may know as well as I.

Magistrate: Well. What have you done towards this?

Martin: Nothing at all.

Magistrate: Why, 'til you or your Appearance.

Martin: I cannot help it.

Magistrate: Is it not *your* master? How comes your Appearance to hurt these?

Martin: How do I know? He that appeared in the shape of Samuel, a glorified Saint, may appear in any ones shape.

It was then noted in her, as in others like her, that if the Afflicted went to approach her, they were flung down to the Ground. And, when she was asked the reason of it, she said, *I cannot tell; it may be, the Devil bears me more Malice than another.*

V. *Bernard Peache* testifi'd, That being in Bed, on the Lord's-day Night, he heard a scrabbling at the Window, whereat he then saw *Susanna Martin* come in, and jump down upon the floor. She took hold of this Deponent's Feet, and drawing his Body up into an Heap, she lay upon him near two Hours; in all which time he could neither speak nor stir. At length, when he could begin to move, he laid hold on her Hand, and pulling it up to his Mouth, he bit three of her Fingers, as he judge, unto the Bone. Whereupon she went from the Chamber, down the stairs, out at the Door. This Deponent thereupon called unto the People of the House, to advise them of what passed; and he himself did follow her. The People saw her not; but there being a Bucket at the Left-hand of the Door, there was a drop of Blood found upon it; and several more drops of Blood upon the Snow newly fallen abroad: There was likewise the print of her 2 feet just without the Threshold; but no more sign of any Footing further off.

XI. *Jervis Ring* testified, That about seven years ago, he was oftentimes and grievously oppressed in the Night, but saw not who troubled him; until at last he Lying perfectly Awake, plainly saw *Susanna Martin* approach him. She came to him, an forcibly bit him by the Finger; so that the Print o the bite is now, so long after, to be seen upon him.

XII. But besides all these Evidences, there was a most wonderful Account of one *Joseph Ring*, produced on this occasion.

This Man has been strangely carried about by *Daemons*, from one *Witch-meeting* to another, for near two years together; and for one quarter of this time, they have made him, and keep him Dumb, tho' he is now again able to speak. There was one *T.H.* who having, as 'tis judged, a design of engaging this *Joseph Ring* in a snare of Devilism, contrived a while, to bring this *Ring* two Shillings in Debt unto him.

Afterwards, this poor man would be visited with unknown shapes, and this *T.H.* sometimes among them; which would force him away with them, unto unknown Places, where he saw Meetings, Feastings, Dancings; and after his return, wherein they hurried him along through the Air, he gave Demonstrations to the Neighbours, that he had indeed been so transported. When he was brought unto these hellish Meetings, one of the first Things they still did unto him, was to give him a knock on the back, whereupon he was ever as if bound with Chains, incapable of stirring out of the place, till they should release him. He related, that there often came to him a Man, who presented him a *Book*, whereto he would have him set his Hand; promising to him, that he should then have even what he would; and presenting him with all the delectable Things, Persons, and Places, that he could imagine. But he refusing to subscribe, the business would end with dreadful Shapes, Noises and Screeches, which almost scared him out of his Wits. Once with the Book, there was a Pen offered him, and an Ink-horn with Liquor in it, that seemed like Blood: but he never touched it.

This Man did now affirm, That he saw the Prisoner at several of these hellish Rendezvous.

Note, this Woman was one of the most impudent, scurrilous, wicked Creatures in the World; and she did now throughout her whole Tryal, discover her self to be such an one. Yet when she was asked, what she had to say for her self? Her chief Plea was, *That she had lead a most virtuous and holy Life.*

Boston: John Dunton, 1693.

THOMAS BRATTLE'S LETTER

Thomas Brattle, a Cambridge businessman, had been from the first outraged by the accusations and arrests in Salem and the illegal way in which the trials were being conducted. He had joined with several other prominent men in the area to negotiate behind the scenes to stop the trials or at least see that they proceeded in acredible manner. But the appointment of a respectable board of judges to conduct the trials in a regular manner had not brought reason and common sense to the proceedings.

Brattle's letter, delivered to several influential men in the area, is a critical analysis of the events in Salem. He dares to accuse the judges and magistrates there, not only of stupidity, but of unequal justice, in selectively arresting the accused.

FROM "LETTER OF THOMAS BRATTLE, F.R.S." (1692)

October 8, 1692.

First, as to the method which the Salem Justices do take in their examinations, it is truly this: A warrant being issued out to apprehend the persons that are charged and complained of by the afflicted children, (as they are called); said persons are brought before the Justices, (the afflicted being present.) The Justices ask the apprehended why they afflict those poor children; to which the apprehended answer, they do not afflict them. The Justices order the apprehended to look upon the said children, which accordingly they do; and at the time of that look, (I dare not say by that look, as the Salem Gentlemen do) the afflicted are cast into a fitt. The apprehended are then blinded, and ordered to touch the afflicted; and at that touch, tho' not by the touch, (as above) the afflicted ordinarily do come out of their fitts. The afflicted persons then declare and affirm, that the apprehended have afflicted them; upon which the apprehended persons, tho' of never so good repute, are forthwith committed to prison, on suspicion for witchcraft. . . .

I would fain know of these Salem Gentlemen, but as yet could never know, how it comes about, that if these apprehended persons are witches, and, by a look of the eye, do cast the afflicted into their fitts by poisoning them, how it comes about, I say, that, by a look of their eye, they do not cast others into fitts, and poison others by their looks; and in particular, tender, fearful women, who are beheld by them, and as likely as any in the whole to receive an ill impression from them. This

Salem philosophy, some men may call the new philosophy; but I think it rather deserves the name of Salem superstition and sorcery, and it is not fitt to be named in a land of light as New-England is. . . .

Now for the proof of the said sorcery and witchcraft, the prisoner at the bar pleading not guilty.

1. The Afflicted persons are brought into Court; and after much patience and pains taken with them, do take their oaths, that the prisoner at the bar did afflict them: And here I think it very observable, that often, when the afflicted do mean and intend only the appearance and shape of such a one, (say G. Proctor) yet they positively swear that G. Proctor did afflict them; and they have been allowed so to do; as tho' there was no real difference between G. Proctor and the shape of G. Proctor. This, methinks, may readily prove a stumbling block to the Jury, lead them into a very fundamental errour, and occasion innocent blood, yea the innocentest blood imaginable, to be in great danger. Whom it belongs unto, to be eyes unto the blind, and to remove such stumbling blocks, I know full well; and yet you, and every one else, do know as well as I who do not.

• • •

4. They are searched by a Jury; and as to some of them, the Jury brought in, that [on] such or such a place there was a preternatural excrescence. And I wonder what person there is, whether man or woman, of whom it cannot be said that, in some part of their body or other, there is not a preternatural excrescence. The term is a very general and inclusive term.

As to the late executions, I shall only tell you, that in the opinion of many unprejudiced, considerate and considerable spectatours, some of the condemned went out of the world not only with as great protestations, but also with as good shews of innocency, as men could do. . . .

Many things I cannot but admire and wonder at, an account of which I shall here send you.

1. I do admire some particular persons, and particularly Mrs. Thatcher of Boston, should be much complained of by the afflicted persons, and yet that the Justices should never issue out their warrants to apprehend them, when as upon the same account they issue out their warrants for the apprehending and imprisoning [of] many others.

This occasions much discourse and many hot words, and is a very great scandal and stumbling block to many good people; certainly distributive Justice should have its course, without respect to persons; and altho' the said Mrs. Thatcher be mother in law to Mr. Corwin, who is one of the Justices and Judges, yet if Justice and conscience do oblige them to apprehend others on the account of the afflicted their complaints, I cannot see how, without injustice and violence to conscience, Mrs. Thatcher can escape, when it is well known how much she is, and has been, complained of.

. . . Now, that the Justices have thus far given ear to the Devil, I think may be mathematically demonstrated to any man of common sense: And for the demonstration and proof hereof, I desire, only, that these two things may be duly considered, *viz.*

1. That several persons have been apprehended purely upon the complaints of these afflicted, to whom the afflicted were perfect strangers, and had not the least knowledge of imaginable, before they were apprehended.

2. That the afflicted do own and assert, and the Justices do grant, that the Devil does inform and tell the afflicted the names of those persons that are thus unknown unto them. Now these two things being duly considered, I think it will appear evident to any one, that the Devil's information is the fundamental testimony that is gone upon in the apprehending [of] the aforesaid people.

But altho' the Chief Judge, and some of the other Judges, be very zealous in these proceedings, yet this you may take for a truth, that there are several about the Bay, men for understanding, Judgment, and Piety, inferior to few, (if any,) in N.E. that do utterly condemn the said proceedings, and do freely deliver their Judgment in the case to be this, *viz.* The hon'ble Simon Bradstreet, Esq. (our late Governor); the hon'ble Thomas Danforth, Esq. (our late Deputy Governor); the Rev'd Mr. Increase Mather, and the Rev'd Mr. Samuel Willard. Major N. Saltonstall, Esq. who was one of the Judges, has left the Court, and is very much dissatisfied with the proceedings of it. Excepting Mr. Hale, Mr. Noyes, and Mr. Parris, the Rev'd Elders, almost throughout the whole Country, are very much dissatisfyed. Several of the late Justices, *viz.* Thomas Graves, Esq. Noah Byfield, Esq. Francis Foxcroft, Esq. are much dissatisfied; also several of the late Justices; and particular, some of the Boston Justices, were resolved rather to throw up their commissions than be active in disturbing the liberty of their Majesties' subjects, merely on the accusations of these afflicted, possessed children.

Finally, the principal Gentlemen in Boston, and thereabout, are generally agreed that irregular and dangerous methods have been taken to these matters.

Many of these afflicted persons, who have scores of strange fitts in a day, yet in the intervals of time are hale and hearty, robust and lusty, as tho' nothing had afflicted them.

Collections of the Massachusetts Historical Society, rpt. 1835, Series 1, vol. 5, pp. 61–81.

SEWALL'S APOLOGY AND DIMMESDALE'S CONFESSION

Samuel Sewall, state legislator, prominent New England business-man, and student of divinity, seemed on the surface to be an excellent choice to serve as jurist in the trials. The diary he left shows him to be a good-hearted, dependable, generous, reasonable man. He had always held a position of great influence in the community and seemingly had both the respect and affection of those who knew him. But he obviously went along with the judges who were out for blood in this affair and, becoming caught up in the hysteria himself, never seemed to object to the tactics of the court or to the executions of the accused. He acted as one with the panel of persecutors, even though his own minister in Boston, Samuel Willard, was vehemently opposed to the trials from the first and helped some of the accused escape. Though this was even at the time considered one of the most astounding moments in world history, Sewall records almost nothing about the Salem witch trials in his diary.

The court had been disbanded and the arrests had ceased by the spring of 1693. The general public had reversed its opinion of the trials, seeing the magistrates and judges as the villains and the accused as innocent victims. Again, it was not so much because the circumstances had changed as because perceptions had changed. Without recording any of his soul-searching in his diary, Sewall by 1696 had also reversed himself and decided to take a public stand to make amends. On January 14, 1697, which had been proclaimed a fast day, Sewall gave the following written statement to his minister, Samuel Willard, as Willard walked by him to the pulpit. As Willard began to read the statement, Sewall walked to the pauper's pew of the church, stood during the reading, and bowed at the end.

Two issues pertinent to *The Scarlet Letter* come to mind in reviewing the case of Samuel Sewall. First, as we have seen, is the reversal of sentiments regarding those in authority as opposed to their victims. Second, the public confession of Sewall bears some resemblance to Dimmesdale's confession. For both men—learned in the scriptures, pillars of their churches, pious, and righteous—

public confession of guilt had to be a very difficult thing. But there are also conditions that diminish the importance of both confessions. In the first place, both seem to arise from motives other than a true realization of having done wrong or sense of sorrow for the pain they had caused. Dimmesdale likely senses that he is dying and may very well confess as last-minute "insurance" to give himself an outside chance of going to heaven. Sewall seems to be confessing because he has had so much terrible luck and obviously hopes that a confession will turn things around. Also, since Dimmesdale knows that he is near death, he will not now have to suffer humiliation and punishment by the community for what he has done. Similarly, Sewall can now apologize without fear of censure from the authorities because the whole view of the witch trials has changed. One might argue (uncharitably) that Sewall has just seen the way the wind blows and is now going along with the prevalent attitude, just as he did in the trials.

FROM *THE DIARY OF SAMUEL SEWALL* (1697)

Copy of the Bill I put up on the Fast day; giving it to Mr. Willard as he pass'd by, and standing up at the reading of it, and bowing when finished; in the Afternoon.

Samuel Sewall, sensible of the reiterated strokes of God upon himself and family; and being sensible, that as to the Guilt contracted upon the opening of the late Commission of Oyer and Terminer at Salem (to which the order for this Day relates) he is, upon many accounts, more concerned than any that he knows of, Desires to take the Blame and shame of it, Asking pardon of men, And especially desiring prayers that God, who has an unlimited Authority, would pardon that sin and all other his sins, personal and Relative: And according to his infinite Benignity, and Sovereignty, Not Visit the sin of him, or of any other, upon himself or any of his, nor upon the land: But that He would powerfully defend him against all Temptations to Sin, for the future; and vouchsafe him the efficacious, saving Conduct of his Word and Spirit.

Daniel Neal, *History of New England* 2 vols. (London: J. Clark and R. Ford, 1720), 2: 536.

TOPICS FOR WRITTEN OR ORAL EXPLORATION

1. Note in the case of Sarah Good the undertone of disapproval of her lack of respect for authority. Write a paper on witchcraft as the ultimate rebellion against both civil and religious authority.

2. From the excerpts of testimony against Sarah Good, write a profile of the characteristics of the person accused: social status, personality, habits, disposition, economic level, and so on.

3. Write dialogue, set in the corner of a prison cell, between a person accused of witchcraft and a member of her/his family in which they explore and argue the advisability of the accused's confessing and naming names of others. Do the accused have a responsibility to do anything to save themselves in order to take care of their families? Is there a higher moral responsibility to speak the truth and not injure anyone else? The ideal argument may be between an accused person determined to speak the truth and a family member who tries to convince the accused to save his or her own skin.

4. The playwright Arthur Miller wrote of the communist investigations of the 1950s as witch hunts. Various other groups have been accused of other kinds of witch hunts in the 1990s, with regard to child molestation, for example. What do these so-called witch hunts have in common with the Salem trials? Can you think of other examples?

5. Consider the connection between so-called witch hunts and scapegoating. Define the scapegoat carefully. What characteristics do scapegoats share with witches?

6. From the excerpts you have read here, what do you think may account for the young girls' afflictions? (Note that in *The Scarlet Letter* Hawthorne refers to what others call Mistress Hibbins's witchery as "insanity.")

7. Stage a witch trial using excerpts from the various cases presented here. However, give the accused a defense attorney who can cross-examine witnesses, object to the testimony and questions of the judges, and present a closing statement in defense of the accused.

8. In looking again at "Young Goodman Brown," consider and write a paper on Brown as a stereotypical Puritan who begins to think everyone a witch. Make reference to the actual cases that occurred in 1692.

9. One critic has argued that Brown is (as the story goes) "the chief horror" of the scene. Note in a paper the reversal that has occurred so that the original villains in the trials are now regarded as victims— Hawthorne calls them "martyrs"—while those who were then considered "godly" are now the villains. Note as well how that reversal

is apparent in "Young Goodman Brown" and *The Scarlet Letter*: the "godly" becoming the villains and at least some of those associated with witchcraft becoming sympathetic characters.

10. In regard to this reversal of the expected roles of the witch and the witch-hunter, make an argument, well supported from the novel, that the "Black Man," as the Puritans called Satan, lives in the town as an accepted and respected member of the community rather than in the forest.

11. Examine the irony that Pearl is repeatedly called, by narrator and characters, an offspring of the Black Man. Note who calls her this and why. Remember, in exploring this question, that it was believed that female witches had had sex with the devil.

12. One important issue in the witch trials was the admission of "spectral evidence": accusers said that they had seen the "specters" of the accused flying through the air or appearing and disappearing suddenly. This was treated as if the accusers had seen the flesh-and-blood person at the scene of a crime. Note the place of spectral evidence in "Young Goodman Brown."

13. How, in *The Scarlet Letter*, do characters reveal *themselves* through their points of view? Note especially how they see and evaluate Hester, the "A," and Pearl.

14. Using your analysis of the novel and what you know and can find out about the Salem witch trials, write a hypothetical scenario in which Hester is accused of witchcraft.

SUGGESTED READINGS

From Nathaniel Hawthorne's tales: "Young Goodman Brown," "Alice Doane's Appeal," and "Main Street."

The History of the Puritans

Adair, John Eric. *Founding Fathers*. London: J. M. Dent, 1982. *Aspects of Puritan Religious Thought*. New York: AMS Press, 1982.

Bartlett, Robert Merrill. *The Faith of the Pilgrims*. New York: United Church Press, 1978.

Bercovitch, Sacvan. *The Puritan Origins of the American Self*. New Haven: Yale University Press, 1975.

Bradford, Alden. *History of Massachusetts*. 3 vols. Boston: Richardson and Lord, 1822–1829.

Bradford, William. *Bradford's History "of Plimoth Plantation."* Boston: Wright and Potter, 1901.

Byington, Ezra Hoyt. *The Puritan in England and New England*. New York: B. Franklin, 1972.

Conde, Maryse. *I, Tituba, Black Witch of Salem*. Charlottesville: University Press of Virginia, 1992.

Cragg, Gerald R. *Puritanism in the Period of the Great Persecution*. New York: Russell and Russell, 1971.

Delbanco, Andrew. *The Puritan Ordeal*. Cambridge, Mass.: Harvard University Press, 1989.

Dunlea, William. *Anne Hutchinson and the Puritans*. Pittsburgh: Dorrance, 1993.

Hall, David D. *Puritanism in Seventeenth-Century Massachusetts*. New York: Holt, Rinehart and Winston, 1968.

Middlekauff, Robert. *The Mathers*. New York: Oxford University Press, 1971.

Miller, Perry. *American Puritans: Their Prose and Poetry*. Garden City, N.J.: Doubleday, 1956.

————. *Errand into the Wilderness*. Cambridge, Mass.: Belknap Press, 1956.

————. *The New England Mind*. Cambridge, Mass.: Harvard University Press, 1953.

————. *The Puritans*. New York: American Book Co., 1938.

Morgan, Edmund Sears. *The Puritan Family*. Boston: Trustees of the Public Library, 1956.

————. *Visible Saints*. New York: New York University Press, 1963.

Morison, Samuel Eliot. *Builders of the Bay Colony*. Boston: Houghton Mifflin, 1930.

————. *The Puritan Pronaos*. New York: New York University Press, 1936.

Powers, Edwin. *Crime and Punishment in Early Massachusetts*. Boston: Beacon Press, 1966.

Reintz, Richard. *Tensions in American Puritanism*. New York: Wiley, 1970.

Smith, Chard Powers. *Yankees and God*. New York: Hermitage House, 1954.

Spurgin, Hugh. *Roger Williams and Puritan Radicalism in the English Separatist Tradition*. Lewiston, ME: E. Mellen Press, 1989.

Tyler, Moses Coit. *A History of American Literature, 1607–1765*. New York, 1878. Repr., 1993.

Ziff, Larzer. *Puritanism in America*. New York: Viking Press, 1973.

Anne Hutchinson and the Antinomian Crisis

Adams, Charles Francis. *The Antinomian Controversy*. New York: Da Capo Press, 1976.

Battis, Emery. *Saints and Sectaries: Anne Hutchinson and the Antino-

mian Controversy in the Massachusetts Bay Colony. Chapel Hill: University of North Carolina Press, 1962.

Bremer, Francis J., ed. *Anne Hutchinson, Troubler of the Puritan Zion*. Huntington, N.Y.: R. E. Krieger, 1981.

Cameron, Jean. *Anne Hutchinson, Guilty or Not?* New York: Peter Lang, 1994.

Crawford, Deborah. *Four Women in a Violent Time*. New York: Crown, 1970.

Hall, David D., ed. *The Antinomian Controversy*. Middletown, Conn.: Wesleyan University Press, 1968.

Huber, Elaine. *Women and the Authority of Inspiration*. Lanham, Md.: University Press of America, 1985.

Lang, Amy Schrager. *Prophetic Woman*. Berkeley: University of California Press, 1987.

Williams, Selma R. *Divine Rebel: The Life of Anne Marbury Hutchinson*. New York: Holt, Rinehart and Winston, 1981.

Winthrop, John. *A Short Story of the Rise, Reign, and Ruin of the Antinomian Familists and Libertines*. London: Ralph Smith, 1644.

Witchcraft

Boyer, Paul, and Stephen Nissenbaum, eds. *Salem-Village Witchcraft: A Documentary Record of Local Conflict*. Boston: Northeastern University Press, 1993.

Burr, George Lincoln, ed. *Narratives of the Witchcraft Cases, 1648–1706*. New York: Charles Scribner's Sons, 1914.

Gragg, Larry Dale. *The Salem Witch Crisis*. New York: Praeger, 1992.

Levin, David, ed. *What Happened in Salem?* New York: Harcourt, Brace, 1960.

Mappen, Marc, ed. *Witches and Historians*. Huntington, N.Y.: R. E. Krieger, 1980.

Mather, Cotton. *The Wonders of the Invisible World*. Boston: Printed by Benj. Harris for Sam Phillips, 1693.

Records of Salem Witchcraft, copied from the original documents. [Compiled by W. Elliot Woodward.] Reprint. New York: Da Capo Press, 1969.

7

"The Custom-House": Hawthorne, the Nineteenth Century, and *The Scarlet Letter*

Hawthorne's controversial preface to *The Scarlet Letter*, "The Custom-House," once considered vaguely "introductory" but nevertheless irrelevant to the novel itself (and in fact often omitted), is now regarded as essential to its understanding. First, it clearly dramatizes the author's own vocational struggle as an imaginative writer in a profession scorned by his Puritan ancestors and carried out here, in this dust-ridden custom house, in what he sees as a land of the dead, a society dominated by the past, disdainful (like the Puritans) of an idle life devoted to fiction, and inclined to honor only commercial success: not to make money here is to exist without honor, status, or vocation. Second, the story of Nathaniel Hawthorne among these people in the nineteenth century is clearly linked by analogy with that of Hester, Dimmesdale, and Pearl in the seventeenth century.

Looking first at "The Custom-House" as Hawthorne's struggle for existence, the narrator clearly presents this as a fight between spiritual life and death, the struggle of creativity and imagination—the essential life of an author—even to survive in this land of dust and shadows, this place that casts a sterile hand upon everything bright or human. The writer has left the reclusive life of the literary world in Concord, isolated but distinctly alive, to come to this bustling world of commerce, to make a *living*, to earn basic money for food and shelter. But in the process he has, ironically, entered a dead, torpid world, altogether removed from life—at least from what he considers life.

The situation is in fact an old and familiar one. A man burning with ideas finds himself among a crowd of contented human animals and sees himself, like them, becoming a dependent child. And he longs to aspire and soar. At last burst free he does—with *The Scarlet Letter*, a seething, explosive portrayal of instinct, passion, and human values, of sin and repression; a masterful probing of weakness and law in the Puritan world, and of revenge, the nature of love, and nature itself in human society.

For us today, the meaning may seem clear and the situation familiar. For the people of Salem and of the Custom House, so described, it was not so simple or so clear. Both the preface and the novel aroused storms of protest and indignation.

THE LAND OF THE DEAD

From the very first in the preface, both the Custom House and the town of Salem are presented as places of sterility, emptiness, shadows; places of the living dead. To the narrator, Salem is a place of "decayed wooden warehouses," a "not very enlivening prospect," and wharves that have been permitted "to crumble into ruin." Everything within the narrator's view is as dry, cold, and ugly as a corpse: "old wooden houses, the mud and the dust, the dead level of site and sentiment, the chill east wind" (22). And beyond that, the general life of the community is dead as well, its main street "lounging wearisomely through the whole extent of the peninsula" and its once lively trade having been allowed to wither. To cap it all off, the most famous historical site is a place of death: Gallows Hill, where they hanged the "witches" in the seventeenth century. Finally, the Custom House itself is dead:

The room itself is cobwebbed and dingy with old paint; its floor is strewn with gray sand in a fashion that has elsewhere fallen into long disuse; and it is easy to conclude, from the general slovenliness of the place, that this is a sanctuary into which womankind, with her tools of magic, the broom and mop, has very infrequent access. (19)

AGE AND DEATH

Not only is the town a place of decay and death; the people who inhabit it are all but dead themselves: ancient men with one foot already in the grave who, when they come to work at all, spend their time snoozing in tipped-back chairs like lizards in the sun. Everything about the place has the look and the smell of decay. "Oftentimes," he writes, "they were asleep, but occasionally might be heard talking together in voices between speech and a snore, and with that lack of energy that distinguishes the occupants of alms-houses" (5, 18). All are, it seems, ancient and infirm; and the narrator finds that, willy-nilly, he has taken charge of these "aged men" who, now long inured to stagnation and sterility, have themselves become the living dead. Even though they seem, physically, to possess some magic that keeps death at bay (24), their systems are "half-torpid," and their spirits resemble "the phosphorescent glow of decaying wood" (26). Furthermore, these ancient sea captains who have "finally drifted into this quiet nook" know that they should have "given place to younger men" (25); instead they hang on, uselessly, to the very last.

THE LEADERS OF THE CUSTOM HOUSE

The perfect exemplars of this infirmity come in the person of the two leaders: the Collector, a retired soldier and the "oldest inhabitant" of the place, who, at about seventy, is so infirm as to seem scarcely alive; and the Inspector, the "father of the Custom House" (27), a man of eighty who, while still physically robust, has nevertheless seen virtually all his other human qualities vanish. The narrator quips: "Looking at him merely as an animal—and there was very little else to look at—he was a most satisfactory object" (27). The Collector just sits by the fire, barely able to move or speak. His whole life had been soldiering, and when that ended, so did his active life and thought. The old Inspector, on the other hand, is so much an animal that he has lost all humanity:

The original and more potent causes, however, lay in the rare perfection of his animal nature, the moderate proportion of intellect, and the very trifling admixture of moral and spiritual ingredients: these latter qualities, indeed, being in barely enough measure to keep the old gentleman from walking on all fours.

. . . My conclusion was that he had no soul, no heart, no mind; nothing, as I have already said, but instincts . . . with no higher moral responsibilities than the beasts of the field. (28)

HAWTHORNE'S ANCESTORS AND SALEM

Perhaps as the most ominous aspect of the place, however, the narrator comes to see that his own life is influenced and shadowed by the dead, specifically, by his own ancestors, whom he seems to regard with both shame and pride. They were among the cruelest of the Puritans, especially in their harsh treatment of the Quaker women and the Salem "witches." It is they who, looking over his shoulder in his mind's eye, condemn his life as a writer:

Doubtless, however, either of these stern and black-browed Puritans would have thought it quite a sufficient retribution for his sins, that, after so long a lapse of years, the old trunk of the family tree, with so much venerable moss upon it, should have borne, as its topmost bough, an idler like myself. No aim that I have ever cherished would they recognize as laudable; no success of mine—if my life, beyond its domestic scope, have ever been brightened by success—would they deem otherwise than worthless, if not positively disgraceful. "What is he" murmurs one gray shadow of my forefathers to the other. "A writer of storybooks! What kind of a business in life—what mode of glorifying God, or being serviceable to mankind in his day and generation—may that be? Why, the degenerate fellow might as well have been a fiddler!" (21)

LEANING ON SOMETHING OUTSIDE THE SELF

One sees, too, that the reason for these inhabitants' existence of death-in-life is that long ago they relinquished all aspects of independent thought and action. They remain aged children, leaning on the government for support and care—and even thought. And at last they lose even the desire to be self-reliant. When anyone here loses his Custom House job, he becomes totally inept, and instead of functioning, only looks around him "in quest of support external to himself":

An effect—which I believe to be observable, more or less, in every individual who has occupied the position—is, that, while he leans on the mighty arm of the Republic, his own proper strength departs from him. He loses in an extent proportioned to the weakness or force of his original nature, the capability of self-support. (47)

We see a picture here of people who have grown old and half dead without ever having grown up. They have leaned on the past and on authority (like the government) for so long that they can no longer walk on their own.

DYING IN A DEAD PLACE

To the narrator, then, the tragedy of this place becomes clear: soon he will become dead like the others. He has already experienced the dwindling of his creative powers and his brain; and his past life and his reputation as a man of letters are both alike dead in this place. Nobody in the Custom House or in Salem seems to know about Nathaniel Hawthorne, the writer. Worse, however, is his feeling that his creativity is dying here: "A gift, a faculty, if it had not departed, was suspended and inanimate within me. . . . An entire class of susceptibilities and a gift connected with them— of no great richness or value, but the best I had—was gone from me" (35, 46). He believes that his "intellect is dwindling away" (47). In looking at other men around him, he begins to worry that everything that makes him truly human will die, that he will become either a vegetable like the old general or all animal like the old patriarch of the Custom House: "I was likely to grow gray and decrepit in the Surveyorship, and become much such another animal as the old Inspector . . . to make the dinner hour the nucleus of the day, and to spend the rest of it as an old dog spends it, asleep in the sunshine" (48, 49).

He is surrounded always by those two living symbols of his fate: the old Collector, who exemplifies what can happen if he abandons his rightful work in the world, and the old Inspector, embodying what is even worse—the death of all that he values in himself, those very qualities that make him human. Repeatedly he worries about this. He has condemned the Inspector, whom he finds despicable, for operating only from animal instinct, not from any higher qualities. Now he admits that it was instinct that brought him to Salem, not love—even though he had left Transcendental Concord in order to "exercise other faculties of my nature" (35). He also notes that "the best definition of happiness [was] to live throughout the whole range of his faculties and sensibilities!" (49)—in short, not to be only an animal like the old Inspector, or only a glowing coal of spirit like the old Collector, but fully human. After coming here he doesn't feel that he shares "in the united effort of mankind" (47), and wonders "how much longer I could stay in the Custom House, and yet go forth a man" (48).

IMAGINATION, CREATIVITY, AND ART

Contrasted with these elements of death in the preface is the prospect of creativity, especially as it is manifest in his imagination—his vocation as a writer. He gives up his literary creativity (which is his rightful vocational "life") when he leaves Concord and his literary friends to make money in Salem. In "The Custom-House" he looks back with something like nostalgia to that former life, and he yearns to have a creative, imaginative life again.

It is not until he is fired (which he compares to being beheaded), and so thrown out of the land of the dead, that he is able to resurrect himself as a human being and a writer of fiction. Finally, in the last paragraph of the preface, while he contemplates this fully restored life, he replaces the death image of Gallows Hill, where the witches were hung, with the life-giving and renewing image of the town pump, which he believes he has made famous in one of his sketches by that name.

It may be, however, O, transporting and triumphant thought!—that the great-grandchildren of the present race may sometimes think kindly of the scribbler of by-gone days, when the antiquary of days to come, among the sites memorable in the town's history, shall point out the locality of the town pump! (53)

So while the narrator's illustrious forebears may disapprove of his life as a writer, and while the powerful townspeople of his own day may have fired him from his job, he, the artist, believes that as a writer he will outlive them, as, in fact, he has.

"THE CUSTOM-HOUSE" AND
THE NOVEL'S NARRATIVE

"The Custom-House" not only chronicles the author's spiritual suffocation in a stifling environment; it also connects analogously with the novel that follows. In each is a world controlled by age. Old men set in their ways, whose youth is far removed in an ancient past and whose harshness or inertia serve to stifle everything young and creative, determine the tenor of life.

THE SCAFFOLD, THE ATTIC, AND THE SCARLET LETTER

The primary connective occurs when the narrator claims to have climbed into the attic, where, guided by the ghost of the former surveyor, he finds the ragged scarlet letter, along with the story of Hester Prynne in manuscript. Then, placing the faded letter on his breast, he feels it burn (41). The import of this is inescapable: the narrator feels the same inward fire that stirred in Hester Prynne; indeed, metaphorically at least, he wears a scarlet letter of his own. He, like Hester, is a creator, an artist, the kind of person scorned by societies of rigid and immovable old men. Like her, he has been made to feel ashamed of his creations. As Hester thinks that her creation, Little Pearl, is almost a demon, perhaps even the devil's child, so Hawthorne has written a satanic story about his early days of trying to write fiction, appropriately titled "The Devil in Manuscript," in which the main character (who bears Hawthorne's nickname, Oberon) believes that there is something devilish about the stories he has been trying to publish. Hester, taking her cue from the Puritan society in which she lives, also believes that there must be something wrong with the pleasure she takes in the artistry of her sewing. Similarly, the narrator sees his Puritan ancestors shaking their heads in disgust over his artistry as a writer of stories. There is something analogous, too, in Hester's attempt to deny her creative nature by hiding her physical beauty, while the narrator turns his back on his creative vocation to work for money in the Custom House; perhaps in the fact, too, that he continues to deny his creativity, pretending to find the manuscript in the attic, as if he were only an editor, not a writer of fiction. Hawthorne stresses this point at the beginning of "The Custom-House":

It will be seen, likewise, that this Custom House sketch has a certain propriety, of a kind always recognized in literature, as explaining how a large portion of the following pages came into my possession, and as offering proofs of the authenticity of a narrative therein contained. This, in fact—a desire to put myself in my true position as editor, or very little more, of the most prolix among the tales that make up my volume—this, and no other, is my true reason for assuming a personal relation with the public. (16)

Like Hester, who is persecuted by the Puritans for her creativity, the narrator believes that his culture persecutes him for his vocation—forcing him to give up writing to support his family in a dead, noncreative world, and then allowing incompetents to shame him by throwing him out.

SURVIVAL

Both these accounts, especially as they involve the narrator and Hester, are stories of survival. While Hester suffers intensely, suppressing her passionate nature, losing her faith, and becoming in many ways deluded about herself and her situation, she is still able to survive; she even grows in strength in Boston, returning at last to take up a new mission. The narrator of "The Custom-House," however, seems troubled by his inability to survive in Salem, this nineteenth-century land of the dead, as, say, the young clerk is able to do. He fears that if he remains he won't survive as a full human being but will become instead no more than an animal; and he worries that his creative powers have not survived. In short, he fears that the place itself has triumphed over him.

DENYING ONE'S OWN TRUTH

The narrator's denial of his past (one might say his "true") vocation as a creative writer and his pretense that he is only an editor of *The Scarlet Letter* link him inevitably with Dimmesdale, who also attempts to deny his creative nature by denying that he is Pearl's father. But while Dimmesdale consciously seeks to be something more than human in trying to simulate sainthood, the narrator of the preface is terrified that he will become less than human. Dimmesdale wants to be an angel, but the narrator wants to live throughout the full range of his human faculties.

There is also a similarity between Dimmesdale's mounting the scaffold at the end to publicly claim Pearl as his daughter and Hester as his lover and the narrator's imaginary ascent to the Custom House attic to decide that he will write the story of Hester Prynne, reclaiming his own true relationship to his art. Both find, however, that the society they live in and their relationship to that society have damaged their ability to lead "true" lives or leave behind images of their "true" selves; many in Dimmesdale's congregation refuse to believe him, and the narrator, who pretends to be merely an editor rather than a writer, finds that the story he tells is gloomier and less elevating than he would like it to be because of his stay in the land of the dead.

REVENGE

One of the most surprising parallels between the novel and the preface is the similarity between the narrator of "The Custom-House" and the villain of the novel, Chillingworth. Both men use deception and "black magic" to achieve revenge. Chillingworth uses his "black art" to control Dimmesdale, the target of his vengeance. The narrator of the preface uses his "black art" of writing to hold up to public ridicule the town of Salem as well as the men who worked in the Custom House and who managed to get him fired. And as one critic, Louisa DeSalvo, has pointed out, the narrator has another motivation for his vengeance: Charles Upham, a politically powerful resident of Salem, could have averted Hawthorne's firing but instead did nothing.

PUBLIC REACTION TO "THE CUSTOM-HOUSE"

From a modern perspective, it is curious that it was not the subject matter of adultery and a misbehaving minister that caused such controversy when *The Scarlet Letter* appeared, but rather the portrayal of Salem as an ugly, dying city and the people in the Custom House as a collection of incompetent buffoons. To get the full impact of Hawthorne's revenge, however, one need only reread his description of the Custom House employees, many of whom work for only a few weeks in the year, and when they do appear seem completely to mess up whatever they try to do, and may even steal from the government. Added to that is his devastating portrait of the old Surveyor. Judging from the public reaction in Salem, the sketch did all the damage that Hawthorne seemingly wanted it to do. In an additional preface to the second edition of *The Scarlet Letter*, he gleefully refers to the "unprecedented excitement" caused by publication of "The Custom-House," claiming that he achieved a lively "effect of truth," and stubbornly refuses to withdraw "The Custom-House" sketch. Instead, despite objections, he emphatically states that he will "republish his introductory sketch without the change of a word" (xiv). Like Chillingworth, Hawthorne wears an "A" for avenger without apology.

In addition, like Chillingworth, he accomplishes his vengeful purpose with a good deal of deception by disclaiming any hurtful motive. In the beginning of his sketch, he emphasizes that the *only* purpose of "The Custom-House" is to explain how he came to write the story of Hester Prynne: "this, and no other, is my true reason for assuming a personal relation with the public" (16). The preface to the second edition is even more deceptive, as he asserts that, upon review, he finds "The Custom-House" to be written with remarkably "good humor." Further, "as to enmity, or ill feeling of any kind, personal or political," he utterly disclaims such motives, asserting that he could not have written it "in a better or a kindlier spirit" (xiii). This is scarcely the impression that most Salemites received, including the one who in 1850 wrote the review that follows.

In conclusion, the story of Nathaniel Hawthorne in "The Custom-House" is a fitting introduction to *The Scarlet Letter* in that he wears an "A" himself—not only for "author," but Hester's and Dimmesdale's "A" for "artist" and Chillingworth's "A" for "avenge." And like all three of his characters, he has not at every turn been "true" to what he is and what he intends. There are, in fact, subtle—and perhaps sometimes deceptive—levels of meaning in both "The Custom-House" and the novel.

FROM "A REVIEW OF 'THE CUSTOM-HOUSE' " (MARCH, 1850)

. . . Whether from an undue sensitiveness on account of his removal, or from what other reason we know not, he seeks to vent his spite on something or somebody, by small sneers at Salem, and by vilifying some of his former associates, to a degree of which we should have supposed any gentleman, to say nothing of a man of ordinary feeling, refinement, and kindliness of heart, incapable.—Indeed, while reading this chapter on the Custom House, we almost began to think that Hawthorne had mistaken his vocation—that, instead of indulging in dreamy transcendentalism, and weaving exquisite fancies to please the imagination and improve the heart, he would have been more at home as a despicable lampooner, and in that capacity would have achieved a notoriety which none of his tribe, either of ancient or modern times, has reached. We were almost induced to throw down the book in disgust, without venturing on *The Scarlet Letter*, so atrocious, so heartless, so undisguised, so utterly inexcusable seemed his calumnious caricatures of inoffensive men, who could not possibly have given occasion for such wanton insults.

What can be more heartless and irreverent, after ridiculing the infirmities of aged men, two of whom he admits have been discharged thro' his own influence, than the following passage? [quotes passage describing old workers]

This strange antipathy to the aged manifests itself even in *The Scarlet Letter*.

But the most venomous, malignant and unaccountable assault is made upon a venerable gentleman, whose chief crime seems to be that he loves a good dinner, has preserved a youthful flow of cheerfulness, and can tell a graphic story. . . . Why this gentleman should be dragged so rudely and abusively before the public, and his and his children's feelings lacerated and outraged so unjustifiably, is a mystery beyond our power to fathom. The only thing we can liken it to, in refinement of cruelty, is the fell purpose with which old Roger Chillingworth sets about wrecking his vengeance on Arthur Dimmesdale. . . .

Salem Register, March 21, 1850, 2: 1–2.

"A" IS FOR ANCESTRY

> The figure of that first ancestor, invested by family tradition with a dim and dusky grandeur, was present to my boyish imagination as far back as I can remember. . . . He was a soldier, legislator, judge; he was a ruler in the Church; he had all the Puritanic traits, both good and evil. He was likewise a better persecutor; as witness the Quakers, who have remembered him in their histories. . . . His son, too, inherited the persecuting spirit, and made himself so conspicuous in the martyrdom of the witches, that their blood may fairly be said to have left a stain upon him.
>
> "The Custom-House," 20, 21

In certain ways one might well argue that *The Scarlet Letter* is one of the most heavily autobiographical works of nineteenth-century fiction. In the first place, of course, it is prefaced by what the author/narrator calls the result of an autobiographical impulse to tell the story of his three-year residence in Salem as a Custom House officer. Moreover, as we find in that prefatory sketch, he links his own life to that of the characters in *The Scarlet Letter*.

The sketch seems, among other things, to be his way of examining his ancestral past—a past that became the raw material for *The Scarlet Letter*. About the only conclusion that can be stated with some certainty here, however, is that his view of his ancestors was extremely complex. In studying the novel in light of Hawthorne's background, readers have arrived at different disparate conclusions about his view of his Puritan past.

Obviously, he felt pride in the importance of his New England family. William and John Hathorne were among the most powerful and respected businessmen and public officials of the time, a matter of both pride and shame for the author. As he points out in "The Custom-House," the importance of his ancestors in early Salem stands in marked contrast to the present insignificance of his family. He claims too that he shares several important qualities with his ancestors. He doesn't tell us directly what these qualities are, but we can assume that they include something at least of his gloomy view of human nature and his tendency toward intense introspection.

Several questions arise about the impact that his ancestry had on *The Scarlet Letter*:

- To what extent does Hawthorne identify himself with the Puritans' victims—Hester, the Quakers, the Indians, the Antinomians—mentioned in *The Scarlet Letter*?
- Is his sympathetic presentation of Hester's story his way of trying to make up for what his ancestors had done?
- By showing that Hester is not killed or whipped in public or banished from the colony, and by showing that she is deluded about her penance, is he trying to make his ancestors appear less cruel than they really were?

To approach these questions, it is useful to know something about the two ancestors Hawthorne mentions in the preface to *The Scarlet Letter*, William and John Hathorne. First of all, Hawthorne's background (to which he refers in *The Scarlet Letter*), was steeped in what he would call the blackest hues of Puritan culture, and somehow his changing of the spelling of his family name from Hathorne to Hawthorne seems more significant than just the adding of a "w" for the sake of appearance. Something of moral ambivalence about the family becomes apparent from the start.

WILLIAM HATHORNE

William Hathorne arrived on New England soil with the first wave of Puritans around 1632. They settled just northwest of Boston in Salem, where the coastline gave promise of being able to support a bustling seaport. William was a figure of considerable importance in New England. As Hawthorne describes him in "The Custom-House," he was "a soldier, legislator, judge; he was a ruler in the Church" (20).

> This woman has brought shame upon us all, and ought to die. Is there no law for it? Truly there is, both in the Scripture and the statute-book. Then let the magistrates, who have made it of no effect, thank themselves if their own wives and daughters go astray!
>
> *The Scarlet Letter*, 59

Two facts about William Hathorne's career are especially pertinent to *The Scarlet Letter*. First, as we have seen in Chapter 4, it was William Hathorne who, dissatisfied with the lax way in which the colony was carrying out punishment for adultery, came into direct conflict with the more tolerant Governor John Winthrop and succeeded in making death the required sentence for adultery. The figure of William Hathorne looms not only in the introductory sketch, "The Custom-House," but also in *The Scarlet Letter* itself, where his harsh arguments are, ironically, put into the mouths of old women, who are disgusted that the lenient magistrates have not sentenced Hester to death, as mandated by law.

Not only did this Puritan ancestor have a direct hand in writing the harsh criminal codes of the community; he was also instrumental in carrying through the punishments. In his sketch "Endicott and the Red Cross," Hawthorne describes a variety of these punishments in Salem—punishments his ancestor would have been in charge of exacting, including that of wearing the scarlet letter. And in a sketch entitled "Main Street" (referring to that street in Salem), he attributes one of the more horrible examples of a public beating to William Hathorne.

WILLIAM HATHORNE AS QUAKER PERSECUTOR

> The Puritan could not but remember that this was the very spot, which had been made accursed a few hours before, by the execution of the Quakers, whose bodies had been thrown together into one hasty grave, beneath the tree on which they suffered.
>
> "The Gentle Boy"

> It might be that an Antinomian, a Quaker, or other heterodox religionist, was to be scourged out of town.
>
> *The Scarlet Letter*, 57

> She saw the children of the settlement, on the grassy margin of the street or at the domestic thresholds, disporting themselves in such grim fashions as Puritanic nurture would permit; playing at going to church, perchance; or at scourging Quakers.
>
> *The Scarlet Letter*, 96

The second fact about William Hathorne's past, and one that Hawthorne mentions in "The Custom-House," is his infamy as a persecutor of Quakers, in what was undoubtedly one of the most shameful chapters in Puritan history, and one that was riveted in Hawthorne's imagination. He made this the subject of a chapter in his child's history of New England, *Grandfather's Chair*; he confesses William Hathorne's participation in this persecution in "Main Street"; and he wrote a short story on the clash between Puritan and Quaker entitled "The Gentle Boy." This story is about a Quaker woman who (like Anne Hutchinson's friend, Mary Dyer) insists on entering Puritan Boston even after several Quakers have been hanged. She leaves behind in Boston her child, who is adopted by a kindly man and woman who do not fit in well with the Puritans and who, like many Puritans in reality, were sympathetic to the Quakers. Finally, in "The Custom-House" he mentions that William Hathorne's cruelties are well documented in Quaker histories; and in *The Scarlet Letter* he alludes twice to Puritan persecution of Quakers, paralleling their suffering with Hester's and perhaps with his own suffering as a writer, scorned for his "idle" profession by nineteenth-century sons of the Puritans.

In any case, one cannot ignore the intensity of Hawthorne's ancestral involvement in this chapter in Puritan history. Let us look briefly at the context of this religious clash before examining the Quaker version of William Hathorne's place in their history.

QUAKERS CONFRONT PURITANS

Quakerism, as it emerged in England in the 1650s, was actually an offshoot of Puritanism. George Fox, the most prominent Quaker leader, taught that every person had the seed of Christ or a true light within him or her, and that if one listened to and respected this light, he or she would go to heaven. This contradicted the Puritan idea that only a few elect people, chosen before the creation of the world, would be saved. It also threatened the authority of the clergy, because one did not need an educated clergy to get to know this inner light or truth. Furthermore, scripture was not the only (or even the principal) way of knowing God. Inner revelation could be truer than the Bible. There was clearly potential for a clash between Puritans and Quakers in the New World. In fact, given the strong beliefs of both, it was inevitable.

The Quakers first came to New England in 1656. By 1662 the Puritans had hanged four of them on Boston Common, and many others had been whipped in public, fined, mutilated, and banished. Hundreds had been imprisoned. The Hutchinson controversy of the 1630s in many ways prepared for the persecution of the Quakers. In the first place, Hutchinson and her friends had made many converts to their slant on Puritanism. Virtually the entire First Church of Boston, except John Wilson, its pastor, were supporters of Anne Hutchinson, for example.

Although strict laws were immediately enacted in the Massachusetts Bay Colony to ban both Quakers and their books, even tougher measures were continually being added: ship's masters who brought Quakers as passengers were fined; people who kept Quakers in their homes were fined or imprisoned; and if Quakers returned after having been banished, they were to have an ear cut off. If they persisted, another ear was to be cut off. If they still returned, the law stated that their tongue was to be bored with a red-hot iron. Other Quakers, in addition to the above punishments, were at various times brutally whipped, at least one so severely that a doctor who examined the victim thought he would die.

PERSECUTION OF MARY DYER

In September 1659, Mary Dyer, a member of the Boston church who had supported Anne Hutchinson and had become a convert to Quakerism, was arrested along with two men who were Quakers. All were banished and told that they would be executed if they returned. All three did return, and on October 18, 1659, all were sentenced to death. They were marched to the gallows on Boston Common on October 27. Both men were hanged. But as Mary Dyer stepped onto the ladder, she was drawn back and given another chance, supposedly because she was still officially a member of the Reverend Wilson's church, and because her son and her husband had made eloquent pleas for her life. So she was once more thrown out of the colony. Meanwhile, the bodies of her two companions were thrown into an unmarked pit on Boston Common, and observers who objected were themselves beaten.

In May of the following spring, Mary Dyer returned to Boston to preach. She was promptly arrested, and on June 1, 1660, she was hanged. The Reverend John Wilson, her former pastor, was on hand to hurl curses at her as she ascended the ladder.

Mary Dyer, Quaker Missionary, being led to the gallows in Boston, Massachusetts, by Puritan militia. "At her appearing, the multitude was hushed, awed by that air she wore," illustration by Howard Pyle for *McClure's Magazine* XXVIII, 4 (November 1906); courtesy of Friends Historical Library of Swarthmore College, Swarthmore, Pennsylvania.

ANN COLEMAN AND WILLIAM HATHORNE

One other Quaker, William Leddra, was hanged on the Common, on March 14, 1661. By this time, however, both English and New World Quakers had mounted a strong appeal to the English king, Charles II, to issue an order commanding that the executions be stopped. This the king did. No further Quakers were executed, but nonetheless punishments were still occasionally brutal. For example, after the king's order halting the executions, the Puritans passed the Cart and Whip Act. By means of this law, Quakers appearing in the Massachusetts Bay Colony would be dragged behind a cart in each settlement, successively, and whipped through the streets until they reached the boundaries, where they were thrown out and left to pursue their own way if they were capable. One Quaker, Ann Coleman, was brutally beaten in this fashion on the orders of William Hathorne.

The following document is from a 1702 Quaker assessment of William Hathorne's part in these events (one of those "Quaker histories" in which Nathaniel Hawthorne notes that his ancestor is "remembered").

FROM GEORGE BISHOP, *NEW ENGLAND JUDGED BY THE SPIRIT OF THE LORD* (1659)

(As addressed directly to Puritan leaders in the Massachusetts Bay Colony)

And whilst I am hereupon, let me give you two more instances, viz., those of Edward Wharton and Samuel Gaskin, who were arrested for not coming to your meetings; and were had to Ipswiich court and fined, the one five pounds ten shillings, and the other eight pounds,—one of them being a young man, and apparently having no visible estate. William Hathorn, though he was but an assistant in the Court, gave judgment against him, and advised, "That if he had not, nor would not pay, they must send him to Barbadoes and sell him, to pay it." And this was when the Court knew not on what to levy the fines. And this is the said Hathorn of whom I have before spoken, who turned from the tenderness that was once in him to please you, to get an employment whereby to live; and, having got it, thus turned against his tender principles and his friends, to whom he was once tender, to sell them for slaves, as he did in other particulars.

One case of which, in a warrant sent to the Constable of Salem under his hand, in these words, I shall instance:—

You are required, by virtue hereof, to search in all suspicious houses for private meetings; and, if they refuse to open the doors, you are to break open the door upon them, and return the names of all ye find to Ipswich Court. (92, 93)

"William Hathorn"

But at this time he missed, though he shall not miss his judgment from the hand of the Lord, who will assuredly meet with him, and give him his portion with the rest of those who persecute His Truth. . . .

A Court being soon to be held at Salem, by Simon Bradstreet, Daniel Dennison, and William Hathorn, three bloody persecutors, against the sitting of this Court there was a town-meeting for the choosing of constables, which that it might be effectually done, that the innocent might suffer and their laws be as bloodily executed, as they were made by them, and in their hearts, William Hathorne desired them to choose one Philip Cromwel, "Because," said he, "he will scour the Quakers," (see, a bloodthirsty persecutor! how he is not ashamed, in the face of the country, to put forth his desired thirst of persecution,) who, being chosen, was heated by this Hathorn and John Higginson, priest of Salem, who blasphemously said, "That the Quakers' light was a stinking vapour from hell" (242).

Jeremy Tiblets, constable, having received the warrant, he was bid to have Edward away, and tie him to the cart's tail and whip him through the town. To which Edward manfully answered, as he was passing from them, "Friends, I fear not the worst you may be suffered to do unto me; neither do I seek for any favour at your hands." And to William Hathorn he said, "Oh, William, William! the Lord will surely visit thee." So he was tied to a pair of cartwheels with a great rope about his middle, and a number of people to draw them about, where the executioner cruelly whipped him as in the warrant; and, having loosed him, told him, "That he must prepare to receive the like at the next town," which was about fourteen miles from thence, through the woods; which being a long way for a man to travel on foot, whose back was so torn already, to serve their pleasure, in his own execution, he told them, "He should not go, unless they provided a horse for him, or that they dragged him thither."

Thus it fared with Edward Wharton, for his testimony to the Truth and against your persecution. I shall now give an account of some others, on whom your cruelty lighted at Salem by the hand of the said wicked Hathorn, whose cruelty is farther drawn forth in what follows.

This said Hathorn, before he was a magistrate, bore testimony against persecution and restraining conscience in the days of Oliver Cromwell, in one of your meeting-houses at Salem, saying, "That if such an act," which you were then about, (viz., To restrain from preaching but by allowance of certain persons,) "should take place in New England, he looked upon it as one of the most horrid acts that ever was done in New England; and would be as great a token of God's forsaking New England, as any." And yet, after long waiting, coming to be a magistrate, what a bloody persecutor hath he been of the Truth!

Not long after Edward Wharton's executions as aforesaid, Joseph Nicholson, John Liddal, Jane Millard, and Ann Coleman were, by the said Hathorn's warrant, apprehended, and so cruelly whipped through Salem, Boston, and Dedham, that one of them, viz., Ann Coleman, was near death, being well-nigh murdered. She was a little woman, and her back, as hath been said, was crooked, and your executioner had her fast in a cart at Dedham, Bellingham, your deputy, having seen Hathorn's warrant, bidding them "Go on," and saying, "The warrant was firm;" and so encouraging the matter, he so unmercifully laid her on with the rest, that, with the knots of the whip, he split the nipple of her breast, which so tortured her, that it had almost cost her life, which she sometimes thinking might have been the consequence, was willing, if she should have died, that her body should have been brought and laid before Bellingham, with a charge from her mouth, "That he was guilty of her blood." But it pleased the Lord that she recovered, though it was long after that she was thus cruelly handled.

Now Hathorn, to do his brother Goggins a courtesy, as Pilate did Herod when he had Jesus before him, at the said Goggins' desire, ordered, that the aforesaid should not be whipped through Boston, but through Cambridge, where the said Goggins, one of your magistrates, lives, who desired "That his brother Hathorn would send some of the Quakers through that town, that he might take order for their whipping there." (279–281)

London: T. Sowle, 1703.

JOHN HATHORNE

His son, too, inherited the persecuting spirit, and made himself so conspicuous in the martyrdom of the witches, that their blood may fairly be said to have left a stain upon him. So deep a stain, indeed, that his old dry bones, in the Charter Street burial ground, must still retain it, if they have not crumbled utterly to dust!

"The Custom House," 21

Judge John Hathorne, William's son, was equally infamous, for it was he who presided over the Salem witch trials, and it was he, according to some accounts, who was instrumental in seeking death for the accused; finally, it was he who never expressed any doubts about the righteousness of his actions. Long after the hysteria had subsided, his name continued to command an eerie place in the witchcraft trials because of a legendary curse which, Hawthorne claimed, one of the "witches" placed upon him before she was hanged—a curse to which Nathaniel refers in the preface to *The Scarlet Letter* and which he used in the composition of his next novel, *The House of the Seven Gables.*

The following excerpt is significant in the study of *The Scarlet Letter* for two reasons. First, it reveals something of the extent of John Hathorne's involvement in the witch trials; and, second, it shows the interpretation placed upon John Hathorne's involvement by Nathaniel Hawthorne's archenemy, Charles W. Upham, whom he blamed for costing him his job in the Salem Custom House.

UPHAM ON JOHN HATHORNE

Upham had been lecturing on Salem witchcraft for a number of years and had published some of the lectures in 1831. There was little stress on John Hathorne's role in the hysteria in this early volume. However, in the history he published in 1867, some seventeen years after *The Scarlet Letter*, Upham found John Hathorne to be one of the Puritan leaders who irresponsibly excited the general populace and the accusers to a frenzy, railroading through convictions in order to give themselves importance at a time when their power as officials was dwindling. Upham's interpretation of the interrogation, which was chiefly conducted by John Hathorne, reveals Hathorne to be (as Hawthorne wrote of Young Goodman Brown) "the chief horror of the scene." John Hathorne had come to the investigation in great self-important pomp; he had then pre-judged all the accused, swallowing the ravings of the young accusers without question, and had bullied, terrorized, and worn down the unfortunate suspects. Hawthorne at an earlier time considered Upham a friend and praised his research on Salem witchcraft in his story "Alice Doane's Appeal." Though Hawthorne and his family acknowledged their ancestor's role as magistrate and as one of the panel of judges who investigated and then condemned the witches, they seem not to have believed that Hathorne played the vital role that Upham insists he had in his history. For some reason Nathaniel seemed to acknowledge William Hathorne's part in the Quaker persecutions more readily than John Hathorne's part in the witch hangings, although he did not ignore or seek to white-wash this historical event. There seems to be evidence that the Hawthornes suspected before the publication of *The Scarlet Letter* just how much of a villain John Hathorne would be in Upham's later book (based on his continuing lectures and research). Whether or not Hawthorne agreed with Upham's characterization of John Hathorne, he and his family were not happy that Upham, who had borne responsibility for Nathaniel's being fired from the Salem Custom House, had gone out of his way to embarrass them by informing the world of what a scoundrel their ancestor was. Had rumors of the nature of Upham's publication reached the Hawthorne family in 1849, they may well have added fuel to Nathaniel's venomous introduction to *The Scarlet Letter* and his refusal to cut or modify it in later editions.

DEFENDING HIS ANCESTORS?

> At all events, I, the present writer, as their representative, hereby take shame upon myself for their sakes, and pray that any curse incurred by them . . . may be now and henceforth removed.
>
> *The Scarlet Letter*, 21

Of additional interest is the possibility that Hawthorne may have had the Puritans in *The Scarlet Letter* levy an easier penalty on Hester (easier than the prescribed death penalty or the usual punishment of public flogging and banishment from the colony) in order to make his ancestors appear less cruel than they actually were.

FROM CHARLES W. UPHAM, *SALEM WITCHCRAFT WITH AN ACCOUNT OF SALEM VILLAGE, AND A HISTORY OF OPINIONS ON WITCHCRAFT AND KINDRED SUBJECTS* (1867)

For some time the girls held back from mentioning names; or, if they did, it was prevented from being divulged to the public. . . . The continued pressure upon the "afflicted children," the earnest and importunate inquiry, on all sides, "Who is it that bewitches you?" opened their lips in response, and they began to select and bring forward their victims. . . .

As all was ripe for the development of the plot, extraordinary means were taken to give publicity, notoriety, and effect to the first examinations. On the 1st of March the two leading magistrates of the neighborhood, men of great note and influence, whose fathers had been among the chief founders of the settlement, and who were Assistants,—that is, members of the highest legislative and judicial body in the colony, combining with the functions of a senate those of a court of last resort with most comprehensive jurisdiction—John Hathorne and Jonathan Corwin, entered the village, in imposing array, escorted by the marshal, constables, and their aids, with all the trappings of their offices; reined up at Nathaniel Ingersoll's corner, and dismounted at his door. . . . (12)

It will be noticed that the examination was conducted in the form of questions put by the magistrate, Hathorne, based upon a foregone conclusion of the prisoner's guilt, and expressive of a conviction, all along on his part, that the evidence of "the afflicted" against her amounted to, and was, absolute demonstration. . . . In this, and in all cases, it must be remembered that the account of the examination comes to us from those who were under the wildest excitement against the prisoners; that no counsel was allowed them; that, if any thing was suffered to be said in their defense by others, it has failed to reach us; that the accused persons were wholly unaccustomed to such scenes and exposures, unsuspicious of the perils of a cross-examination, or of an inquisition conducted with a design to entrap and ensnare; and that what they did say was liable to be misunderstood, as well as misrepresented. We cannot hear their story. All we know is from parties prejudiced, to the highest degree, against them. Sarah Good was an unfortunate and miserable woman in her circumstances and condition: but, from all that appears on the record, making due allowance for the credulity, extravagance, prejudice, folly, or malignity of the witnesses; giving full effect to every thing that can claim the character of substantial force alleged against her, it is undeniable, that there was not, beyond the afflicted girls, a particle of evidence to sustain the charge on which she was arraigned; and that, in the worst aspect of her case, she was an object for compassion, rather than punishment. Altogether, the proceedings against her, which terminated with her execution, were cruel and shameful to the highest degree. (16, 17)

The foregoing illustrates the unfairness practised by the examining magistrate. He took for granted, as we shall find to have been the case in all instances, the guilt of the prisoner, and endeavored to entangle her by leading questions, thus involving her in contradiction. By the force of his own assumptions, he had compelled Sarah Good to admit the reality of the sufferings of the girls, and that they must be caused by some one. (22)

... Every effort was made by the examining magistrate [Hathorne], aided by the officious interference of the marshal, or other deluded or evil-disposed persons,—who, like him, were permitted to interpose with charges or abusive expressions,—to overawe and confound, involve in contradictions, and mislead the poor creature, and force her to confess herself guilty and accuse others.... The excitement was kept up, and spread far and wide, by the officers and magistrates riding in cavalcade, day after day, to and from the town and village; and by the constables, with their assistants, carrying their manacled prisoners from jail to jail in Ipswich, Salem, and Boston. (36, 37)

[The following refers to the questioning of Martha Corey]

... It is almost amusing to see how the pride of the magistrates was touched, and their wrath kindled, by what she was reported to have said, "that the magistrates' and ministers' eyes were blinded, and that she would open them." It rankled in Hathorne's breast: he returns to it again and again, and works himself up to a higher degree of resentment on each recurrence. (50)

Boston: Wiggin and Lunt, 1867.

TOPICS FOR WRITTEN OR ORAL EXPLORATION

1. In "The Custom-House," note the narrator's comment that anyone who leans on someone else for too long a time, whether it be an individual or an institution, becomes unable to be an independent adult. Write a theme in refutation or support of his view.

2. Consider that the forces of life and creativity are at war with death-in-life in "The Custom-House." Is this also true of *The Scarlet Letter*? Explain.

3. Do you see anything in contemporary life that tends to pull in the direction of death-in-life? Does the dominance of the machine and technology do this, as critics have argued on occasion? Have a debate on this, the ground rules of which would be establishing just what death-in-life in a society constitutes.

4. Can you recall any other instance in history in which "the sins of the fathers are visited upon the children"? Consider, for example, other nineteenth- and twentieth-century atrocities, those who participated in them, and their children.

5. Hawthorne in "The Custom-House" makes several references to living throughout the full range of his faculties. Write a theme in which you define what you think this means, using specific examples. Do you agree or disagree with him that this is a good thing? Explain.

6. According to Hawthorne, what are the characteristics of someone who isn't fully human?

7. The narrator says that his children will be born in and live in places other than his hometown, Salem. Have two people debate the hometown issue—one arguing the merits of remaining (or returning to live) in one's hometown and the other arguing that it is almost always best to leave.

8. If you have ever held a job, try your own hand at writing a sketch of your experience, including portrayals of co-workers.

9. Write about someone you know who was "meant to" or really wanted to spend his or her life doing one thing, but ended up working at something else.

10. What forces in contemporary life inhibit young persons from doing what they really want to do with their lives?

11. Scholars have commented on the similarity between Catherine in "The Gentle Boy" and the historical figure of Mary Dyer, the Quaker executed on Boston Common. Referring to history, do your own analysis of the historical basis of Hawthorne's story.

12. After conducting research on Mary Dyer, write on the common characteristics and situations of Mary Dyer/Catherine and Hester. Note especially their relationship to members of the community.

13. Consider in writing that religious fanaticism by both Puritans and Quakers receives Hawthorne's disapproval in "The Gentle Boy"—a fanaticism to which the child, Ilbraham, is sacrificed. When does religious belief become fanatical, from your point of view? Give your reasons for your belief. Note as well that both sides believe that they have a monopoly on "truth."

14. While Catherine in "The Gentle Boy" deserts her child in order to pursue her religious mission, Hester fights to keep her child with her. Pearl "saves" her. Contrast the two stories of motherhood. Note particularly the scene of Catherine in the church and Hester in the governor's mansion.

15. Write an essay on the figure of the Reverend Wilson as he appeared in the stories of both Anne Hutchinson and the Quakers, and his fictionalized appearances in *The Scarlet Letter*.

16. Write and produce a one-act drama of the Quaker story in Massachusetts Bay, basing your work on library research and choosing your materials carefully. You can use your imagination in creating the drama, but try not to violate the spirit of the actual events.

SUGGESTED READINGS

From Nathaniel Hawthorne's tales: "The Gentle Boy" and "Main Street."

8

"A" Is for Artist: The Creative Struggles of Nathaniel Hawthorne

EARLY LIFE

By the time Nathaniel Hawthorne was born to Salem sea captain Nathaniel Hathorne and his wife, Elizabeth Manning-Hathorne, on the fourth of July in 1804, the glory of the family (which is mentioned in "The Custom-House") had faded. His father died at sea when Nathaniel was three years old, and he and his sister were reared by a reclusive mother whose brothers extended financial support. One of his uncles afforded him an education at Bowdoin College in Brunswick, Maine. Here he blossomed socially, becoming interested in national politics and making lifelong friends. One of these was fellow student Henry Wadsworth Longfellow, who would become a noted American poet and scholar. Another was a future president of the United States, Franklin Pierce. In later years, Pierce and other Democrats could always be depended upon to help secure government jobs for the struggling writer—jobs like the one in the Salem Custom House.

THE DIFFICULTY OF BEING A WRITER IN AMERICA

Even in his college days, Hawthorne had already decided that he was meant to be a writer. It has always been difficult to earn one's living solely as a writer, but for an American in the nineteenth century, with no status and no financial support, it was a hard profession to follow. In addition to the universal problem of trying to eke out a bare subsistence on a modest income, like many novelists, Hawthorne faced the matter of national condescension and prejudice. In the view of the general English reader of the time, and especially in the mind of the educated English aristocracy, America (artistically speaking) was a raw frontier inhabited by bumpkins too insufficiently refined or insufficiently buttressed by long literary traditions to produce great art. For work of true distinction, one looked only to Europe and the British Isles, or to ancient history; they alone were truly respectable; they alone had that civilized touch of greatness. So the work of American writers rarely sold well and was rarely treated seriously.

Publishers in both England and America were more inclined to publish those English writers—like the fabulously successful Charles Dickens—who were respected by the English-speaking public. The problem was compounded, too, by the laxity of international copyright laws. American publishers could often profitably publish works of successful British writers without paying royalties. This was considered a better business risk than taking a chance on some little-known American writer who would have to be paid and probably would not sell anyway.

> No aim that I have ever cherished would they recognize as laudable; no success of mind . . . would they deem otherwise than worthless, if not positively disgraceful.
>
> "The Custom-House," 21

Another widespread attitude that hampered writers, to a certain extent in England but very much so in nineteenth-century America, was the conviction, strongly reinforced by the Puritan legacy, that fiction was a time-waster and intrinsically immoral. Only loafers wrote stories and encouraged others to waste their time reading instead of working. Moreover, fiction had been frowned upon by the Puritans and continued to be suspect in the nineteenth century: all fiction, inherently, was "untrue"; it was "lies." And readers could get trapped in a false world, could fall in love with falseness. The Puritans in particular believed that the imagination (that critical faculty which was in use in writing and reading fiction) was a tool of the devil, who led people into evil falsehoods in order to control their lives. The other human faculties, like reason and emotion, along with experience, were checks on one another; but the imagination could operate alone and create devilish monsters that were completely outside the realm of possibility. It was assumed that readers were often tempted by fiction to become dissatisfied with their lot in life. Poor people would try to rise above their position, for example, a most serious offense, and women would become dissatisfied with their home lives.

In addition, the subject matter of fiction was frequently considered to be immoral and irreligious: stories of sinful love and tales in which sacred topics were the subject of fun and parody.

TRYING TO MAKE IT AS A WRITER

So, in deciding as early as his student days to write fiction, Hawthorne had taken on a very difficult task. But he was a determined young man; he began his first novel, *Fanshawe*, published in 1828, even before graduating from Bowdoin in 1825. His lack of confidence, however, is shown in his decision to publish it anonymously—and to keep the authorship a secret for the rest of his life.

After graduating from Bowdoin, Hawthorne moved back into his mother's house in Salem. Here he lived for ten years, learning his vocation as a fiction writer and reading omnivorously. During these years, he came to know all the discouragements that American writers encountered, experiencing such anguishing self-doubts that he destroyed some of his manuscripts.

Also during this period, he met and fell in love with Sophia Peabody, whose family lived in Salem at the time. Their courtship was an incentive for him to find another way of making a living, for when publishers paid him anything at all, it was a mere pittance. Through his political connections, he was given a position in the Boston Custom House; he held the job for less than two years, and even from the first the pay was scarcely a living wage.

> After my fellowship of toil and impracticable schemes with the dreamy brethren of Brook Farm . . .
>
> "The Custom-House," 35

Finally, he thought he had come upon an ideal solution: a group of philosophers, calling themselves the Transcendentalists, had made arrangements to open a community called Brook Farm just south of Boston, in what is now West Roxbury. These intellectuals were in fact only one of many groups who were setting up their own communes in the United States at this time. Their plan was to attract people who would be willing to pitch in to do the farm labor. They would live off the land, share all the farm goods and profits, and enjoy a great deal of freedom with regard to their religion and social arrangements. The plan was to include only a few initial investors, each to have a room in the existing farmhouse. Later each would have the opportunity to build a family cottage on the land. Hawthorne saw this as a way to be able to marry and support a family; here he could do his share of the farm work in exchange for food and housing, but still have the time in the evening to write. Thus, in 1841, he invested an initial sum of money in the venture and moved into the farmhouse.

Unfortunately, it soon became obvious to him that he could not unite the vocations of farming and writing. He wrote his fiancee that he just couldn't shovel manure all day and then write fiction at night. Also, the always intensely private Hawthorne apparently found it painful to join a kind of group family. And while he remained close friends with individual Transcendentalists for the rest of his life, his own private philosophy was radically different from theirs, a fact that no doubt caused additional strain while living with them in such close proximity. After only a few months at Brook Farm, he abandoned his plans and withdrew.

> . . . after three years within the subtile influence of an intellect like Emerson's; after those wild, free days on the Assabeth, indulging fantastic speculations beside our fire of fallen boughs with Ellery Channing; after talking with Thoreau about pine trees and Indian relics in his hermitage at Walden . . .
>
> "The Custom-House," 35

In 1842 he and Sophia were married and were able to set up their own little commune. Hawthorne found a Revolutionary War–era house in Concord available for rent. It was only a stone's throw from the famous battlefield in the town. A small rural village just northwest of Boston with trees, hills, and a winding river, Concord was the center of Transcendentalism. Here lived many of the great thinkers of the day: Ralph Waldo Emerson, Bronson Alcott (father of Louisa May, the author of *Little Women*), and Henry David Tho-

Painting of Nathaniel Hawthorne by Charles Osgood, 1840. Courtesy, Peabody Essex Museum, Salem, Massachusetts.

reau, the author of *Walden*. For some four years, it was an ideal situation for the young writer. Rent for the fine old house was nominal, and the orchards, the gardens, and the river, located behind the house, yielded almost all they needed to live on. In addition, Sophia had a small allowance from her family. This, plus the equally small income derived from Hawthorne's tales, supplied all their needs, even as they began to have children. Here Hawthorne enjoyed the friendship of the other writers in the area and had ample time for his own literary pursuits. He would often write of the years in the Old Manse (so named for its former use as a home for various ministers of the gospel) as a time spent in Eden.

OUT OF EDEN, INTO SALEM

This idyllic life came to an end in 1845, when the owners of the Old Manse decided to discontinue renting the property. Their decision came at a time when Nathaniel needed to find other ways of supporting a growing family.

> . . . the new Surveyor was not a politician, and though a faithful Democrat in principle, neither received nor held his office with any reference to political services.
>
> "The Custom-House," 24

He turned again to his friends in politics to help him secure a suitable position. It was a rough time for Sophia and Nathaniel, who had to live with relatives for a time while he put his writing on hold and scrambled to find a job. Finally, in 1846, after months of unpleasant negotiations, a relieved Hawthorne secured a political appointment as a surveyor for the Custom House in Salem. This provided the family with a decent living and a respectable position in the town where his illustrious ancestors had lived and where he himself had grown up as the son of a poor widow and had lived for twelve years as a struggling, penniless writer.

In "The Custom-House," he alludes to his ancestry, his childhood in Salem, his Brook Farm days, and time spent in the Old Manse. Primarily, however, he develops the story of his three-year stay in the Salem Custom House itself, where he tried to come to terms with a vocation he felt he had abandoned and where his creative juices had gone dry.

> So little adapted is the atmosphere of a Custom House to the delicate
> harvest of fancy and sensibility, that, had I remained there through
> ten Presidencies yet to come, I doubt whether the tale of *The Scarlet
> Letter* would ever have been brought before the public eye.
>
> "The Custom-House," 43

Several things marked his life in Salem. First was his inability to
be as active and creative a writer as he had been in the Old Manse.
Joining the work force and having to deal with the mundane people and duties of the business world seemed to give him writer's
block. Second, there was change in his relationship with an old
friend, Charles Upham, who turned against him. And finally, when
the political party known as the Whigs was voted into power in
the election of 1848, he, as a Democrat in a federal job, was
abruptly fired from his position.

> The moment when a man's head drops off is seldom or never, I am
> inclined to think, precisely the most agreeable of his life.
>
> "The Custom-House," 50

Despite his avowal in "The Custom-House" that his firing was
for the best, he was devastated, and encouraged his Democratic
friends to wage a campaign on his behalf to retrieve his job. It was,
however, to no avail. Hawthorne was intensely embittered at the
town of Salem, at Charles Upham, and at the Custom House officials, who had been pleased to see him fired.

GETTING BACK TO WRITING AGAIN

Legend has it that Hawthorne came home one day and announced that he had been fired, whereupon Sophia replied,
"Good. Now maybe you can write that book you've been thinking
about." Supposedly she had saved enough money to allow him to
devote his time to writing once again. The result was *The Scarlet
Letter* in 1850.

> Much to the author's surprise, and (if he may say so without addi-
> tional offence) considerably to his amusement, he finds that his
> sketch of official life, introductory to The Scarlet Letter, has created
> an unprecedented excitement in the respectable community imme-
> diately around him.
>
> Preface to the Second Edition of *The Scarlet Letter*, xiii

Although the novel was generally very well received, the people of Salem were incensed at the prefatory sketch, "The Custom-House," which seemed to give Hawthorne no small degree of pleasure. The strange preface to the second edition of *The Scarlet Letter*, dated March, 1850, shows him unmoved by protests against "The Custom-House"—which, he writes, he will continue to use as a preface to the novel without changing a word.

Eventually, the Hawthornes moved to western Massachusetts, where he completed two further novels: *The House of the Seven Gables*, in which he continued to skewer his Salem enemies, and *The Blithedale Romance*, in which he gave an unflattering account of Brook Farm and, by the way, of Orestes Brownson, who had given *The Scarlet Letter* a negative review. (His is one of the reviews of the novel included in Chapter 7.)

SUSPENDING HIS ART AND MAKING A LIVING

At this time, his old friend, Franklin Pierce, was running for president of the United States. Hawthorne, who now had something of a reputation as a writer, wrote the official campaign biography of Pierce in 1852; like all such biographies, it was intended as much to garner votes as to inform. Upon Pierce's election, Hawthorne was rewarded with an appointment as consul to Liverpool, England. He and his family moved to England in 1853, where they remained for five years. During this time, he ceased to write fiction. Not until he left his consularship was he able to complete his last novel, *The Marble Faun*.

THE MELANCHOLY END OF A CAREER AND A LIFE

The Hawthorne family returned to the United States in 1860, after five years in Liverpool and two years of travel in Europe, to settle again in Concord. His life there until his death in 1864 was not particularly happy. He was ill with what was supposedly cancer; he was unable to write fiction; he seemed to be out of step with the prevailing political climate; and he was deeply saddened by the Civil War. He died while on a pleasure trip with his old friend Franklin Pierce.

"A" IS FOR ART

> While thus perplexed . . . I happened to place it on my breast. It
> seemed to me—the reader may smile, but must not doubt my word—
> it seemed to me then that I experienced a sensation not altogether
> physical, yet almost so, as of burning heat; and as if the letter were
> not of red cloth, but red-hot iron. I shuddered, and involuntarily let
> it fall upon the floor.
>
> "The Custom House," 41

With this scene in "The Custom-House," momentarily wearing
the scarlet letter on his breast, Hawthorne identifies himself with
Hester. He also is a victim of his society, as he sees it: Puritan
culture has condemned the very essence of his vocation—the creative imagination and fiction itself. Hester is punished for creating
Pearl, and he feels himself punished for creating fiction, itself a
"bastard" form of writing in the eyes of the Puritans. Hawthorne
may have been overly sensitive on this matter, but this was not
mere imagination. His impression of how the Puritans and nineteenth-century society felt about fiction and fiction writers was
based on irrefutable evidence.

SEVENTEENTH-CENTURY SUSPICION OF ART

Puritans in the seventeenth century were suspicious of the imagination because they saw it as an element that could get out of
control. The imagination was, in fact, an instrument of the devil.
By means of the imagination a person could pretend to be like
God and create an imaginary world—the supreme heresy. Consid-
ering these three things together, imaginative art was the same as
witchcraft in the eyes of the Puritans.

> "What is he?" murmurs one gray shadow of my forefathers to the
> other. "A writer of storybooks! What kind of a business in life—what
> mode of glorifying God, or being serviceable to mankind in his day
> and generation—may that be? Why, the degenerate fellow might as
> well have been a fiddler!"
>
> "The Custom-House," 21

Except when the imagination was used to convey orthodox Puritan religious beliefs (as it does in Wigglesworth's *Day of Doom*),
the Puritans condemned poetry and fiction, and outlawed drama.

The dangers inherent in the use of the imagination meant that the fiction writer was not only an immoral, useless, lazy person himself, but one who corrupted other people as well by teaching readers to be impious and immoral and encouraging them to neglect useful work in order to read fiction.

NINETEENTH-CENTURY DISAPPROVAL OF FICTION

What did these Puritan notions have to do with a fiction writer in the nineteenth century? Puritan attitudes toward imaginative literature persisted right up to Hawthorne's time. Businessmen regularly warned aspiring young merchants not to waste their time reading fiction. Primarily, however, warnings were directed to young women, who constituted the largest group of novel readers. It was widely thought that such reading gave women a false view of the world, made them dissatisfied with their place in the world, and, in general, corrupted their minds and morals. Rarely does one find a book of advice to young people that does not warn them to stay clear of fiction.

Partly as a result of this view, fiction writers found it hard to pursue their vocation. Moralists, who had much influence with the public, urged people not to buy novels or read short fiction in magazines. Although many people ignored these warnings and read fiction anyway, it was difficult for a fiction writer to make a living by his or her craft or to secure respectability in nineteenth-century society. Hawthorne was one of the few to gain the respect of the public, but that did not come for some time after *The Scarlet Letter* was published.

The first documents in this chapter reflect the Puritan view, first of Hester's art and then of Hawthorne's. These are followed by excerpts from the writings of Timothy Dwight and Noah Webster that show the persistence of Puritan attitudes toward art in the nineteenth century.

The final documents consist of reviews of *The Scarlet Letter* that appeared in 1850 and 1851. While most of the reviews in literary magazines and daily newspapers at the time were very favorable, a few found fault not only with "The Custom-House" for ridiculing Salem's leaders, but with the work itself because it was a novel, thus revealing a distrust of all fiction.

THE PURITAN VIEW OF HESTER'S VOCATION

It was the art—then, as now, almost the only one within a woman's
grasp—of needlework. . . . To Hester Prynne it might have been a
mode of expressing, and therefore soothing, the passion of her life.
Like all other joys, she rejected it as a sin.

The Scarlet Letter, 87

As we saw in Chapter 1, Hawthorne's identification with Hester is
strengthened in that she is also an artist in a society that views the
full exercise of her art, as a creator of beautiful embroideries and
laces, as sinful. Although the occasional use of finery by the leaders
of society is condoned, the beautiful garments she creates are
deemed sinful.

We get the first hint of this when she emerges from the prison
after having richly embroidered the scarlet symbol with gold
thread. This ornate needlework is considered vain and unPuritan-
like, even unlawful:

It was so artistically done, and with so much fertility and gorgeous
luxuriance of fancy, that it had all the effect of a last and fitting decoration to the apparel which she wore; and which was of a splendor
in accordance with the taste of the age, but greatly beyond what was
allowed by the sumptuary regulations of the colony.

The Scarlet Letter, 60

And we learn in "Hester at Her Needle" that, though the Puritan
code preached simplicity in all things, Hester was kept busy making ornate clothing for the town leaders for use in ceremonies of
various kinds—except weddings. She herself loved beautiful things
with a passion.

The following passage from the 1651 *Records of the Massachusetts Bay* reflects the Puritan view of the fruits of Hester's vocation.

FROM "LAWS AGAINST EXCESS IN APPAREL," *RECORDS OF THE
MASSACHUSETTS BAY IN NEW ENGLAND* (1651)

Although several declarations and orders have been made by this Court
against excess in apparel, both of men and women, which have not taken
that effect as were to be desired, but, on the contrary, we cannot but to

our grief take notice that intolerable excess and bravery hath crept in upon us, and especially amongst people of mean condition [that is, poor people], to the dishonor of God, the scandal of our profession, the consumption of estates, and altogether unsuitable to our poverty; and although we acknowledge it to be a matter of much difficulty, in regard of the blindness of men's minds and the stubbornness of their wills, to set down exact rules to confine all sorts of persons, yet we cannot but account it our duty to commend unto all sorts of persons the sober and moderate use of those blessings which, beyond expectation, the Lord hath been pleased to afford unto us in this wilderness, and also to declare our utter detestation and dislike that men or women of mean condition should take upon them the garb of gentlemen, by wearing gold or silver lace or buttons, or points at their knees, or to walk in great boots, or women of the same rank to wear silk or tiffany hoods or scarfs, which though allowable to persons of greater estates, or more liberal education, yet we cannot but judge it intolerable in persons of such like condition: it is therefore ordered by this Court, and the authority thereof, that no person within this jurisdiction, or any of their relations depending upon them, whose visible estates, real and personal, shall not exceed the true and indifferent value of two hundred pounds, shall wear any gold or silver lace, or gold and silver buttons, or any bone lace above two shillings per yard, or silk hoods or scarfs, upon the penalty of ten shillings for every such offence, and every such delinquent to be presented by the grand jury. And forasmuch as distinct and particular rules in this case, suitable to the estate or quality of each person, cannot easily be given, it is further ordered by the authority aforesaid, that the selectmen of every town, or the major part of them, are hereby enabled and required from time to time to have regard and take notice of apparel in any of the inhabitants of their several towns respectively, and whosoever they shall judge to exceed their ranks and abilities in the costliness or fashion of their apparel in any respect, especially in the wearing of ribbons or great boots, (leather being so scarce a commodity in this country,) lace points, and silk hoods or scarfs, the select men aforesaid shall have power to assess such persons so offending in any of the particulars above mentioned in the country rates at two hundred pounds estates, according to that proportion that such men use to pay to whom such apparel is suitable and allowed, provided this law shall not extend to the restraint of any magistrate or public officer of the jurisdiction, their wives and children, who are left to their discretion in wearing of apparel, or any settled military officer or soldier in the time of military service, or any other whose education and employments have been above the ordinary degree, or whose estates have been considerable, though now decayed. (60, 61)

Boston: William White, 1853.

THE PURITAN VIEW OF
HAWTHORNE'S VOCATION

The Puritans would also have scorned Hawthorne's vocation as a sin. The eighteenth century brought advances in printing, along with the emergence of the novel and an increase in the size of the reading public. But none of these changes quieted the suspicion of literature on the part of the Puritan clergy. In 1726 the Reverend Cotton Mather, in *Manuductio Ad Ministerium* (Instructions for Other Ministers), heatedly castigated poetry, drama, and fiction.

Mather, then, put "*Plays*, as well as the *Romances* and *Novels* and *Fictions*" in a subcategory of poetry, most of which he castigated in language just as inflammatory as that used by English Puritans to condemn the theater, using his own imagination in the acceptable instructive manner to compare fictions to toads and dragons of the devil.

The question presents itself: If imaginative literature, chiefly intended for recreation, was seen to "sensibly indispose" *ministers*, the intended readers of Mather's treatise, how much more of a threat did it pose to those ordinary folk who weren't dedicated to lives in the church? Consequently, how acceptable could be the calling of someone like Hawthorne, whose work produced such immoral effects on the lives of others, even on those fortified with divinity school educations?

FROM COTTON MATHER, *MANUDUCTIO AD MINISTERIUM* (1726)

Be not so set upon POETRY, as to be always poring on the PASSIONATE and MEASURED Pages. Let not what should be sauce rather than FOOD for you, Engross all your Application. Beware of a BOUNDLESS and SICKLY Appetite, for the Reading of POEMS, which now the RICKETY Nation swarms withal: And let not the CIRCEAN Cup intoxicate you. But especially preserve the CHASTITY of your Soul from the Dangers you may incur, by a Conversation with MUSES that are no better than HARLOTS.

Indeed, not meerly for the IMPURITIES which they convey, but also on some other Accounts, the POWERS OF DARKNESS have a LIBRARY among us, whereof the POETS have been the most NUMEROUS as well as the most VENEMOUS Authors. Most of the Modern PLAYS, as well as the ROMANCES and NOVELS and fictions, which are a sort of POEMS, do belong to the CATALOGUE of this cursed Library . . . THEY ARE NA- TIONAL SINS, AND THEREFORE CALL FOR NATIONAL PLAGUES: AND IF GOD SHOULD ENTER INTO JUDGMENT ALL THE BLOOD IN THE NATION WOULD NOT BE ABLE TO ATONE FOR THEM. (42)

How much do I wish that such Pestilences, and indeed all those worse than EGYPTIAN TOADS . . . might never crawl into your Chamber! The UNCLEAN SPIRITS that COME LIKE FROGS OUT OF THE MOUTH OF THE DRAGON, AND OF THE BEAST; which GO FORTH unto the young People of THE EARTH, and expose them to be dealt withal as the Enemies of *GOD*, in THE BATTLE OF THE GREAT DAY OF THE ALMIGHTY. As for those WRETCHED SCRIBBLERS of MADMEN, My Son, TOUCH THEM NOT, TASTE THEM NOT, HANDLE THEM NOT: Thou wilt PERISH in the USING of them. They are, THE DRAGONS WHOSE CONTAGIOUS BREATH PEOPLES THE DARK RETREATS OF DEATH. To much better Purpose will an Excellent but an Envied BLACKMORE feast you, than those Vile rapsodies. (43)

Boston: Printed for Thomas Hancock, 1726.

DISAPPROVAL OF FICTION IN
HAWTHORNE'S TIME

Despite the passage of nearly two centuries and the end of the Puritan church as it existed in the time of Hester and John and William Hathorne, many of its influences remained, chief among which was the disapproval of creative literature. Moralists and teachers in the nineteenth century had a special interest in keeping young girls from becoming dissatisfied with their limited positions in life. A young girl who read a romance might become dissatisfied with the farmer she had planned, with her family's blessing, to marry, or, in reading of a woman who had traveled far and wide, she might become dissatisfied with staying at home and having babies. Similarly, businessmen and others were interested in keeping young male workers from wasting time reading novels when they should be out making money. Reading fiction was a bad habit. The following documents include the kinds of opinions about fiction Hawthorne would have read throughout his young life and career. The first is an excerpt from a book of memoirs by the Reverend Timothy Dwight, who served as president of Yale College. It is followed by a letter by language specialist and educator Noah Webster, from a collection of his work published in 1843.

FROM TIMOTHY DWIGHT, "LETTER ON FASHIONABLE EDUCATION" (1821)

[Speaking of a poorly educated boy] Novels, plays, and other trifles of a similar nature, are the customary subjects of his investigation. Voyages, travels, biography, and sometimes history, limit his severe researches. By such a mind thinking will be loathed, and study regarded with terrour. In the pursuits, to which it is devoted, there is nothing to call forth, to try, or to increase, its strength. Its powers, instead of being raised to a new degree of energy, are never exercised to the extent, in which they already exist. . . . Destitute of that habit of labouring, which alone can render labour pleasing, or even supportable, he dreads exertion as a calamity. The sight of a Classic author gives him a chill: a lesson in Locke, or Euclid, a mental ague.

Thus in a youth, formed, perhaps, by nature for extensive views, and manly efforts, sloth of mind is generated, dandled, and nursed, on the knee of parental indulgence. A soft, luxurious, and sickly character is spread over both the understanding and the affections; which forbids their growth, prevents their vigour, and ruins every hope of future eminence, and future worth.

If these observations are just, they furnish every parent an easy and sure directory for the intellectual education of his children. If he wishes them to possess the greatest strength, of which they are capable, he must induce them to the most vigorous mental exertions. The reading education, which I have described, will never accomplish the purpose.

On girls, this unfortunate system induces additional evils. . . . The Reading of girls is regularly lighter than that of boys. . . . When the utmost labour of boys is bounded by history, biography, and the pamphlets of the day: girls sink down to songs, novels, and plays.

Of this reading what, let me ask, are the consequences? By the first novel which she reads, she is introduced into a world, literally new; a middle region between "this spot which men call earth," and that which is formed in Arabian tales. Instead of houses, inhabited by mere men, women and children, she is presented with a succession of splendid palaces, and gloomy castles. . . .

With this ideal world the unfortunate girl corresponds so much and so long, that she ultimately considers it as her own proper residence. With its inhabitants she converses so frequently, and so habitually, that they become almost her only familiar acquaintance.

But she must one day act in the real world. What can she expect, after having resided so long in novels, but that fortunes and villas and Edens, will spring up every where in her progress through life, to promote her enjoyment. She has read herself into a heroine, and is fairly entitled to all the appendages of this character. . . .

With these views, how disappointed must she be by the rugged course of nature? How untoward must be the progress of facts? How coarsely must the voice of truth grate upon her ear?

Between the Bible, and novels, there is a gulf fixed, which few novel readers are willing to pass. The consciousness of virtue, the dignified pleasure of having performed our duty, the serene remembrance of an useful life, the hope of an interest in the Redeemer, and the promise of a glorious inheritance in the favour of God, are never found in novels. . . . The admission of fiction, and of philosophical as truly as of poetical fiction, demands nothing, but the luscious indulgence of fancy. . . .

I know, that this education is merely a refinement of the imagination; of an imagination, already soft, and sickly; of a sensibility, already excessive.

Timothy Dwight, *Travels; in New-England and New-York* (New Haven: Privately published, 1821), pp. 513–519.

FROM NOAH WEBSTER, "LETTER TO A YOUNG GENTLEMAN
COMMENCING HIS EDUCATION" (1843)

In selecting books for reading, be careful to choose such as furnish the best helps to improvement in morals, literature, arts and science; preferring profit to pleasure, and instruction to amusement. A small portion of time may be devoted to such reading as tends to relax the mind, and to such bodily amusements as serve to invigorate muscular strength and the vital functions. But the greatest part of life is to be employed in useful labors, and in various indispensable duties, private, social, and public. Man has but little time to spare for the gratification of the sense and the imagination. I would therefore caution you against the fascinations of plays, novels, romances, and that species of descriptive writing which is employed to embellish common objects, without much enlarging the bounds of knowledge, or to paint imaginary scenes, which only excite curiosity, and a temporary interest, and then vanish in empty air.

The readers of books may be comprehended in two classes—those who read chiefly for amusement, and those who read for instruction. The first, and far the most numerous class, give their money and their time for private gratification; the second employ both for the acquisition of knowledge which they expect to apply to some useful purpose. The first gain subjects of conversation and social entertainment; the second acquire the means of public usefulness and of private elevation of character. The readers of the first class are so numerous, and the thirst for novelty so insatiable, that they must be deluged with tales and fiction; and if you suffer yourself to be hurried along with the current of popular reading, not only your *time*, but your *mind* will be dissipated; your native faculties, instead of growing into masculine vigor, will languish into imbecility. Bacon and Newton did not read tales and novels; their great minds were nourished with very different aliment.

Noah Webster, *Collection of Papers on Political, Literary and Moral Subjects* (New York: Webster and Clark, 1843), pp. 299–300.

PUBLIC RECEPTION OF *THE SCARLET LETTER*

The following excerpts are from reviews of *The Scarlet Letter* published soon after its publication. The old Puritan bias against fiction, which continued into the nineteenth century, and which Hawthorne mentions in "The Custom-House" and dramatizes in *The Scarlet Letter*, betrays itself in reviews of his novel. Most of the negative reviews, it will be noticed, come from religious periodicals, and their chief objection is that the adultery has not been portrayed as sufficiently evil. The *Christian Register* objects that Hester's and Dimmesdale's adultery is not made to look sinful enough and that through their guilt and sorrow the adulterers never reach any religious peace. Nor does it seem that any religious peace or redemption is possible. The *Christian Inquirer* complains that the book is melodramatic and has "neither a natural nor a Christian conscience," in that Dimmesdale and Hester "do not repent" and are just as bad at the end of their lives as they were at the beginning. Hawthorne's old friend at Brook Farm, Orestes Brownson, writes in his religious magazine that the story of adultery, even though there were many cases of it in Puritan times, is not a fit subject for fiction, nor, he says, does Hawthorne ever show how terrible the adulterers' sin was. The reviewer for the *Church Review* believes Hawthorne has done the public a disservice in writing about adultery and making it romantic.

One reviewer for the *North American Review,* who was obviously not up on his Puritan history, objects to the novel because Hawthorne locates "his picture of gross impurity and sacrilegious vice where no shadow of reproach, and no breath but of immaculate fame, had ever rested before."

FROM "THE SCARLET LETTER" (1850)

But, morally, we doubt whether the annals of literature furnish a single instance of success in any work, where the one act around which the whole interest of the narrative gathers and on which it all depends, is an act of moral pollution. As in The Heart of Mid-Lothian, such an act may incidentally add to the moral interest and instruction of the story, but not when it is the one thing on which the imagination is obliged to rest from beginning to end. The intensity of the interest only increases the painfulness of the emotion. Another moral objection to the Scarlet Letter is, that while falsehood is very justly made through the conscience the source of the most fearful torture and self-approach, the crime which falsehood is employed to cover up is not presented in such a way as to awaken the same kind of self-condemnation and horror. . . .

But as a Christian narrative, detailing the experience of a Christian man and woman, falling away from their purity, and struggling to get back again, it is utterly and entirely a failure. The peculiar office of Christianity in the conversion of sinners and their restoration to purity and peace is nowhere recognized throughout the volume. . . . The soul in consequence never rises to a religious peace. Nor is there any intimation that such a result is possible. The author nowhere recognizes the transforming and redeeming power of that Christian faith through which the spiritually dead may yet live and the lost be restored,—through which the most sinful may be converted and leave their sins behind, and regenerated, purified and sanctified in their affections, may walk in newness of life, and amid the wreck of earthly hopes find a peaceful satisfaction in a life of religious fidelity, in offices of Christian charity, in a sense of God's pardoning mercy and his constant love.

The great office of Christ, as a Redeemer, is overlooked. The remedial character of his religion is not understood. The grace of God in the soul, purging away its iniquities and leading it through many sorrows up the mountain of purification, till the rays of divine love rest upon it, and it has gained the victory over all its enemies, is a power which finds no place in Mr. Hawthorne's religious tales.

Christian Register, April 13, 1850, p. 58.

FROM "THE SCARLET LETTER" (1850)

In regard to the moral tone of this book, it seems to us somewhat strained where it is good, and only natural where it is questionable. The retributive principle in it is theatrically exaggerated. Remorse is represented as having all its agony, without any of its uses. The guilty suffer, confess that they suffer justly, live lives of voluntary penance, do works of utmost usefulness and die deaths of poetical justice—but do not *repent;* are just as bad at the close as at the beginning of their guilty career—and what is worse, just as *good,* for aught we see, after their crime, as before it. . . . Their suffering, while it is made severe enough, is not made to carry the reader's sense of justice with it; and their remorse, while it produces all the effects of penitence in every thing else, does not produce it where we see no reason for its not doing so—in respect to the crime itself. . . . We seem to see no hearty condemnation of the crime in the author's heart, and are not permitted to feel it in our own.

The conscience of the book is neither a natural nor a Christian conscience, but a sort of cross between the classic and the romantic conscience. We are not, with some of our contemporaries, offended with the falsification of the history of the time; for we do not imagine the Scarlet Letter will be regarded as documentary authority. We are more disturbed by the caustic, cynical, perhaps even bitter tone of parts of it. . . .

The essentials of the Scarlet Letter will forever prevent its taking a high and permanent place in the public heart. . . . it will not survive a temporary importance.

Christian Inquirer, May 25, 1850, 2: 4–6.

FROM ORESTES BROWNSON, "LITERARY NOTICES AND CRITICISMS" (1850)

. . . The story is told with great naturalness, ease, grace, and delicacy, but it is a story that should not have been told. . . . Crimes like the one imagined were not unknown even in the golden days of Puritanism, and are perhaps more common among the descendants of the Puritans than it is at all pleasant to believe; but they are not fit subjects for popular literature, and moral health is not promoted by leading the imagination to dwell on them. There is an unsound state of public morals when the novelist is permitted, without a scorching rebuke, to select such crimes, and invest them with all the fascinations of genius, and all the charms of a highly polished style. In a moral community such crimes are spoken of as rarely as possible, and when spoken of at all, it is always in terms which render them loathsome, and repel the imagination.

. . . He nowhere manages . . . to make their suffering excite the horror of his readers for their crime. . . . The minister, her accomplice, suffers also, horribly . . . but not from the fact of the crime itself, but from the consciousness of not being what he seems to the world, from his having permitted the partner in his guilt to be disgraced, to be punished, without his having the manliness to avow his share in the guilt, and to bear his share of the punishment. Neither ever really repents of the criminal deed; nay, neither ever regards it as really criminal, and both seem to hold it to have been laudable, because they *loved* one another,—as if the love itself were not illicit, and highly criminal. No man has the right to love another man's wife, and no married woman has the right to love any man but her husband. Mr. Hawthorne in the present case seeks to excuse Hester Prynne, a married woman, for loving the Puritan minister, on the ground that she had no love for her husband, and it is hard that a woman should not have some one to love; but this only aggravated her guilt, because she was not only forbidden to love the minister, but commanded to love her husband, whom she had vowed to love, honor, cherish, and obey. The modern doctrine that represents the affections as fatal, and wholly withdrawn from voluntary control, and then allows us to plead them in justification of neglect of duty and breach of the most positive precepts of both the natural and the revealed law, cannot be too severely reprobated.

. . . They hug their illicit love; they cherish their sin; and after the lapse of seven years are ready, and actually agree, to depart into a foreign country, where they may indulge it without disguise and without restraint. Even to the last, even when the minister, driven by his agony, goes so far as to throw off the mask of hypocrisy, and openly confess his crime, he shows no sign of repentance, or that he regarded his deed as criminal.

Brownson's Quarterly N.S. 4 (October 1850), pp. 528–532.

FROM ARTHUR CLEVELAND COXE, "THE WRITINGS OF HAWTHORNE" (1851)

Why has our author selected such a theme? Why, amid all the suggestive incidents of life in a wilderness; of a retreat from civilization to which, in every individual case, a thousand circumstances must have concurred to reconcile human nature with estrangement from home and country; or amid the historic connections of our history with Jesuit adventure, savage invasion, regicide outlawry, and french aggression, should the taste of Mr. Hawthorne have preferred as the proper material for romance, the nauseous amour of a Puritan pastor, with a frail creature of his charge, whose mind is represented as far more debauched than her body? Is it, in short because a running undertide of filth has become as requisite to a romance, as death in the fifth act of a tragedy? . . . yet we honestly believe that "the Scarlet Letter" has already done not a little to degrade our literature, and to encourage social licentiousness: it has started other pens on like enterprises, and has loosed the restraint of many tongues, that have made it an apology for "the evil communications which corrupt good manners." . . .

We shall entirely mislead our reader if we give him to suppose that "the Scarlet Letter" is coarse in its details, or indecent in its phraseology. This very article of our own, is far less suited to ears polite, than any page of the romance before us; and the reason is, we call things by their right names, while the romance never hints the shocking words that belong to its things, but, like Mephistopheles, insinuates that the archfiend himself is a very tolerable sort of person, or nobody would call him Mr. Devil. . . . "the Scarlet Letter" is delicately immoral.

. . . She responds—"never, never! What we did had a *consecration of its own,* we felt it so—we said so to each other!" This is a little too much—it carries the Bay-theory a little too far for our stomach! "Hush, Hester!" is the sickish rejoinder; and fie, Mr. Hawthorne! is the weakest token of our disgust that we can utter. The poor bemired hero and heroine of the story should not have been seen wallowing in their filth, at such a rate as this.

Church Review 3 (January 1851) pp. 506–510.

FROM ANDREW PRESTON PEABODY, "NATHANIEL HAWTHORNE" (1853)

. . . As illustrative of history, his stories are eminently untrustworthy; for, where he runs parallel with recorded fact in his narrative of events, the spirit that animates and pervades them is of his own creation. Thus, in the "Scarlet Letter," he has at once depicted the exterior of early New England life with a fidelity that might shame the most accurate chronicler, and defaced it by passions too fierce and wild to have been stimulated to their desolating energy under colder skies than of Spain or Italy. At that same time, he has unwittingly defamed the fathers of New England, by locating his pictures of gross impurity and sacrilegious vice where no shadow of reproach, and no breath but of immaculate fame, had ever rested before. He thus has violated one of the most sacred canons of literary creation. A writer, who borrows nothing from history, may allow himself an unlimited range in the painting of character; but he who selects a well-known place and epoch for his fiction, is bound to adjust his fiction to the analogy of fact, and especially to refrain from outraging the memory of the dead for the entertainment of the living.

North American Review 76 (January 1853), pp. 232–233.

TOPICS FOR WRITTEN OR ORAL EXPLORATION

1. Write an essay on Hester as artist, using what the narrator has to say about her art as a seamstress and the Massachusetts Bay law prohibiting artful dress.

2. Write an analysis of the various eighteenth- and nineteenth-century objections to fiction.

3. Are these characteristics of fiction, which moralists found objectionable, true of *The Scarlet Letter*?

4. Write an analysis of one of the lengthier critical reviews of *The Scarlet Letter*. Can you determine anything about the personality and values of the reviewer? Make an argument refuting or supporting the ideas in the review.

5. Are any of the values or opinions about fiction reflected in these reviews, held by anyone today, as far as you know?

6. Are any of the same moralistic judgments applied to other aspects of contemporary culture, such as certain types of music or art? Discuss.

7. The debate on certain types of music or art does rage on. Stage a debate over one of these issues. Late twentieth-century issues to choose from might be the controversy over the photographs of the photographer Robert Mapplethorpe or the controversy over rock or rap music.

8. More than one reviewer condemns *The Scarlet Letter* because neither Hester nor Dimmesdale is properly remorseful and because their crime is not presented as a horrible one. Stage a debate on these two points.

9. Write a letter to the editor of the *North American Review* in which you correct the reviewer's historical facts about the Puritans.

SUGGESTED READINGS

Hawthorne's Life

DeSalvo, Louise. *Nathaniel Hawthorne*. Atlantic Highlands, N.J.: Humanities Press International, 1987.

Ferguson, Helen Myatt. *Nathaniel Hawthorne and Charles Wentworth Upham*. Ann Arbor: University Microfilms, 1980.

Mellow, James. *Nathaniel Hawthorne in His Times*. Boston: Houghton Mifflin, 1980.

Upham, Charles Wentworth. *Lectures on Witchcraft*. Boston: Carter, Hendee and Babcock, 1831.

Attitudes Toward Art

Galloway, W. F. "The Conservative Attitude Toward Fiction 1770–1830."
    PMLA 55 (December 1940): 1041–1059.
Orians, G. Harrison. "Censure of Fiction." *PMLA* 35 (1937): 195–215.
Tyne, Stephen H. "Men of Business: Their Perplexities and Temptations."
    In *The Man of Business Considered in His Various Relations.* 4
    vols. New York: Anson D.F. Randolph, 1857: 4: 1–52.

Quakers

Dalglish, Doris N. *People Called Quakers.* Freeport, ME: Books for Li-
    braries Press, 1969.
Dove at the Window: Last Letters of Four Quaker Martyrs. Lincoln, Mass.:
    Penmaen Press, 1973.
Ingle, H. Larry. *First Among Friends: George Fox and the Creation of
    Quakerism.* New York: Oxford University Press, 1994.
Plimpton, Ruth Talbot. *Mary Dyer: Biography of a Rebel Quaker.* Boston:
    Branden, 1994.

The Scarlet Letter: Issues in the 1980s and 1990s

While *The Scarlet Letter* is set in the seventeenth century, we have seen that in some ways, especially in the public perception of art and the woman question, it sheds light on the nineteenth century, when it was published. Many of the issues it raises also have relevance in the last decades of the twentieth century. Some of those issues include:

- the single mother
- the immoral minister
- the custody of children and biological parents
- the separation of church and state
- corporal punishment

While the student is encouraged to pursue all of the topics independently, the issues of the single mother and the immoral minister will be examined in some detail here, after a brief discussion of some of the other newsworthy issues of the 1990s relative to *The Scarlet Letter.*

THE SEPARATION OF CHURCH AND STATE

> . . . a people among whom religion and law were almost identical.
> *The Scarlet Letter,* 58

In *The Scarlet Letter* church and state are one. The colony was founded by religious men for a religious purpose. The legislature and the courts were advised by ministers and made laws affecting religion. Church attendance and proper observance of the Sabbath were mandated by law. The most serious crime imaginable, heresy, was an offense against both the church and the state. To preach beliefs incompatible with the state religion, Puritanism, like those of the Quakers, the Baptists, or even the Antinomians, was punishable by public beatings and banishment, and in the case of the Quakers, even death. Sexual misbehavior like Hester's, which violates a religious code, is treated as a state crime. And union of church and state is shown in the religious character of political holidays; the high point of Election Day in *The Scarlet Letter* is the sermon preached by Arthur Dimmesdale.

The danger of expressing unconventional religious views in this church/state is suggested in Dimmesdale's vicarious but secret thrill in hearing Chillingworth's dangerous religious speculations. Hester also has to keep her radical religious speculation to herself. Otherwise, the narrator says, she would suffer a fate much worse than that she suffers because of her adultery.

The British crown began to force some separation between church and state in the Massachusetts Bay Colony even before the American Revolution, and by 1776 separation of church and state had become an ideal, if not a reality, of the revolution. The newly established country would allow freedom of religion without favoring or establishing any religion or forcing a religion on anyone.

Treading the thin line between allowing the free practice of religion and not allowing anyone to force his or her views on others has not always been easy. Persistent problems have arisen in the last decades of the twentieth century, especially in regard to public prayer (or mandated periods of time for prayer) in public schools and at public school graduations or legislative sessions, and in regard to the use of public facilities (like schools) by religious organizations.

Those who are vigilant about keeping church and state separate have neither the desire nor the ability to interfere with the silent prayer of the individual citizen in any arena; nevertheless, frequent violations of the separation of church and state happen when public prayers are offered or when officially sanctioned times for public prayer are set aside in state-supported institutions. One such case occurred in December 1993 in a high school in Jackson, Mississippi, when a principal gave his permission for students to read prayers over a school intercom. He was suspended from his duties.

Another case surfaced in June 1994, when some U.S. senators became alarmed, fearing that new Equal Employment Opportunity Commission guidelines to protect workers from religious harassment would limit freedom of religious expression. Would the new guidelines mean that workers could not wear religious symbols or invite co-workers to church? Where, it was asked, are the lines to be drawn?

CORPORAL PUNISHMENT

> It might be that a sluggish bond-servant, or an undutiful child, whom his parents had given over to the civil authority, was to be corrected at the whipping-post.
>
> *The Scarlet Letter*, 57

As we have seen, although Hester escapes the usual punishment for adultery and fornication, being branded or whipped, the tradition of corporal punishment is very much a part of the society in which she lives. And she comes very close to being on the receiving end of brutal physical punishment when she is made to stand on the scaffold instead. Some female spectators talk of putting "the brand of a hot iron on Hester Prynne's forehead" (59), and she stands on a spot where many have been "corrected at the whipping-post" (57).

Spankings or whippings were a regular part of "correction" in the public schools almost until the middle of the twentieth century. But by the 1990s, incidents of corporal punishment had dwindled dramatically. An international incident involving corporal punishment occurred in 1993 and 1994 when an American teenager living in Singapore was arrested for vandalism. The punishment for this crime was caning—being struck on the bare behind with a bamboo cane. The boy and his family claimed that they were told by Singapore officials that if he confessed to the crime, he would not be caned. But the boy's confession, the objections of the president of the United States and other U.S. officials, and constant publicity in the media failed to avert the caning.

In the context of rampant youthful crime in the United States, opinions about the incident were decidedly mixed, some people arguing that severe corporal punishment was needed to stem the tide of crime. With the publicity given the incident, many other articles appeared in the public press over whether any corporal punishment, whether severe or mild, whether administered by the school, the state, or the parents, could, as a violent act, ever have other than lasting bad effects.

CHILD CUSTODY

> It had reached her ears that there was a design on the part of some of the leading inhabitants, cherishing the more rigid order of principles in religion and government, to deprive her of her child. . . . If the child . . . were really capable of moral and religious growth and possessed the elements of ultimate salvation, then, surely, it would enjoy all the fairer prospect of these advantages by being transferred to wiser and better guardianship than Hester Prynne's.
>
> *The Scarlet Letter*, 101

The question of whether a child should remain with (or be returned to) its biological parent is no less a controversy in the twentieth century than it was for Hester Prynne in *The Scarlet Letter*. The reasons for taking Pearl from Hester were several. The only one that would be considered valid today was that relocating the child was in Pearl's best interests. Hester, as a fallen woman, it was thought, would be a bad influence on Pearl. Furthermore, it was suspected that she was not providing the child with a proper religious education. The other two reasons were peculiar to Hester's Boston: the society would consider separating mother and child if it considered the arrangement to be bad for the community as a whole. It was also thought that—good mother though Hester might be—Pearl was interfering with Hester's rehabilitation, or penance: "On the supposition that Pearl, as already hinted, was of demon origin, these good people not unreasonably argued that a Christian interest in the mother's soul required them to remove such a stumbling block from her path" (101). Though this is the initial reason given for taking Pearl from Hester, ironically, the opposite is true. Pearl is what saves Hester from abandoning herself to the darkest elements of human nature.

In the governor's mansion, a little impromptu custody hearing is conducted, the Reverend Wilson acting as a specialist in putting questions to Pearl, and Governor Bellingham acting as judge. The criterion they apply is not whether Hester is a good mother, but whether she is teaching Pearl the tenets of Puritanism. Pearl, being the contrary child that she is, refuses to cooperate, and the decision is initially rendered against Hester. At this point Hester is prepared to sacrifice her former lover, the Reverend Dimmesdale, if he does not act as a witness in her behalf. In short, she blackmails him—"Look to it!" she says. In other words, if you don't step in to prevent these men from taking my child, I'll be forced to reveal that you are her father.

The conflict over child custody is older than Solomon and continues to the present day. In the 1990s, for example, two unusual cases received extensive national attention. One was the case of Baby Jessica, who had been born to an unmarried man and woman, seemingly relinquished by the mother, and then placed with a couple eager to adopt a child. However, when the child was several years old, the mother and father married and went to court to have their natural child returned. Eventually, after many legal maneuvers, the child was taken from its adoptive parents and placed with its biological parents.

Another highly publicized case involving rights of adoptive and biological parents occurred in the 1990s when it was discovered that two babies had been switched at birth twelve years before. One of the children had died, and tests had revealed that she was not the biological child of the parents who had raised her. The parents then sought custody of their biological daughter, who had been raised by another couple, the biological parents of the girl who had died. After much ill-feeling, the biological parents and the widowed man who had reared her received joint custody. But the daughter, unhappy with the joint custody arrangement, took her biological parents to court to "divorce" them. After hearing her testimony, the court agreed to grant her wish. In another strange turn of events, only a few months later, the daughter appealed to the court for permission to leave the father who had reared her to live with her biological parents.

A divorced parent frequently challenges the custody of an ex-partner on a variety of grounds, none of which have much to do with "abuse" or "fitness." Less frequently, either an ex-spouse or an agency of the state has challenged the continuance of a child with a parent for reasons of religion or sexual preference. For example, in a number of instances, homosexuals have been challenged as fit parents of their biological children.

Challenges on religious grounds in the late twentieth century usually involve children living with one biological parent in a religious cult where some kind of abuse may be taking place. One such instance occurred in the Branch Davidian religious cult in Waco, Texas, where the parents of very young girls were collaborating in the sexual abuse of their daughters by the cult leader.

A case that addresses several issues in *The Scarlet Letter*, custody included, was reported in the May 15, 1994, *Boston Globe*. Here the biological father pled for custody of his children, who were being reared by their mother in a religious cult. Other issues pertinent to the novel that arose in this case included administering corporal punishment and the refusal of the sect to allow the children to use their imaginations.

The father's objections were that the children were being subjected to brutal corporal punishment and were being refused a standard general education. They were being educated only for menial jobs within the church's industries.

The mother and the church, on the other hand, argued that she has been denied custody of some of their children because of a bias against her religion, which teaches that children as young as six months old should be struck with a switch to instill obedience, and which forbids the children experiences the church finds harmful, like the use of the imagination. The court eventually found in favor of the father, allowing the mother visitation rights outside the cult.

ALONE AND MOTHERING AN ILLEGITIMATE CHILD

> And my child must seek a heavenly Father; she shall never know an
> earthly one.
>
> *The Scarlet Letter*, 74

The basic story of *The Scarlet Letter* is that of a woman rearing an illegitimate child alone. She has no friends and little confidence in her own goodness, and enjoys not even the simplest pleasures in life. Her child is labeled the child of the devil.

Shame and guilt were the inevitable consequences of unwed motherhood for well over three hundred years after the seventeenth century, the time of *The Scarlet Letter*. For example, young women who became pregnant (married or not) in high school and even in college, surprisingly enough, were ordered to withdraw. It was not until the 1970s after use of the birth control pill became widespread and the "sexual revolution" came about that this situation began to change. By the 1980s, with little or no stigma attached, unwed motherhood among teenage girls had become epidemic.

Despite the existence of thousands of unwed mothers in America, what can only be described as a "flap" regarding unwed motherhood erupted in the spring of 1992 during the presidential campaign when Vice President Dan Quayle castigated a character on a television program (Murphy Brown) for having a baby out of wedlock. Vice President Quayle accused the television networks of contributing to immorality and a general breakdown in family values indicative of an unsavory lifestyle. Quayle's point, and one on which Hester's Puritan community acted, was that the unwed mother was both a symbol of immorality and a threat to the values of the community. Note, for example, how even members of the community who are recipients of her charity act as if Hester will infect them if they get too close to her, and how she becomes the symbolic subject of the sermons of various ministers, as the embodiment of evil.

In the Murphy Brown case, the writers and producers of the show, attempting to counter criticism, argued that Murphy Brown was just a character who was pregnant with her ex-husband's child and should have made Quayle happy in that she had opted not to have an abortion, which Quayle thought was wrong. Many joined in the fray throughout the summer, proving that, despite the sexual revolution, the issue of the unwed mother is very much alive.

Included here are an excerpt from a *New York Times* story on how unwed mothers are depicted in movies, a newspaper account of the Quayle/Murphy controversy, and a commentary by an African American columnist on illegitimate births among teenagers.

FROM "UNWED MOTHERS: THE SCARLET LETTER RETURNS IN PINK"

By SUSAN CHIRA

From the 1930's to the 50's, the rules were ironclad, and those who broke them were punished accordingly. Unwed motherhood was a disgrace. But flashes of sympathy for the heroine eased the shame of the scarlet letter, and the penitent mother could gain redemption by suffering. Then the sexual revolution tossed out most conventions, and film makers in the 60's and 70's scrambled to keep up. The pill uncoupled sex from pregnancy, sex before marriage grew commonplace, and abortion became legal. But motherhood out of wedlock remained taboo.

While unwed motherhood may be common in real life these days, it is still treated gingerly on the screen. Unwed motherhood in today's films runs the gamut from a comic plot device ("Three Men and a Baby," "Look Who's Talking") to a reexamination of women's lives and choices, most notably in several recent films by women directors. There is even talk of a remake of "The Scarlet Letter," starring Demi Moore as Hester Prynne.

Although having a child outside of marriage can now be a conscious choice, movies more often than not still brand it a bad one. More than 60 years after Helen Hayes was shown turning to prostitution in "The Sin of Madelon Claudet," movies still reflect society's pervasive discomfort with unwed motherhood, even as politicians and pundits battle over the links between teenage motherhood and welfare and family values.

"We all have mixed feeling about this," said Molly Haskell, an author and film critic. "We see the real fruits of unbridled sexuality among teenagers. It's what everyone feared, that young people really aren't able to take responsibility. There are very legitimate reasons for these taboos, and for Hollywood's often straitlaced observance of them. What seems unfair is that women have always had to carry the burden."

Katha Pollitt, a writer on feminist topics, argues that movies have not drawn a distinction between unwed mothers capable of raising a baby and those who are not. Maturity, not marriage, is the issue, she suggested.

"You should have a baby when you're a grown-up," she said. "It's fascinating to me that, given how much the idea of becoming a single mother by choice is in the culture, that there aren't movies about it."

New York Times, January 23, 1994, p.13.

FROM "QUAYLE DEPLORES ERODING VALUES; CITES TV SHOW"

By DOUGLAS JEHL

Vice President Dan Quayle on Tuesday blamed the Los Angeles riots on a breakdown of American family values and accused prime time television of contributing to moral decay by making a heroine of a character who bore a baby out of wedlock.

In a stern admonition on behalf of traditional mores, Quayle said the "lawless social anarchy" that erupted in Los Angeles emerged from a broader breakdown that has fostered a "poverty of values."

He said the plight of urban America has not been helped by the portrayal this week on TV's "Murphy Brown" of the title character "mocking the importance of fathers by bearing a child alone, and calling it just another 'lifestyle choice.'

"Marriage is probably the best anti-poverty program there is," Quayle said in a speech for the Commonwealth Club of San Francisco, a copy of which was released in Washington.

Told about Quayle's comments, a senior Bush campaign official replied only, "Oh, dear."

The CBS network said that its Monday night episode of "Murphy Brown," the season finale in which she gave birth to a son, was watched, in whole or part, by 38 million people. It was the second highest rated episode in the series' history, topped only by last fall's special one-hour season premiere in which Murphy Brown learned definitely that she was pregnant.

CBS said it had no comment on Quayle's remarks, but Diane English, creator of "Murphy Brown," said, "If the vice president thinks it's disgraceful for an unmarried woman to bear a child without a father, then he'd better make sure abortion remains safe and legal."

A spokeswoman for Gov. Bill Clinton of Arkansas said the popularity of "Murphy Brown" reflects the fact "millions of Americans think she has something relevant to say."

"The world is a much more complicated place than Dan Quayle wants to believe," Clinton campaign press secretary Dee Dee Myers said. "He should watch a few episodes before he decides to pop off."

Quayle voiced his concerns about unwed motherhood as he suggested that the Los Angeles riots were "directly related to the breakdown of family structure, personal responsibility and social order in too many areas of our society.''

He cited statistics showing sharp increases in illegitimacy and crime rates among black Americans to suggest that within the nation's underclass, the most troublesome poverty is ''fundamentally a poverty of values.''

Quayle also noted that the poverty rate for families headed by a single mother is six times higher than the rate among families headed by married couples. But the vice president devoted his address more to the diagnosis than to cures for the nation's urban woes.

Los Angeles Times, May 20, 1992, pp. A1, A14.

FROM ''ONE LAST COLUMN: WRITER DETAILS WHERE HE FAILED''

By BILL MAXWELL

I'm most disappointed by the area's black leaders' lack of vision, their unwillingness to publicly stand firm against self-destructive behavior, their general cowardice, their refusal to use their considerable influence to foster self-reliance, their blatant worship of popularity.

For example, everyone knows that low-income babies born out of wedlock stand a better than average chance of always living in poverty, that these mothers virtually condemn themselves and their children to a lifetime of hardship. Yet, local black leaders lack the nerve and sense of morality to tackle this issue. Why? Because such talk is unpopular.

If they went on the stump with this issue, many black girls would pay attention. And some would change their behavior. But our leaders don't speak out publicly. Why? Because they would be accused of being enemies of the people.

New York Times, June 26, 1994.

THE IMMORAL MINISTER

I, your pastor, whom you so reverence and trust, am utterly a pollution and a lie!

The Scarlet Letter, 140

One-half of *The Scarlet Letter* is about someone other than Hester who wears the scarlet "A." Though the reader as well as the community thinks of only Hester as a wearer of the scarlet letter, we know early on that Dimmesdale, the minister so beloved in the village, also wears the same letter on his heart, that he has committed adultery with her, and that the tombstone with the armorial "A" on it is Arthur Dimmesdale's tombstone as well.

Yet the unexpected jolt that the reader is given as Hester's partner in sin is discovered is that this crime, which the society calls the vilest of the vile, the blackest of the black, has been committed by a minister of the church. We have already traced Dimmesdale's shameful steps as he deals with his crime of adultery and cowardly and ambitious deception: his way of trying to insure that Hester won't name him as father, his telling her in the forest that he has always been terrified of discovery, his attempts at beating his human nature out of his body and gaining peace of mind with phoney confessions. By the end of his life, the reader views Dimmesdale's lying to the public and to himself as a greater sin than his adultery.

Throughout the years, Arthur Dimmesdale has been the prototype of the minister discovered in a sexual scandal. Many of those indiscreet clergymen who followed Dimmesdale—both real and fictional—have shared strikingly similar characteristics. First is insatiable ambition, the drive to climb to the top of their profession. In so doing, they must take great pains to conceal their sexual misbehavior. Most of these men, at the same time, make a concerted effort to cultivate a public image of saintliness. And all enjoy a very real kind of power over their parishioners, who idolize them. As a result, an astonishing number of their followers refuse to believe charges of sexual misbehavior or easily forgive them and defend them from their detractors, as Dimmesdale's congregation does even after he has confessed.

Dimmesdale's real nineteenth-century counterpart was one of the most prominent ministers of that century, Henry Ward Beecher, brother of novelist Harriet Beecher Stowe. Beecher was involved in a highly publicized trial for adultery with at least two of his married parishioners. Daily transcripts of the court proceedings ran in the New York newspapers.

One of the more famous members of Dimmesdale's brotherhood in fiction is Elmer Gantry, a popular tent evangelist in Sinclair Lewis's novel by the same name, who is found to be a womanizer. Gantry, a likable, charismatic sort, refrains from presenting himself as saintly, as Dimmesdale does, but he still succeeds in living two lives: one as a leader of simple people who exercises great power over his audiences' hearts and pocketbooks as an extraordinarily moral man of God, and the other as an unprincipled man who spends another life in pursuit of women and booze.

The documents that conclude this chapter are from the 1990s, when other members of Dimmesdale's brotherhood fell from power and grace. The stage was set for scandal in the late 1980s and 1990s when evangelists greatly increased the immense power they already held over the hearts and souls of their believers through the use of television, gaining greater exposure, fame, and money than Elmer Gantry would ever dream of. They had not only the usual power of any pastor; they were also television stars. The television ministry became big business; many of these men were not only paid substantial salaries for their television appearances, but also came to control huge corporations that, in turn, owned the television shows they appeared on and sometimes even television stations, along with other allied businesses. They lived in extraordinary personal luxury, owning posh houses, luxury cars, and extravagant jewelry and clothes. Again and again, it was proved that the insignificant amount of money they returned to the people went to spreading the word of their own ministries and not to relieving the poor.

Two of the most famous of these men, Jim Bakker and Jimmy Swaggart, were discovered to have participated in illicit sex.

ARTHUR DIMMESDALE, JIM BAKKER, AND JIMMY SWAGGART

In late March 1987, the country was astonished when Jim Bakker, a well-known and controversial television evangelist who was already under investigation for irregularities in his soliciting and spending of money, admitted that he had had a sexual liaison with a church secretary, a revelation all the more shocking because his wife, Tammy Faye, was a very visible member of the evangelistic team.

In light of this information, the Reverend Bakker was stripped of his church duties, and a full-scale investigation of his personal and financial life was launched by his religious denomination and the government of the United States. The range of his sexual misconduct escalated beyond the single incident as the investigation continued. The government immediately moved to seize Bakker's businesses, including a religious theme park, as well as houses, cars, and expensive personal effects to cover income tax and other debts.

Other television evangelists were divided over the incident, some continuing to offer their sympathy to Bakker, most keeping their distance from the affair, and others condemning him unconditionally. The most vitriolic in his condemnation was a Louisiana television evangelist, Jimmy Swaggart, also the leader of a multimillion-dollar ministry, who, it was reported, had notified authorities of Bakker's sexual liaison in the first place. Bakker was subsequently arrested on charges of fraud and income tax evasion, found guilty, and sent to prison.

As if this scandal were not enough of a blow to the evangelistic movement, on February 19, 1988, a shocking story broke about Swaggart himself. The evangelistic soap opera became even more complicated when it was learned that another minister, Marion Gorman, who had himself been accused by Swaggart of conducting numerous adulterous affairs, had provided church authorities with evidence against Swaggart.

Even though Swaggart was never found to have done anything criminal, his story was much more sordid than Jim Bakker's. Prostitutes, cooperating with photographers, were able to provide video, audio, and eyewitness evidence that the Reverend Swaggart was a frequent and somewhat kinky visitor to houses of ill repute.

Note in the following articles the similarities between the cases of these two fallen idols and Dimmesdale. They enjoy immense stature in their congregations. They seem to be closer to God than ordinary people. Note the revelation of adultery, the attempt at a cover-up, the flocks' reluctance to believe their misbehavior, the belief that Satan had a hand in attempting to thwart the work of the church, and the fear that the incident would discredit all television evangelism.

The scene between Chillingworth and Dimmesdale in the chapter entitled "The Leech and His Patient" and the first five paragraphs of the conclusion reveal the rationalizations that a minister can concoct to defend bad behavior, as well as the blindness of congregations to the transgressions of their leaders. Again, the discussion of *The Scarlet Letter* brings us to the way we view others and the way we present ourselves to the world.

FROM "BAKKER, EVANGELIST, RESIGNS HIS MINISTRY OVER
SEXUAL INCIDENT"

By WAYNE KING
Washington, March 20—The Rev. Jim Bakker, a leading television evangelist, has resigned his ministry, asserting that he was maneuvered into a sexual encounter six years ago and subsequently blackmailed.

Mr. Bakker, a protege of the Rev. Pat Robertson, a founding father of television ministries, has become one of the nation's most prominent broadcast evangelists in the decade since he assumed the spiritual and financial leadership of the PTL Club in Fort Mills, S.C. He has repeatedly drawn the attention of Federal investigators because of his fund-raising techniques, which yield more than $100 million annually.

His leadership of the PTL ministry—the letters stand for Praise the Lord and People That Love—will be assumed by the Reverend Jerry Falwell. Mr. Falwell is host of his own widely viewed television ministry program, "The Old Time Gospel Hour," and is founder of the conservative lobby Moral Majority.

In an emotional statement to the *Charlotte Observer* on Thursday, Mr. Bakker said he had been "wickedly manipulated by treacherous former friends" who "conspired to betray me into a sexual encounter" in Florida in December, 1980. As a result, he said, he "succumbed to blackmail" to protect his ministry and family.

Mr. Bakker and his wife, Tammy Faye, have for a decade been co-hosts of a daily talk program now called "The Jim and Tammy Show," distributed to hundreds of stations around the country through the PTL network.

On March 6, Mrs. Bakker, who was often moved to tears of religious feeling on the program, disclosed on the show, in a videotaped appearance from California, that she was undergoing treatment at a Palm Springs clinic for drug dependency.

In his statement to *The [Charlotte] Observer* on Thursday, Mr. Bakker said that he, too, was under treatment. "My and Tammy's physical and emotional resources have been so overwhelmed that we are presently under full-time therapy at a treatment center in California," he said.

Woman Denies Blackmail

Mr. Bakker (pronounced baker) did not disclose the amount of money involved in the purported blackmail. The *Observer* reported that a lawyer for the evangelist had paid a woman $115,000, although the source of the money was not made clear.

The *Observer* identified the woman as Jessica Hahn, who at the time of the incident was a 21-year-old church secretary from Oklahoma. The newspaper said she had acknowledged to it that an incident had occurred but had not provided details except to say that there had been "no blackmail, no extortion."

The PTL organization reported revenue of $129 million last year. It employs 2,000 people and operates a 2,300-acre religious theme park, Heritage USA, at Fort Mills.

Mr. Bakker's resignation came on the heels of disclosures last week by the officials of his religious denomination, the Assemblies of God, that a formal investigation was under way into allegations of sexual misconduct by the minister.

A church leader said today that the scandal had hurt the church. The Rev. Everett Stenhouse, assistant general superintendent of the International Assemblies of God, said church leaders could reject Mr. Bakker's resignation and instead strip him of his ministries.

In his statement, Mr. Bakker acknowledged that he had paid to hush up a sexual encounter. He was not specific about the nature of the incident. But he said, "I categorically deny that I've ever sexually assaulted or harassed anyone."

He went on to "sorrowfully acknowledge" that "in an isolated incident I was wickedly manipulated by treacherous former friends and then-colleagues who victimized me with the aid of a female confederate."

"In retrospect," he went on, "it was poor judgment to have succumbed to blackmail. But when extortionist overtures were made, I was concerned to protect and spare the ministry and my family. Unfortunately, money was paid in order to avoid further suffering."

The Devil in the Computer

Over the years since 1974, when Mr. Bakker took over the PTL ministry, the success of the fund-raising and the Bakkers' ostentatious way of life drew scrutiny, although inquiries by both the Federal Communications Commission and the Internal Revenue Service found no cause for legal action.

At various times the Bakkers drove matching Rolls-Royces, purchased a $375,000 condominium in Florida and spent $80,000 more equipping it with gold plumbing fixtures, and vacationed on an ocean-going cruiser.

On one occasion, when the Internal Revenue Service questioned book-keeping practices that left $13 million in PTL revenue accounted for incompletely or not at all, Mr. Bakker suggested that "the devil got into the computer" used for record-keeping.

The Justice Department concluded in March, 1983, that there was no evidence that the PTL Club misused funds it solicited.

New York Times, March 21, 1987, pp. 1, 33.

FROM "PREACHERS' BATTLE TRANSFIXING THE SOUTH"

By ROBIN TONER

Charlotte, N.C., March 25— . . . On Monday, Mr. Bakker said he had re-signed to avert a hostile takeover of PTL by "a well known individual" who knew about his troubles. On Tuesday, Mr. Bakker's lawyer said it was Mr. Swaggart who had plotted to oust Mr. Bakker. Mr. Swaggart denied those accusations. But he was harshly critical of Mr. Bakker, saying on the ABC News program "Nightline" Tuesday night that the "entire debacle" involving Mr. Bakker was "a cancer that needed to be excised from the body of Christ."

Lining up with Mr. Bakker, meanwhile, was Mr. [Oral] Roberts, who has recently gained considerable attention himself for announcing that God had told him to raise $8 million by March 31 or he would be "called home." Also sympathetic to Mr. Bakker was Mr. Falwell, who agreed to replace Mr. Bakker as head of PTL.

But Mr. Falwell did not join in the attack on Mr. Swaggart. Mr. Falwell was quoted in The Charlotte Observer today as saying he did not believe Mr. Swaggart was involved in any takeover plot.

Some experts on evangelism and television ministries said the week of turmoil would take its toll in the way people view these ministries. "This is not going to destroy individual ministries as such, but the immediate impact on all of them will be significant," said Jeffrey Hadden, a professor of sociology at the University of Virginia who wrote the book "Prime Time Preachers."

Mr. Hadden said the events of recent days feed the "Elmer Gantry image" that many people had of television evangelists, although he said audiences of individual ministers would probably not be affected.

The Rev. Bob Dugan of the National Association of Evangelicals said, "I think probably a lot of people will take a closer look at where they invest their money." He and others active in the evangelical movement said they were concerned that the PTL turmoil would be unfairly connected to the evangelical movement as a whole, which in recent years has gained increasing recognition and political influence. . . .

New York Times, March 26, 1987, p. A16.

FROM "PASTOR TELLS OF GUILT OVER INTRODUCING PAIR"

By ROBIN TONER

Rochester, March 28 (AP)—The evangelist who brought the Rev. Jim Bakker together with a young woman for what became a sexual encounter says he has been tortured with guilt.

"I am guilty," the evangelist, John Wesley Fletcher, told about 500 people at Faith Temple on Friday.

Mr. Fletcher, a traveling preacher from Oklahoma City, said he had been bothered since he introduced Mr. Bakker to the woman, Jessica Hahn, in a hotel room in Clearwater Beach, Fla., on Dec. 6, 1980.

• • •

Mr. Fletcher was once a minister of the Assemblies of God, but was dismissed years ago "for some kind of ministerial misconduct," church officials have said. Mr. Bakker is also affiliated with the Assemblies of God.

New York Times, March 29, 1987, p. 24.

FROM "BAKKER'S TROUBLES TEST FAITH AT RELIGIOUS RESORT"

Fort Mills, S.C., March 27— . . . "The workings of God are not as man sees it," said Joyce Barchus, a book-keeper from Manchester, N.H., who was spending her vacation at Heritage for the third year in a row. "What seems a tragedy will turn out to be good."

Mrs. Barchus said she did not know "what the Lord has in store" for the Bakkers, but she said she believed these troubles would bring more people to God. Like other visitors here, she spoke with smiling conviction and was eager to talk, viewing it as an opportunity to "witness" her faith before the outside world.

Request for Contributions

On today's PTL television broadcast, the Rev. Richard Dortch, who succeeded Mr. Bakker as the program's host and the organization's president, urged his viewers to show their faith by increasing their support of Heritage and PTL, which stands for Praise the Lord and People That Love.

"Everybody is saying to us, 'How can we help?' " Mr. Dortch said. "First of all, you can pray. Secondly, you can come and visit us." The evangelist told his audience to "vote" for PTL by sending in contributions.

New York Times, March 29, 1987, p. 24.

FROM "TV MINISTRY LISTS '85 INCOME"

Baton Rouge, La., May 1 (AP)—The Jimmy Swaggart Ministries had revenue of nearly $128.5 million in 1985, according to the auditor of the evangelical organization.

Jim Guinn, a Dallas-based auditor who has kept financial records since 1978, estimated the organization's 1986 revenue at $142 million. . . .

• • •

The Rev. Jimmy Swaggart, his wife, Frances, son, Donnie, and daughter-in-law, Debbie, hold four of the ministries' seven board positions. The organization, which is based here, would not disclose their salaries. But Mr. Swaggart has said he was paid less than $100,000 a year.

New York Times, May 2, 1987, p. 23.

FROM "SWAGGART IS SUBJECT OF INVESTIGATION BY HIS CHURCH"

Springfield, Mo., Feb. 19. (AP)—The Rev. Jimmy Swaggart, the television evangelist, is under investigation by his church, the Assemblies of God, a church spokeswoman said today. Newspaper and broadcast reports said the inquiry involved allegations of sexual misconduct.

$140 Million Ministry

The ABC News program "Nightline," citing sources it did not identify, reported that church officials at the meeting were shown photographs that were said to show Mr. Swaggart with a "known prostitute" at a New Orleans motel. The Nightline report said a church official told ABC News that the photos were "open to interpretation."

Nightline said the photos were provided to the church officials by Marvin Gorman, a New Orleans preacher who has been feuding with Mr. Swaggart.

Bakker Is "Shocked"

Mr. Gorman filed a $90 million suit accusing Mr. Swaggart and others of plotting to ruin his ministry with false reports of adulterous affairs, but a judge dismissed the suit in September, saying it was a religious dispute that did not belong in court. He is pastor of the Metropolitan Christian Life Church in Metairie, outside New Orleans. Calls to his church today were not answered.

Mr. Swaggart was among Mr. Bakker's chief accusers.

New York Times, February 20, 1988, p. 22.

FROM "SWAGGART SAYS HE HAS SINNED, WILL STEP DOWN"

By WAYNE KING

Baton Rouge, La., Feb. 21—The Rev. Jimmy Swaggart, who last year condemned a fellow television evangelist, Jim Bakker, as "a cancer on the body of Christ," today confessed to sins of his own and begged to be forgiven.

But he also referred, in the plural, to "incidents" that led to his confession to church authorities Thursday in Springfield, Mo., where the Assemblies of God governing council sits.

Scornful Description

Turning his lip in scorn, the self-styled "old-fashioned, Holy Ghost-filled, shouting, weeping, soul-winning, Gospel-preaching preacher," would glower through his horn-rimmed glasses and shout for deliverance from "pret-ty lit-tle boys with their *hair* done and their *nails* done, who call themselves *preachers*."

Few doubted that he referred to Mr. Bakker, who was also a member of the Assemblies of God.

Last year Mr. Swaggart was accused by Roy Grutman, Mr. Bakker's attorney, of having set off the scandal that toppled Mr. Bakker from the PTL ministry by passing on to officials of the Assemblies of God the allegations of Mr. Bakker's sexual liaison with the church secretary, Jessica Hahn.

A source with knowledge of the latest matter said that Marvin Gorman, a television evangelist from New Orleans, had given church officials information that initiated the inquiry into Mr. Swaggart's conduct.

In 1986, Mr. Gorman admitted committing "an immoral act" with a woman. He asserted, however, that Mr. Swaggart had unjustly accused him of numerous adulterous affairs, and he sued Mr. Swaggart, seeking $90 million. That suit was dismissed by a judge who said the dispute was a religious one that did not belong in court. Mr. Gorman is appealing the dismissal.

New York Times, February 22, 1988, pp. 1, 14.

FROM "THE PHALLIC PULPIT"

By GARRY WILLS

Of all the men running for President in 1988, only two were forced, by the birth dates of their children, to admit to having had sex with their wives before marriage—and those two, Pat Robertson and Jesse Jackson, were the only preachers in the race. To some, that might seem odd; but not to those who know preachers. The pulpit has always been a libidinous zone. Jimmy Swaggart and Jim Bakker are not likely to surprise people familiar with the sexual exploits of Paul Tillich or Martin Luther King. Or of Henry Ward Beecher. Or, for that matter, of Peter Abelard, the twelfth-century theologian who was castrated for his affair with Eloise, the niece of his ecclesiastical superior. The ranks of the ministry would be considerable if Abelard's punishment followed regularly on Abelard's sin.

Believers, in time, become inured to pastoral lust, less shocked than outsiders when Jimmy Swaggart has to wash his sins away in copious tears. It is the outsider who cannot understand why so many forgive and forget these offenses, or why it does not seem hypocritical for preachers to keep denouncing the very sins they succumb to. Thus Michael d'Antonio, after an intelligent survey of modern evangelicals' activities, concludes that recent scandals are leading to "the inevitable collapse of the Christian Right." But Randal Balmer, after an equally intelligent look at much of the same material, finds it amusing that journalists repeat the error of thinking the downfall of a famous preacher means the end of religion. Balmer, brought up an evangelical, knows from experience that "faith is shaped by many forces." Outsiders see only the salient preacher or two on television, not the dense religious undergrowth that produces leaders and influences generation after generation.

New York Review of Books, December 21, 1989, p. 20.

TOPICS FOR WRITTEN OR ORAL EXPLORATION

1. Compare the attitudes of your own community toward unwed mothers with the attitude in Hester's time.

2. Examine *The Scarlet Letter* carefully for proofs of the union of church and state that would not be tolerated today.

3. Look in newspaper indexes (or computer information files) for a controversy over religious liberty in the past year. Write a paper on the instance.

4. Have a debate on the issue of allowing religious groups to use public school property after school hours.

5. Research an instance of controversy over child custody in the last year. Compare and contrast it with Hester's situation.

6. Detail what you consider to be valid reasons for removing a child from its biological parents. If there are marked differences in the lists of different students, debate the differences.

7. Can you think of any valid reason for removing a child from its mother, for the good of the *mother* or of the *state*, as is proposed in *The Scarlet Letter*?

8. There was great controversy over the Singapore caning of an American teenager for vandalism, many people in the United States approving of the punishment. Have a debate on whether the United States should reinstate any form of corporal punishment. Don't overlook the fact that statistics may contribute to your argument.

9. Discuss in a paper the relevance of Hawthorne's "Be True, Be True" to the cases of the Reverends Jim Bakker and Jimmy Swaggart.

10. Compare and contrast the cases and characters of Dimmesdale and Swaggart, specifically.

11. Imagine you have landed a job that you desperately need. Your boss invites you to attend church with him or her. The church aggressively recruits new members, and you strongly disagree with its teachings. (Have a specific group in mind, which for discussion purposes can be labeled the ABC Church.) How do you handle the situation? Would you feel that the mere invitation resulted in placing religious pressure on you? If it can be staged without identifying specific churches, have a debate on whether a law prohibiting bosses from inviting subordinates to church would (1) interfere with the free expression of the boss's religion or (2) infringe on the employee's religious liberty.

12. Similarly, imagine that you attend a school in which almost all the

other students and teachers belong to a religious group other than your own—Catholic, if you are Protestant or Jewish; or Protestant, if you are Catholic or Jewish, for example. Would such circumstances affect your views on allowing public prayer in schools? Debate the issue.

13. Are there legal reasons why a student cannot pray silently in school at any time? If not, why would anyone want an amendment to the Constitution to allow prayer in public schools? Discuss.

14. Research two separate but related issues: teen pregnancy in America in the 1990s, and child-rearing by single adult women. Debate the two issues separately. Do not ignore the question of the implications for society as a whole.

Glossary

alchemy   a kind of chemistry that involved the use of magic.

Anabaptists   Protestants who denied the validity of infant baptism, baptized believers only, and advocated the complete separation of church and state. An early term for Baptists.

Antinomians   a name given by the Puritans to a group, led by Anne Hutchinson, who believed that the Puritan leaders had strayed from the Calvinist emphasis on God's grace (as opposed to man's good deeds and outer displays of piousness).

Baptists   Protestants who denied the validity of infant baptism, baptizing believers only.

celibacy   abstention from sexual relations

Congregationalists   in early New England another term for Puritans, especially those who settled Massachusetts Bay—the area around Boston.

corporal punishment   punishment delivered on the body, such as whipping.

covenant theology   Calvinist theology based on the view that biblical history can be explained by a series of God's covenants.

Elect   those human beings who were chosen by God (before the beginning of time) to be saved from hell. These are not people who have done good deeds to *deserve* salvation. Rather, they are those whom God has *wanted* to save.

Election Sermon a sermon preached on the occasion of an election in Puritan New England. Illustrates the union of church and state in Massachusetts. It was a high honor for a minister to be asked to preach such a sermon.

the Fall refers to Adam and Eve being driven out of Eden into a world of suffering, sin, death, and damnation.

fate destiny; that which is inevitable or predetermined.

First Covenant called the Covenant of Works; the first contract between God and humankind, whereby God promised Adam and Eve a good and simple life within the protection of the Garden of Eden, and they promised Him obedience in return.

free will actions arise from personal choice rather than divine determination.

grace the gift of God. In Puritan theology, it referred to the fact that human beings are only saved from damnation by the grace or gift of God, not by their own efforts.

heterodox not in accordance with established doctrines; unorthodox doctrines or opinions.

natural depravity the sin with which a human being is born. Since the Fall, it is human nature to be evil. Same as original sin.

oligarchy form of government in which power is vested in a few persons; usually a government of the aged.

Original Sin the sin with which a human being is born. Since the Fall, all human beings are born evil, that is, with the tendency to be sinful.

penance punishment undergone for wrongdoing.

penitence state of being regretful for wrongdoing, and trying to make up for wrongdoing.

Quakers (the Society of Friends) a religious group founded by George Fox which believed that God spoke to individuals through an "inner light."

Second Covenant called the Covenant of Grace; a covenant made after the Fall between God and Jesus Christ by means of which a very few people would be saved from damnation.

Separatists Puritans who believed that their church must separate from the Church of England. Separatists founded Plymouth, Massachusetts, and are generally called the Pilgrims.

spectral evidence evidence of a spiritual rather than a physical nature. So even though a woman might actually be sitting in church, a neighbor could testify that her "specter" came into his house at the same time and tortured him.

works good deeds. According to the Second Covenant, human beings could not save themselves from hell by works, or by doing good deeds.

Index

About the Author

CLAUDIA DURST JOHNSON is Professor of English at the University of Alabama, where for 12 years she chaired the Department of English. She is Series Editor of the Greenwood Press "Literature in Context" series, which includes *Understanding The Scarlet Letter*. She is the author of two other volumes in the series, *Understanding To Kill a Mockingbird* (Greenwood Press, 1994) and *Understanding Huckleberry Finn* (forthcoming). She is also author of *To Kill a Mockingbird: Threatening Boundaries* (1994), *American Actress: Perspective on the Nineteenth Century* (1984), (with Vernon Johnson) *Memoirs of the Nineteenth-Century Theatre* (Greenwood, 1982), *The Productive Tension of Hawthorne's Art* (1981), and (with Henry Jacobs) *An Annotated Bibliography of Shakespearean Burlesques, Parodies, and Travesties* (1976), as well as numerous articles on American literature and theatre.